DIRECTING THE PLAY

DIRECTING
THE PLAY

A Source Book of Stagecraft

By

GEORGE II, DUKE OF SAXE-MEININGEN,
ANDRE ANTOINE, OTTO BRAHM, DAVID BELASCO,
ADOLPHE APPIA, GORDON CRAIG, JACQUES COPEAU,
VSEVOLOD MEYERHOLD, GEORGE BERNARD SHAW,
EUGENE VAKHTANGOV, ARTHUR HOPKINS,
LOUIS JOUVET, B. E. ZAKHAVA, TYRONE GUTHRIE,
JOSHUA LOGAN, KONSTANTIN STANISLAVSKY,
MAX REINHARDT, LEOPOLD JESSNER,
JEAN-LOUIS BARRAULT, BERTOLT BRECHT,
ELIA KAZAN and HAROLD CLURMAN

Edited with an Illustrated History of Directing by
TOBY COLE and **HELEN KRICH CHINOY**

THE BOBBS-MERRILL COMPANY, INC.
INDIANAPOLIS   *Publishers*   NEW YORK

First Edition

ACKNOWLEDGMENTS

The editors thank the following persons who contributed uncommon information on aspects of the subject at hand: Eric Bentley, Marie-Hélène Dasté, Tamara Daykarhanova, Alexander M. Drummond, John Gassner, Andre van Gyseghem, William W. Melnitz, Donald Oenslager, Kurt Pinthus, Michel Saint-Denis, Robert Sencer, Lee Simonson, Lee Strasberg and Samuel M. Waxman.

Translations of material previously unavailable in English were made by Joseph M. Bernstein, Louis Lozowick and Zina Voynow. Mordecai Gorelik and Ralph Steiner kindly consented to the use of illustrative material.

We thank Alfred A. Knopf for the use of quotations from *The Fervent Years* by Harold Clurman, and Harcourt, Brace & Company for passages from *Moscow Rehearsals* by Norris Houghton and *The Stage Is Set* by Lee Simonson, as well as the many publishers who gave their permission, as noted in the text, to reprint from their publications.

Particular acknowledgment is made of the kindness of Lee Strasberg, who put his extraordinary private theatre collection at our disposal, and of the enthusiasm for our project on the part of Else Pinthus, Librarian of the Brander Matthews Dramatic Museum Library at Columbia University, whose co-operation facilitated our work immeasurably.

Finally, we owe a great debt to those of our family circle who, without being named, must know how much they helped to make this book.

TOBY COLE
HELEN KRICH CHINOY

PREFACE

Directing the Play is offered as a guide to what has been called the "unknown theatre," the theatre of the director. Here pioneer directors reveal in their own words those concepts and techniques by which they transformed a theatre ridden by Victorian convention into a dynamic modern medium. Their successors, outstanding contemporary craftsmen, explore the manifold problems of current theatre practice. Here the great directors share with us not only their general theatrical wisdom but also their working methods in preparing some of their famous productions.

"The Emergence of the Director," Part I of *Directing the Play*, provides the historical context for the selections that follow. In this survey an attempt has been made to trace the rise of the director from his shadowy origins, and to interpret the search for consummate theatrical form which culminated at the turn of the century in the preeminence of a single craftsman who integrated play, actor, movement and *décor* into an organic theatrical image.

Part II, "Vision and Method," consists of fifteen essays that expound, in his own words, the credo and the craft of the director in triumph. Selections by André Antoine, Otto Brahm, Adolphe Appia, Vsevolod Meyerhold, Jacques Copeau and Eugene Vakhtangov appear for the first time in English. Joshua Logan's "The Art in Yourself" was written especially for this collection, and a lecture delivered by Tyrone Guthrie for the Royal Society of Arts here makes its initial appearance in print. The indispensable classics of the director's art by Gordon Craig, George Bernard Shaw, David Belasco and Arthur Hopkins, among others in this volume, have never before been gathered together. In the penetrating and varied observations of such masters of the stage invaluable instruction on almost every aspect of stagecraft can be found.

The volume concludes with "The Director at Work," which offers

the closest approximation to observing the director in action. By means
of verbatim transcripts of rehearsals, eyewitness reports, and pages
from promptbooks and personal notebooks, work on eight famous productions is brought to life. Elia Kazan's analysis of the leading characters in A *Streetcar Named Desire* and Harold Clurman's preliminary
notes for *The Member of the Wedding* were made available by the
directors for publication here. Examples of the production techniques
of Vsevolod Meyerhold, Leopold Jessner, Jean-Louis Barrault and
Bertolt Brecht were translated for this volume. The director's work in
motion pictures, significant as it is, had to be omitted because of the
specialized problems of the medium.

The three-fold organization of this collection, which juxtaposes history, theory and practice, high-lights the striking change in theatre
wrought in a few decades by a handful of visionaries. Disclosing as it
does the aesthetics as well as the techniques of the masters, *Directing
the Play* is offered as a why-to-do-it as well as a how-to-do-it book. The
heritage presented here is more than history; it is the animating spirit
which keeps the theatre alive.

TABLE OF CONTENTS

PAGE

Part I: THE EMERGENCE OF THE DIRECTOR . . . 13

Part II: VISION AND METHOD

GEORGE II, DUKE OF SAXE-MEININGEN
Pictorial Motion 71

ANDRÉ ANTOINE
Behind the Fourth Wall 79

OTTO BRAHM
Style and Substance 92

DAVID BELASCO
Creating Atmosphere 98

ADOLPHE APPIA
Light and Space 111

GORDON CRAIG
The Artist of the Theatre 120

VSEVOLOD MEYERHOLD
Theatricality 136

GEORGE BERNARD SHAW
The Art of Rehearsal 142

JACQUES COPEAU
Dramatic Economy 148

EUGENE VAKHTANGOV
Fantastic Realism 160

ARTHUR HOPKINS
Capturing the Audience 166

TABLE OF CONTENTS (CON.)

LOUIS JOUVET
The Profession of the Director 175

BORIS E. ZAKHAVA
Work with the Actor 183

TYRONE GUTHRIE
An Audience of One 199

JOSHUA LOGAN
The Art in Yourself 210

Part III: THE DIRECTOR AT WORK

KONSTANTIN S. STANISLAVSKY
Director's Plan for *Othello*, Act III, Scene IV . . . 221

MAX REINHARDT
Regiebuch for *The Miracle*, Scenes I and II 242

VSEVOLOD MEYERHOLD
Rehearsals of *The Inspector-General* 259

LEOPOLD JESSNER
Staging of *The Weavers*, Act IV, The Looting Scene . 273

JEAN-LOUIS BARRAULT
Mise en Scène of *Phaedra*, Act II, Scene V 279

BERTOLT BRECHT (by an Anonymous Observer)
Brecht Directs 291

ELIA KAZAN
Notebook for *A Streetcar Named Desire* 296

HAROLD CLURMAN
Some Preliminary Notes for
The Member of the Wedding 311

BIBLIOGRAPHY 323

INDEX 337

LIST OF ILLUSTRATIONS

PAGE

The Swan Theatre (1596) 12

A Medieval Mystery Play 15

Staging of Valenciennes Passion Play (1547) 17

Performance of Molière's *Le Malade Imaginaire* (1673) 19

Perspective Stage Setting for *Il Granchio* (1566) 21

Spectators seated on the stage during an eighteenth century
production 22

Macready as Macbeth 24

Banquet scene from *Macbeth* 27

Poster of the Théâtre Antoine 30

Stanislavsky as Rakitin 34

Trigorin and Nina 36

Multiple flats for escape scene of Boucicault's
Arrah-na-Pogue (1865) 39

Self-Portrait (1919): Gordon Craig 44

Hamlet: "Lights, lights, lights." (1927) 46

Copeau's stage at the Vieux Colombier 49

Notation from first page of Reinhardt's *Regiebuch* for
Danton's Death 51

Interior view of the Grosses Schauspielhaus 53

Vsevolod Meyerhold 56

Constructivist setting for Tairov's production of
The Man Who Was Thursday (1923) 58

Playing area of Okhlopkov's arena staging of *Aristocrats* . . . 60

Bertolt Brecht's *Three-Penny Opera* designed by Caspar Neher . 62

PAGE

Jean-Louis Barrault in *Baptiste* 64

Operating room in the Group Theatre production of
Men in White 66

PART III PHOTOGRAPHS

André Antoine reading to the company at the Théâtre Libre

Stanislavsky and members of the Moscow Art Theatre hear Chekhov read *The Seagull* (1898)

George Bernard Shaw takes a hand in the direction of *Androcles and the Lion*

David Belasco explaining a scene to the company of *Tiger Rose*

Vsevolod Meyerhold rehearsing a scene from his production of *The Final Conflict* (1931)

Max Reinhardt and his *Regiebuch* in action during the 1937 production of *The Eternal Road*

The Group Theatre rehearsing *The Case of Clyde Griffiths* under the direction of Lee Strasberg (1937)

Joshua Logan directs the chorus of *Wish You Were Here* (1952)

Part I

THE EMERGENCE
OF THE
DIRECTOR

THE SWAN THEATRE (1596). DRAWING BY JOHANN DE WITT.

The Emergence of the Director

Less than a hundred years ago the director was only an ideal nurtured by disgruntled critics of the chaotic Victorian theatre. He did not even have a name, for the terms "director," "régisseur," and "*metteur en scène*" had barely begun to acquire their present theatrical meaning. He was imaged as a "disciplinarian" who would superintend the "whole conduct of a piece and exact a rigid but a just decorum." He was conceived as a super stage manager who would be "at one and the same time a poet, an antiquarian and a costumier." When the director did finally appear toward the end of the nineteenth century, he filled so pressing a need that he quickly pre-empted the hegemony that had rested from time immemorial with playwrights and actors. From mysterious recesses behind the scenes the director stamped his individuality on a rich and varied international stage. By his control he defined the complex modern theatre, just as once the words of the poet had fixed the theatrical life of the Elizabethan stage and the personal magnetism of the actor had dazzled eighteenth-century audiences. The appearance of the director ushered in a new and original theatrical epoch. His experiments, his failures and his triumphs set and sustained the stage.

When the animators of modern theatre—Antoine, Stanislavsky, Appia, Craig, Reinhardt, Meyerhold, Copeau—examined the *fin de siècle* theatres, they saw only an appalling absence of homogeneous values in the production itself and in its appeal to the audience. They insisted that if theatre was to retrieve its unique, primitive, communal power, a director would have to impose a point of view that would penetrate play, production and spectators. By his interpretation a director would weld a harmonious art and a cohesive audience out of the disturbing diversity increasingly apparent in our urban, industrial, mass society. By his multifarious activities the director would restore the artistic and social unity that have always been the central demands of the collective art of theatre.

The pristine epochs when writing and staging a play were a single creative process inspired these pioneer directors. Dramatic conception and theatrical performance had gone hand in hand in ancient Greece, medieval Europe, Tudor England, and the France of Louis the Fourteenth. The titans of these eras—Aeschylus, Shakespeare, Molière—had done more than envision a fictive world; they had made that world live on the stage.

The Greek poet symbolized the ideal toward which Gordon Craig's "artist of the theatre" aspired. Nascent directors could see that the Greek poet had been *didaskalos,* or teacher, because he had instructed his performers in the intricate movements of their dance, had rehearsed his poetic strophes with them, had originated costumes and scenic conventions for them. Aeschylus, for example, was the triumphant man of the theatre whom even ancient critics had distinguished for "the brilliant mounting of his plays."

The new director felt himself a lineal descendant of the medieval *maître du jeu.* Baton and book of the play in hand (the image is preserved, for example, in the miniature painted by Jean Fouquet), the *maître du jeu* realized Jacques Copeau's condition that the director handle a text "as a musician reads notes and sings them right at the first sight." The superintendents appointed by the *compagnons* at Valenciennes to stage the Passion in 1547 seemed a primitive version of Max Reinhardt's corps of *régisseurs* and Meyerhold's battery of stage managers. One superintendent was in charge of sets, one prepared the music, one handled the stage effects (the *secrets*) and three arranged the text. Firmin Gémier contemplated with deep emotion the staging of the Mons Passion Play discovered by Professor Gustave Cohen. Sensing in the many pages of this 1501 promptbook the labors of a predecessor, Gémier suggested that these old records be called *Le Livre de conduite du régisseur.*

In the Elizabethan dramatist the director found a more recent and more familiar progenitor. Shakespeare seemed the first modern artist of the theatre. Directors could hear his voice in Hamlet's advice to the players. He was one of them, coaching and coaxing his actors to conform to his standards. Dissatisfied with the physical limitations of their own stages, they could sympathize with Shakespeare's complaint

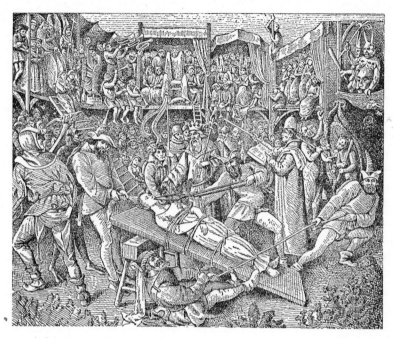

A MEDIEVAL MYSTERY PLAY. DETAIL AFTER THE MINIATURE
BY JEAN FOUQUET.

about his "unworthy scaffold." In each of his great plays they found
a director's *Regiebuch*, a producer's plan.

Molière spoke directly to the modern craftsman from the pages of
his *Impromptu at Versailles*. They could hear him convincing a reluc-
tant actress of the correctness of his casting, follow him as he analyzed
roles or explained fine points of acting technique. They recalled that
his co-worker, the invaluable record keeper La Grange, had said that
Molière's special perfection lay in his handling of *le jeu des acteurs*:
"A glance of the eye, a step, a gesture, these things were observed with
an exactitude that was unknown until then in the theatres of Paris."

In seeking historical precedents for their role, however, the visionaries of the director's art tended to romanticize the past. Often they
forgot that none of the great models had been quite the unfettered
superman of Craig's dreams. Like the modern director, the Greek

poet had been dependent upon his "producers": the archon, who regulated dramatic performances at the Festival of Dionysus, and the choregus, the wealthy citizen who footed the bill. The *maître du jeu* had struggled with a host of amateur players, keeping them in line by imposing heavy fines. The Elizabethan dramatist had often found his job exasperating. Ben Jonson described the poet-director in the "tiring house," prompting the actors aloud, stamping at the book hold-er, swearing for the properties, cursing the poor tireman, railing that the music was out of tune and swearing over every venial trespass the actors committed. Molière, so devoted to the *jeu* of the actors, found himself composing plays to exploit the spectacular potentialities of Mazarin's *Salle des Machines*.

As the emergent director sought to become an artist of the theatre like his great exemplars, he discovered that the comprehensive har-mony of the theatres that he took as his ideal could not have been the simple consequence of autocratic domination. The clue to the unity he admired did not lie in any specific theatrical expedients—the poet-director, the size of the arena, the shape of the platform, the absence of realistic scenery—nostrums that directors frequently offered for a resuscitation of contemporary theatre. The unity existed prior to theatrical creation. The concord sprang from a cohesive society whose common thoughts and emotions found in an "idea of a theatre" a basic vision of human life.

The practices of the Greek theatre, for example, were based, as Francis Fergusson has pointed out, upon "the perspectives of the myth, of the rituals, and of the traditional *hodos*, the way of life of the city." These perspectives provided patterns of response that embraced the audience and the diverse arts of theatre. To their contemporaries the plays of the Greek poets had significance only as performances. "Antique drama was the event, the act itself, not a spectacle," Adolphe Appia concluded. Religious observance and civic pride brought the whole community together yearly to honor the god Dionysus with dramatic presentations. Artists and audiences alike were caught up in the ritual emotion of the occasion. Their collective social experience found its natural expression in the collective art of theatre.

These perspectives basically distinguish the directorial activities of the antique poet from those of his modern counterpart. They took the place of the integrating interpretation to which the director today devotes all his energies. The existence of accepted values and conventional modes of action in and out of the theatre made the director as a

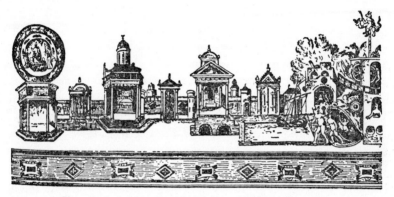

STAGING OF VALENCIENNES PASSION PLAY (1547).

distinct craftsman unnecessary. His basic function is to supply these now-absent values for a segmented society by means of the unifying principle of interpretation.

Thus, for example, the *maître du jeu* who seems so like the modern director is in terms of this definition of the director's task essentially a stage manager only. The medieval drama, which originated in Christian ritual, became an elaborate and complex civic production of the Biblical epic from Creation to the Judgment Day. Someone had to organize the host of amateur players, the profusion of visual and aural displays, and the multitude of scenes of performances that could last for many days. A man who could do this effectively would be in great demand. Jean Bouchet, for example, staged the Passion so successfully at Poitiers in 1508 that his advice was sought throughout France and Belgium. The *Livre de conduite du régisseur* of the Mons Passion Play embodied the work of two specialists, Guillaume and Jehan Delechiere. It is significant that these men were called *conducteurs de secrets*, manipulators of machines for staging such scenic effects as the Deluge or Thunder in Hell with extraordinary literal realism.

The work of these *conducteurs de secrets* was an organizational task of a complexity and magnitude that would appall the modern director. At Mons some six months of preparation preceded the single eight-day performance. Yet the task of the *conducteur de secrets* was simplified by the conventional nature of the materials with which he dealt and by the ritual preparedness of his audience. The script, despite variations, was always basically the same: the Biblical story, familiar to performers and audience alike. The point of view was always basically the same: the performance was an expression and a reinforcement of the values of the medieval world. The stage setting contained the same essential elements, whether the technique used was the English pageant wagon or the simultaneous display of mansions, in the Continental manner. There were Paradise and Hell and between them all the necessary terrestrial stations for the oft-repeated Christian saga. Like the Greek stage before it, this medieval scene pictured a comprehensive view of life that could embrace all the contradictions of human experience. What seem to us destructive antinomies between a lofty symbolism and a naïve realism in their productions were integrated not by the individual interpretation of a director, but by the act of faith that motivated these communal performances.

The Elizabethan theatre, although no longer a religious or a communal enterprise, encompassed the aggregate values of its society. The dramatist used a conventional stage to image an accepted view of life; he used it as a mirror to "show virtue her own feature, scorn her own image, and the very age and body of the time his form and pressure." Groundlings and noblemen surrounded the theatrical microcosm, with its Heavens above and its trap-door Hell, as they gathered at the perhaps symbolically named Globe, which had as its motto *"Totus mundus agit histrionem."*

Molière too had a cohesive, if limited, public. With the protection of the king, he could project a subtle, urbane comedy whose implications satisfied yet went beyond the extravagant and complacent audience for which it was performed. Like his great peers, he worked in terms of the traditional elements of theatre, which for him was the popular ensemble art of the old Italian comedians. For him, therefore, as for the other prototypes of the director "staging did not pose distinct

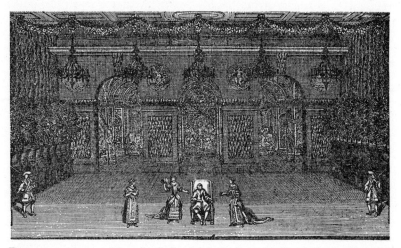

PERFORMANCE OF MOLIÈRE's *Le Malade Imaginaire* (1673). DETAIL.

aesthetic problems. For him," as a French theatre historian noted, "it was concomitant with literary creation. It was an integral part of it."

The director as an artist who, as Lee Strasberg has said, must provide "that angle of viewing the play from which the actions of the characters will appear most plausible, most meaningful . . . most truthful and most exciting" cannot be found in these great theatres to which the modern director has turned for inspiration. These theatres did not need an integrating figure, for they had an *innere Regie*—to adapt a phrase used often by German writers on directing—a unity and control intrinsic to the theatre arts and to the social conception of theatre. Modern theatre tends more and more toward an *äussere Regie*, a unity imposed by historically accurate sets and costumes, by realistic imitation, and ultimately by the external hand of the director charged with finding a collective focus for theatre in an atomized society.

The decay of a universal system of values and a traditional way of life at the beginning of our modern era deprived theatre of its homogeneous and representative public and of its accepted conventions for mirroring a shared human experience. As the audience lost its collective emotion, the diverse arts of theatre lost their internal cohesiveness.

The play yielded its focal position to scenic display and to virtuoso acting. Theatre became as fragmented as the society around it.

In the midst of these revolutionary social changes, however, theatre still sought its ideal condition. If intrinsic unity was no longer possible, then perhaps some substitutes could reintegrate the disjointed arts of a heterogeneous community. In rough historical succession four ideas of theatre emerged as restoratives. Out of Renaissance experimentation came the idea of the pictorial stage; out of eighteenth-century rationalism and nineteenth-century determinism came the facsimile stage; out of twentieth-century discontent came the expressionistic stage and the theatrical stage. The emergence of the director followed these formulas for unity. His genesis lay in the pictorial stage; his first triumphs in the facsimile stage; and his efflorescence in the expressionistic and theatrical stages.

The Renaissance discovery of painted perspective suggested a direct, palpable organizing principle for theatre in an increasingly complex, diversified, rationalistic era. Having lost the communal agreement to accept the stage as a metaphorical, symbolic microcosm, audiences could yet find a replica of the world in the *trompe-l'œil* painted stage. The realistic stage picture could be achieved, however, only by replacing the popular periwigged tragedian displaying the "points" of his histrionic art on a green baize carpet with groups of actors appropriately garbed moving in front of accurately limned backdrops.

The time-honored arts of acting and playwrighting did not possess the capacity for creating the essentially external, visual unity of the pictorial stage. A special art of production was, therefore, developed to organize all the theatrical elements into a relatively harmonious illusory world, and with the art of production came the embryonic director.

As early as the mid-sixteenth century this new art may be glimpsed. In his preoccupation with production, Leone de Sommi, theatrical adviser to the Mantuan court, sounds like a true forerunner of the modern director. In his *Dialogues on Stage Affairs*, De Sommi suggested that "it is far more essential to get good actors than a good play." He went on to insist that his actors must be ready "to follow [his] instructions." An incipient realistic bias is apparent in his remarks. In instructions on acting he stressed verisimilitude; in costuming he emphasized historical accuracy, albeit embellished by splendor and exoticism; in lighting he introduced primitive hints of psychological atmosphere.

PERSPECTIVE STAGE SETTING FOR *Il Granchio* (1566).

But it was only during the century roughly from 1750 to 1850 that an international coterie of theatre artists gradually prepared the domain over which the director would finally have absolute control. As production more and more usurped the power once held by the play itself, they perfected the implements with which the director would work—the rehearsal, the co-ordinated acting group and the external paraphernalia of archaeological sets and authentic costumes and props. Their activities revealed the creative contribution to be made by a single autocrat in charge of production.

David Garrick, for example, as artistic manager at Drury Lane, turned the platform for declamation into a picture stage by dispossessing the gallants from their ancient prerogative of sitting on the stage. He devoted more attention than was usual in the period to rehearsals and casting of minor roles. He encouraged the designer, P. J. de

SPECTATORS SEATED ON THE STAGE DURING AN EIGHTEENTH CENTURY
PRODUCTION. GRAVELOT ENGRAVING.

Loutherbourg, who invented more picturesque and more realistic effects within the proscenium picture frame.

In Germany Konrad Ekhof pointed the way with his concept of the *Konzertierung des Spiels.* In plans prepared for his short-lived Academy for Actors in 1753, he declared that no play was to be produced before it had had an initial reading, that all roles were to be thoroughly analyzed beforehand and that the objective needs of the production were to take precedence over the prejudices and special desires of members of the company.

Friedrich Schroeder, like Garrick, primarily remembered as a portrayer of Shakespearean roles, was a stern taskmaster who showed his company exactly how he wanted them to perform their parts. In his own work he provided the model for them. "It does not occur to me to stand out and be dazzling," he observed, "but to fill out and be the character." Seeking a blending of stage effects, he made use of Ekhof's valuable idea of the initial reading to establish some image of the whole play. Like other nascent producers, he invested each major production with punctilious sets and costumes.

At the turn of the century Johann Wolfgang von Goethe, as supervisor of the Weimar Court Theatre, perfected many techniques of the new art of production. He utilized readings and rigorous rehearsals, stipulating: "One should not permit himself to do anything in rehearsal that he cannot do in the play." In choosing actors he revealed a growing concern for the group as opposed to the starring performer. When he hired a new member of his company, he would let the new actor show his talents and see "how he suited the others; whether his style and manner disturbed [the] ensemble, or whether he would supply a deficiency." Once chosen, the actor had to submit himself to Goethe's absolute control. P. A. Wolff, the best actor to come from his troupe, reported that "on the stage marked out in squares every single position and movement was determined beforehand with the aim of producing a harmonious and pleasing spectacle." Tradition has it that Goethe even used a baton at rehearsals.

Since plays remained essentially untouched by the concept of the pictorial stage, acting, settings and costumes were the primary elements of the art of production. As always the strictly theatrical arts, directly responsive to vicissitudes in audience taste, anticipated changes in the more private creations of the dramatists. "Truth in plays was unobtainable," cried the great French actor Talma at the beginning of the nineteenth century; "I had to be content with putting it into the costumes."

In England, too, "truth" was found in costumes and staging, not in' new plays. Shakespeare's works were often made the vehicle for working out new pictorial values. In "producing" Shakespeare the famous actor-managers of the period took upon themselves tasks that were neither simply those of an actor nor of a manager. John Philip Kemble, for example, had as his objective "a more stately and perfect representation of his plays . . . to attend to all details as well as the grand features, and by aid of scenery and dress to perfect the dramatic illusion."

MACREADY (LEFT) AS MACBETH. CONTEMPORARY PRINT.

Kemble's attention to details was an early attempt to efface the usual careless disorder of the London theatres. His orderly rehearsals must be contrasted with the normal preparation of a play, as described by William Charles Macready in his *Reminiscences:* "It was the custom of London actors, especially the leading ones, to do little more at rehearsals than read or repeat the words of their parts, marking on them their entrances and exits, as settled by the stage manager, and their respective places on stage. To make any display of passion or energy would be to expose oneself to the ridicule or sneers of the green room."

When Macready himself became a manager he too tried to elevate

production standards. For him the rehearsal became an artistic prov-
ing ground, not a walk-through. He tried to blend settings, lighting
and stage groupings. After analyzing Macready's promptbook for
Macbeth Alan Downer concluded: "In his constant emphasis on the
necessity for unity in production, Macready foreshadowed the modern
régisseur."

By the mid-point of the century the tentative beginnings of the
Kembles and the Macreadys began to bear fruit. Samuel Phelps transformed the Sadler's Wells Theatre from an out-of-the-way melodrama
house into the equivalent of a national theatre with an unparalleled
series of Shakespearean revivals. Here his productions were marked by
an evident concern for total integration. In the vivid critical notes of
his contemporary Henry Morley we read, for example, that in A *Midsummer Night's Dream* "Mr. Phelps has never for a minute lost sight
of the main idea which governs the whole play, and this is the great
secret of his success in the presentation of it. . . . Everything has been
subdued as far as possible at Sadler's Wells to this ruling idea."

Charles Kean earned his fame as the "Prince of Managers" because
he, like Phelps, was perfecting the unified pictorial illusion. His
splendid and archaeologically exact sets and costumes were supple-
mented by the orderly movement of supernumeraries as well as leading
players. His productions were unexcelled because, as one critic pointed
out, every aspect "came under the immediate superintendence of Mr.
Charles Kean."

Although the progress from Garrick to Kean established the art of
production and the primacy of the stage picture, none of these precursors of the director was able to achieve consistently the total integration that had emerged as the ideal. Their contributions were the
necessary spadework. The consummation of their efforts was left to an
artistic nobleman of an obscure German duchy, George II, Duke of
Saxe-Meiningen.

May 1, 1874, is a red-letter day in the history of the director, for on
that date the Duke of Saxe-Meiningen brought his unknown troupe to
Berlin to display the unique accomplishments of a director's theatre.
The Duke of Saxe-Meiningen utilized all the innovations we have been

chronicling—intensive rehearsals, disciplined, co-ordinated acting and historically accurate sets and costumes—to create realistic stage pictures. But the Duke went significantly beyond his predecessors in that he attempted a reconciliation between the usually competing illusions of the painted set and the moving actor. In the words of his ardent admirer Lee Simonson, "the human figure in movement was made the pictorial unit." For the occasional moments of pictorial plasticity that one glimpses in the productions of men like Kean, whose work directly influenced him, the Duke perfected a sequence of continuous and integrated movement. Not only did the Duke seek the reconciliation of actor and set, but he also fashioned the text into the pattern of his plastic picture by extensive use of business. He interpreted the text through the medium of all the theatrical arts.

The authority of the Duke as *régisseur*, director, made possible this complex integration. Although he was assisted by his wife and by his stage manager Ludwig Chronegk, he alone was the artistic creator of each production. He designed the sets and costumes, but he went farther and designed every movement and every position on stage. He dictated the very folds of each actor's costume. Everyone in his small theatre had to be subservient to the production, whose form he determined and sustained through an iron discipline. The mob scenes, for which the Meininger were greatly admired, were made possible by this discipline. Each actor had to take his turn as a supernumerary; those who refused were dismissed from the company. The Duke's ensemble was the product of his skill in using actors as theatrical material, rather than the natural result of individual acting talent at his disposal.

Nowhere were the Duke's powers more in evidence than at rehearsals. Here he blended the theatrical arts into a symphony of visual and aural minutiae. No detail could be allowed to destroy the total effect, since these details, rather than the play itself, transformed the stage picture into a successful image of the world. The very first rehearsal was conducted with the actual sets, costumes and properties to be used in performance. With plenty of time to spend on his work, the Duke spared no effort in achieving the exact nuance he envisioned. Aloys Prasch in his "Reminiscences of the Meininger" describes an amusing illustration of this in rehearsals of Ibsen's *The Pretenders*.

The Duke wanted the voices of the besiegers to sound muffled. After several unsuccessful attempts to get the right tone from his actors, he finally had some mattresses brought in and forced the whole cast, men and women, to lie on their stomachs and cry into the mattresses. "In this way," says Prasch, "was the intended effect obtained, and it speaks well for the discipline of the Meininger that on this occasion not one single performer laughed at the comical situation."

With the Duke of Saxe-Meiningen the art of production found its master. His work, which inspired Antoine and Stanislavsky among others, revealed, in the words of Lee Simonson, "the necessity for a commanding director who could visualize an entire performance and give it unity as an interpretation by complete control of every moment of it; the interpretive value of the smallest details of lighting, costuming, make-up, stage setting; the immense discipline and the degree of organization needed before the performance was capable of expressing the 'soul of a play.'"

BANQUET SCENE FROM *Macbeth*. DESIGN BY THE DUKE OF SAXE-MEININGEN.

Until the advent of the art of production the "soul of a play" had resided in the words of the playwright. Now the playwright could be relegated to a secondary position. A shifting panorama of framed pictures provided visual, rather than dramatic, proof that the stage was still a world in miniature. This scenic documentation of reality sustained theatre in an era whose "form and pressure" were becoming more and more difficult to assess.

While production did shape the stage arts into a complex and flexible medium, the attitude of the producer was potentially dangerous. He could claim, as did Henry Irving, exponent of lavish graphic stagings, that "the theatre is bigger than the playwright, that its destiny is a higher one than that of the mouthpiece for an author's theses, and finally that plays are made for the theatre and not theatre for plays." Without the imaginative values of the playwright, however, theatre could be only a show, such as Irving offered, a spectacle, not the social act it had once been.

But the new scenic realism could be made to serve the playwright if it became the milieu, the "experimental situation," in which the writer placed his fictional creatures in order to observe, with scientific detachment, how environment determined character. The doctrine of naturalism, promulgated by Emile Zola, offered this scientific attitude as a new, uniquely modern point of view uniting playwright, production and audience.

In his manifestoes Zola confessed somewhat uneasily that the spirit of the nineteenth century did not supply the kind of communal focus that, for example, had made the theatre of Molière "an exact reproduction of contemporaneous society." Yet he insisted that the "experimental and scientific spirit of the century" would enter the domain of the drama, and that in it lay "its only possible salvation." He outlined the advances in production that were preparing theatre for "science" and "truth." The next step, as he saw it, was for the appearance of plays so written that they would control the external scenic decoration by making it the environment for the presentation of "life itself."

"Either the theatre will become naturalistic or it will not be at all," Zola declared with desperate finality. But when plays written in the new mode began to appear, the public responded to them with shock rather than with sympathy or with "scientific objectivity." It was only when a director, imbued with the naturalistic ideals, gathered a special audience for these plays and performed them on a new facsimile stage that a satisfying theatrical experience became possible.

Despite its emphasis on the playwright, therefore, the facsimile stage, like the pictorial one, found the director an indispensable figure. In the "free theatres" devoted to naturalism the director had his first sustained successes. Here he interpreted new plays in new ways for an organized public. In a world that no longer had a total unity which theatre could reflect, the director created for audiences selected from the mass a limited approximation of the ancient ideal.

André Antoine, first significant French director, put Zola's "man of flesh and bones on the stage, taken from reality, scientifically analyzed, without one lie." The facsimile stage was born when this lowly clerk from a Parisian gas company and his amateur actors performed an adaptation of Zola's *Jacques Damour* in a setting whose furnishings the director himself had carted from his home.

At the Théâtre Libre, model of all "free theatres," Antoine translated Zola's theory of environment into living theatre. In a now-famous letter to the all-powerful critic Sarcey, Antoine raised the central question of the new stage: "In modern works written in a vein of realism and naturalism, where the theory of environment and the influence of exterior things have become so important, is not the setting the indispensable complement of the work?" In this new "theatre of situations" the *metteur en scène*, the director, was essential, Antoine insisted, for unless the naturalistic plays were staged and acted the right way, they would fail, as had Becque's *La Parisienne* at the classic Comédie-Française.

As a director Antoine took his cue from the accomplishments of the Duke of Saxe-Meiningen, absorbing from him the manipulation of the disciplined corps of actors. But he went significantly beyond the plastic picture stage of the Meininger to create the facsimile stage of naturalism. For Antoine the setting had to be more than a harmonious functional background. It had to be the environment that shaped the life and actions of the characters. In describing his directorial procedures, Antoine explained: "First of all, I found it useful, in fact, indispensable, carefully to create the setting and the environment, without worrying at all about the events that were to occur on the stage. For it is the environment that determines the movements of the characters, not the movement of the characters that determines the

POSTER OF THE THÉÂTRE ANTOINE.

environment." After fashioning the complete environment Antoine would then decide where to remove the "famous fourth wall," which would expose a "slice of life" for the audience.

Antoine pursued the new métier of the director rather than accept the plaudits that might easily have come to him as an actor, because to a large extent his mission included more than production; it included literary discovery and defense of new authors. The naturalist's desire for complete theatrical unity tied the director's work to the craft of the playwright to such an extent that Antoine could say, after the failure of his production of Curel's *Les Fossiles*, "I am far happier to have discovered *Les Fossiles* in a pile of manuscripts and to have brought Curel to your attention, than vexed at having played the piece badly." To his contemporaries it seemed that Antoine had "introduced a factor unknown till now in the theatre: the director, defender of the author, of the play, of the ensemble interpretation." Antoine "was an apostle teaching new doctrines," said Curel, "and a master in indicating the way to apply them."

As an "apostle of new doctrines" Antoine was confined not only to one type of play but also to one type of audience. He could not understand why, for example, his real butcher shops and real water fountains fascinated audiences. To him these effects were part of a philosophy; the audience, not always sharing his point of view, simply enjoyed the stage trick. Antoine realized that his theatre was directed toward a select public. It was, in his words, "reserved for an elite."

Yet this "amusing and droll director" with his "foreman's whistle" and his "noms du Dieu" was not content to remain leader of a partisan theatre. Feeling that naturalism was the only possible point of view for modern theatre, Antoine wanted to impose it on all plays given au grand public. He explained his desire to become director of the Odéon, second state theatre, in these terms: "I felt the need to encounter the great plays, the classical and foreign works of art, to try to create for the classics the same movement of progress that I had the good fortune to release for the contemporary repertory." In the years from 1906 to 1916 at the Odéon, Antoine with varying degrees of success stamped his theatrical ideal on les grands ouvrages of Shakespeare and Molière, trying to bring them within the confines of the "slice of life."

Antoine's Théâtre Libre was the model for Otto Brahm, director of the Freie Buehne, Germany's naturalist experiment. Devotion to new plays was even greater in Brahm than it had been in Antoine, since Brahm had been a scholar and critic before he became a director. While still a critic Brahm had observed: "Two capacities are required of the producer in a repertory theatre: he must be capable of both directing and literary discovery." Like Antoine, too, Brahm moved from directing naturalistic plays to doing all plays in the naturalistic manner. When he undertook the supervision of the Deutsches Theater in 1894, Brahm's motives were like those Antoine expressed when he sought his position at the Odéon. Brahm "wanted to produce the classics but not in the traditional and conventional way; his intention was to make them come to life by utilizing the new methods and direction."

Brahm saw his directorial task in terms of work with the actors and playwrights. He tried to tread a path between the weakness of a *"wort régisseur"* like Heinrich Laube, who, Brahm felt, had concentrated "one-sidedly on the listening not the seeing audience," and the limitations of the Meininger, who, he wrote, "unfortunately forgot one thing: to project onto the true-to-life sets of their stage human beings who acted naturally." Although Brahm did insist that the milieu of a play be faithfully represented, he let his aides, Carl Hachmann and Emil Lessing, handle the external facets of production. It is interesting to note that Hachmann and Lessing were listed as "directors" on the programs. Brahm's name did not appear in that capacity, but what became known in Germany as the "Brahm style," the German naturalist style, was nevertheless his creation.

For Brahm the director is a man who must be "sensitive to the inner spirit of a work" and project "in its representation the individual tone and mood born of that certain work and none other. He who wishes to bring a dramatist's creation to stage-life must be capable of perceiving those basic mood-creating tones and of making them resound in the audience through the medium of his performers."

One of Brahm's major tasks in the Freie Buehne was to find actors to accomplish this goal. Unlike Antoine and his troupe of amateurs, Brahm did not have his own company, but used professional stars who would spare time for his productions. It was in part this desire for an acting group that led him to seek the position of producer at the Deutsches Theater. The ensemble was his ideal, as it had been Antoine's and Saxe-Meiningen's. But unlike the last, who achieved co-ordinated effects at the expense of the individual actor, Brahm tried to create the ensemble through the talent of the individual actor.

Neither Brahm nor Antoine used a *Regiebuch*, or production plan, for their performances. Since Brahm preferred to allow the play to take shape during rehearsals, he had no use for detailed, advance preparation. Professor Samuel Waxman, who had access to Antoine's complete files for his study of Antoine and the Théâtre Libre, indicated in a letter to the editors that he did not find any production plans. It seems quite possible that intense respect for the playwright's text prevented both Brahm and Antoine from using it merely as a stimulus to their directorial imagination.

Konstantin Stanislavsky, perhaps the greatest of naturalistic directors, differs from Brahm and Antoine in that his initial concern was with new theatrical form rather than with new dramatic content. His three published production plans for *The Sea Gull, The Lower Depths* and *Othello*, although they reveal great changes in technique, suggest that the play itself was never Stanislavsky's full source of inspiration. In his early work, particularly, the play was only the starting point for directorial elaboration. An assistant once said of him that "a stage direction or a single phrase in a play called forth all sorts of images in his mind and these very often played havoc with the author's text." Stanislavsky, in reminiscing about his production of *The Bells* in 1896, said that he produced the play "not as it was written but as [his] imagination prompted [him]." Indeed he chose this melodrama because it offered great scope for the director's manipulation of stage effects.

In his long career Stanislavsky seems to recapitulate in striking fashion the history of the director. He began as a disciple of the Meininger's pictorial stage, became a facsimile realist devoting his theatre to new authors and went beyond to rediscover the basic sources of theatrical art.

Stanislavsky started out with an ideal of what he called the "producer-autocrat," which he derived from his careful observation of Ludwig Chronegk directing the Meininger on tour in Moscow in 1890. "I began to imitate Chronegk," he wrote, "and with time I became a producer-autocrat myself and many Russian producers began imitating me as I had imitated Chronegk. A whole generation of producer-autocrats arose, but alas, as they did not possess Chronegk's talent, the producers of this new type merely became theatrical managers who treated the actors as if they were props, as mere pawns to be moved about as they liked in their *mise en scènes*."

The talent of Chronegk that Stanislavsky so admired was the creative directorial imagination which, he felt, made possible excellent performances with unskilled actors. "It seemed to me at that time that we amateur producers were in the same position as Chronegk and the Duke of Saxe-Meiningen. We, too, wanted to put on great plays and to reveal the thoughts and feelings of the great playwrights, but as we

STANISLAVSKY AS RAKITIN IN TURGENEV'S *A Month in the Country* (1910). DRAWING BY M. DOBUJINSKY.

had no trained actors we had to relegate all the power to the producer, who alone had to create the performance of the play with the help of scenery, props, interesting *mise en scènes* and his own imagination. That is why the despotism of the Meiningen producer seemed justified to me."

Like the Meininger, Stanislavsky was intrigued by the perfection of external realism. In preparing Alexei Tolstoy's *Czar Fyodor*, for example, he insisted on visiting the actual historical locales and purchasing authentic accessories. Looking back at this early period in his career, he decided: "This artistic truth was at the time merely external; it was the truth of objects, furniture, costumes, stage properties, light and sound effects, the reproduction of the typical features of a stage character and his external, physical life, but the very fact that we succeeded in bringing real, though only external artistic truth on the stage, which at that time knew only artistic falsehood, opened up some new perspectives for the future."

In order to create this external truth, Stanislavsky began his preparations by working out enormously detailed production notes. Then in innumerable rehearsals these plans were translated into stage life. Increasingly the production plan and the rehearsal were becoming the basic implements of the director's craft, because through them the director could most effectively impose his interpretation of a play.

The procedures of external realism were particularly useful to Stanislavsky in preparing the initial production of Chekhov's *The Sea Gull* for the Moscow Art Theatre, since, as he himself admitted, he did not perceive the theatrical values in Chekhov. "I shut myself up in my study," he explained, "and wrote a detailed *mise en scène* as I felt it and as I saw and heard it with my inner eye and ear. At those moments I did not care for the feelings of the actor! I sincerely believed it was possible to tell people to live and feel as I liked them to; I wrote down directions for everybody and those directions had to be carried out. I put down everything in those production notes; how and where, in what way a part had to be interpreted and the playwright's stage directions carried out, what kind of inflections the actor had to use, how he had to move about and act, and when and how he had to cross the stage. I added all sorts of sketches for every *mise en scène*—exits, entries, crossings from one place to another, and so on and so forth. I described the scenery, costumes, make-up, deportment, gaits, and habits of the characters, etc." Any line taken at random from the published production score of the play reveals this scrupulous detail; for example, "Konstantin delivers the whole of his speech while smoking, taking the cigarette out of his mouth, replacing it, inhaling the smoke, and so on."

Although Stanislavsky's *mise en scène* for the play brought the Art
Theatre great success, Chekhov was not completely satisfied. By interpreting the play through his production art Stanislavsky had created
values that the author felt were not in his play. Despite Chekhov's
criticisms the challenge of his plays stimulated Stanislavsky's creative
efforts.

TRIGORIN AND NINA. SKETCH BY STANISLAVSKY FROM HIS PRODUCTION
PLAN FOR *The Sea Gull* (1898).

Through his search for a proper style for the Chekhov plays, and
through his growing concern with the art of the actor, Stanislavsky
moved from the purely external realism of his early work to an inner
verity, to psychological realism. This subtle refinement did not involve
a break with external realism, but rather made it the key to the inner
realism of the play. In his work on Gorky's *The Lower Depths* Stanislavsky felt his methods were changing. He undertook an expedition to
the Khitrov market to find the real-life equivalent of Gorky's locale in
accordance with his usual initial step in preparing a production. This
time he observed the people more than the place. This expedition
made him "aware of the inner meaning of the play."

Stanislavsky's own growing dissatisfaction with the limitations of
external realism coincided with the attempt in Russia as elsewhere to
do away with what a Russian symbolist magazine called "unnecessary
truth." Meyerhold and others were turning from realism to symbolism,
and Stanislavsky, by establishing the Studio on Povarskaya Street

where Meyerhold had a chance to experiment, aided the new move-ment. He himself struck out in new paths, producing plays by men like Andreyev. As part of the general ferment, Stanislavsky invited Gordon Craig, leader of the antinaturalist movement, to visit and work with the Moscow Art Theatre. In 1908 he wrote: "Of course we have returned to realism, to a deeper, more refined and more psychological realism. Let us get a little stronger in it and we shall once more con-tinue our quest. That is why we have invited Gordon Craig. After wandering about in search of new ways, we shall again return to realism for more strength. I do not doubt that every abstraction on the stage, such as impressionism, for instance, could be attained by way of a more refined and deeper realism. All other ways are false and dead."

This path of refined realism led Stanislavsky deeper and deeper into work with the actor, whose human form, he felt after seeing some of Meyerhold's experiments, could not be twisted to comply with ab-stract ideas. From the producer-autocrat, devoted to the facsimile stage, he became, through his work on acting, the producer-instructor, who located the heart of theatre in the actor. This development led him to a new appreciation of the playwright, whom he no longer rele-gated to a mere stimulus for his imagination. Thus in the last years of his active career, from 1927 on, his whole conception of the director underwent a profound change. "No producer," he wrote, "can produce a play unless he first finds its ruling idea. At present the producer of a play in our theatres and even in the Moscow Art Theatre does not care about the ruling idea at all, but builds up his production entirely on all sorts of clever tricks. This is the very negation of the art of the stage. It is true that such clever tricks are usually rewarded by a thunder of applause, which is what the actors want, but it was not for this that Pushkin and Shakespeare wrote."

This change in attitude meant a change in directing technique which is illustrated in the following statement which appears in David Magarshack's biography of Stanislavsky, from which the other transla-tions in this section have been drawn: "Before, a producer planned his *mise en scènes* and the nature of the inner feelings of the *dramatis personae* in his own study. He then went to the rehearsal and told the actor to carry them out. The actor was quite naturally expected to copy his producer. But when I arrive at a rehearsal now, I am no more prepared than the actor and I go through all the phases of his work with him. The producer must approach the play with a mind as fresh and clear as the actor's and then grow together with him." Stanislavsky even discarded his use of elaborate historical study, which had absorbed much of his time in earlier years. "The best analysis of a play," he now said, "is to act it in the given circumstances. For in the process of action the actor gradually obtains mastery over the inner incentives of the actions of the character he is representing, evoking in himself emotions and thoughts which resulted in those actions."

While Stanislavsky remained essentially within the framework of naturalistic tradition, he found a new and profound basis for it in his work with the actor. His quest for the primal source of theatre art, for the simple physical action, linked him with those very artists who ultimately turned against naturalism.

What could result when naturalism was used as mere technique unrelated to new content in plays or to new concepts in acting was evident in the work of David Belasco. In the history of American theatre, David Belasco was the first significant directorial figure. Unlike his European colleagues, who had all begun in revolt against the commercial theatre, Belasco, bred in the commercial theatre, became its leading exponent. His tradition stemmed largely from craftsmen like Dion Boucicault, whose sensational realistic stage effects anticipated cinematic movement, or Tom Robertson, whom Allardyce Nicoll credits with being "the first man in England to conceive of stage realism as a complete whole."

Belasco transformed the lowly position of stage manager into the major role of director through know-how accumulated in years as actor, playwright and play-doctor. Early in his career, in his western days, his directorial activities were lauded by his co-workers: "Your quick apprehension and remarkable analytical ability in discovering and describing the mental intentions of an author are so superior to anything we have heretofore experienced that we feel sure that the position of master dramatic director of the American stage must finally fall on you."

Belasco did become "master dramatic director of the American stage" by bringing to it carefully organized, unified productions. Even so vitriolic an opponent of all that Belasco stood for as George Jean Nathan had to concede: "Mr. Belasco has contributed one—and only one—thing for judicious praise to the American theatre. He has brought to that theatre a standard of tidiness in production and matu-

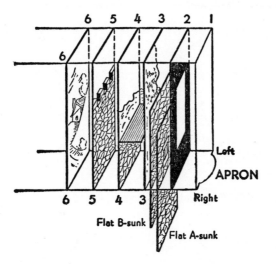

MULTIPLE FLATS FOR ESCAPE SCENE OF BOUCICAULT'S *Arrah-na-Pogue* (1865). (FROM *Stage to Screen* BY NICHOLAS A. VARDAC.)

ration of manuscript, a standard that has discouraged to no little extent that theatre's erstwhile not-uncommon frowzy hustle and slipshod manner of presentation."

Belasco made his mark primarily as master of the mechanics, the externals of theatre. Montrose Moses aptly labeled him "the psychologist of the switchboard," suggesting with this pregnant phrase Belasco's special contribution. The subtle use of lights which transformed fourteen minutes into Cho-Cho-San's night-long vigil for the return of Pinkerton attested, in the words of Belasco's adulatory biographer William Winter, to his "resource and skill in stage management and stage mechanics." While on occasion Belasco paid lip service to the importance of the play and the actors, his description of his directorial practices suggests how basic was his concern with what he himself called "the material things"—the perfect California sunset for *The Girl of the Golden West*, the actual cheap boardinghouse furniture for *The Easiest Way*, the interior of Childs Restaurant in *The Governor's Lady*.

An inventive master of stage techniques, Belasco deserves credit for his many innovations in making stage life real. His major significance as a pioneer director lies in his use of his materials to form a unified production. But his type of facsimile realism was a manner of stage production rather than a thoroughgoing vision. For that reason, perhaps, it was capable of satisfying the popular taste for photographic effects, but it had lost its rationale as a basis for theatrical integration.

As men like Belasco cut the "slice of life" terribly thin, voices cried out in alarm that drama had a purpose loftier than the technical reproduction of physical reality. Even the richer naturalism of the European masters had quickly been rejected as a narrow, partial view of human experience. Thus, despite its essentially modern scientific and objective qualities, the facsimile stage, like the antiquated pictorial one, did not restore to theatre its lost organic unity. Its failure raised pressing questions about the very nature of the theatrical impulse.

The newly emerged director, whom the realistic-naturalistic movement had turned into the central theatrical figure, became the prime mover in the re-examination of theatre art. The men whom we may call the visionaries of the director's art—Appia, Craig, Meyerhold, Copeau—were those who consciously assigned the director this task of rediscovering the wellsprings of theatre. To them we owe the flamboyant image of the "artist of the theatre." The realists had stumbled on the director out of necessity. The rebels proclaimed the director the messiah of a new theatrical synthesis.

Just as Zola stands behind the naturalistic movement, so Richard Wagner stands behind what Sheldon Cheney has called the "synthetic movement." During the mid-years of the nineteenth century Wagner had attacked a decaying theatre because it could not house the "deepest and noblest of man's consciousness." He looked back to the Greeks, whose theatre he saw as the profound expression of the whole people gathered "within the ample boundaries of the Greek amphi-theatre." He asserted that the inherent characteristics of modern society—its degradation of religion, its emphasis on "industrial gain," its denial of art—robbed audience and artist alike of an ennobling idea of theatre. He schematized the cause as the "Art-Antagonistic Shape of Present Life, under the Sway of Abstract Thought and Fashion." Damning the whole social fabric, Wagner looked forward to a revolu-tionary new "art work of the future."

This "art work of the future" would be a *Gesamtkunstwerk*, a com-posite art work, which would fuse all theatrical elements. He offered the word-tone-drama, the music drama, as the magic amalgam not only for uniting the disparate arts of the theatre but also for spanning the gap between art and the folk. He explained the unique advantages of a musical orientation. "A subject," he wrote, "which is comprehended merely by the intelligence can also be expressed merely through the language of words; but the more it expands into an emotional concept, the more does it call for an expression which in its final and essential fullness can alone be obtained through the language of sounds. Hereby the essence of that which the Word-Tone-Poet has to express results quite by itself: it is the Purely Human, freed from all conventions."

Expression of the universal, elemental, inner man was thus disclosed as the theatrical motive in opposition to the naturalist's rational exposure of selected segments of reality. In shifting the theatrical objective from the reproduction of external reality to the externaliza-tion of hidden emotional life, the expressionists increased the demands made on the director. In the absence of a social definition of what was universal or elemental, he alone could define these qualities in the theatrical experience.

Adolphe Appia, Swiss designer and theoretician, made the Wag-nerian ideal the touchstone for a comprehensive scrutiny of theatre art. He suggested that "to derive a play from music does not mean that musical sounds must themselves be the source of the dramatic idea, but merely that the object of music should also be the object of that idea. It is an *interiorization* of the dramatic emotion, prompted by the assurance that music will furnish the means of expressing all that hidden life unhampered." The "hidden life" was too complex to be revealed by the realistic theatre of conversation. Appia's *art vivante* demanded emotional participation such as he admired in the antique theatre. His basic question was: "How can we once more live art instead of merely contemplating works of art?"

In translating this philosophical concern into technical exposition, Appia laid the groundwork for modern stage practice. Although it is impossible here to outline all the theatrical issues with which he was concerned, we can suggest his chief preoccupation. How, he asked, can theatre be turned into a "supreme union of all art" when the various theatrical elements are irreconcilably divided into time and space arts? In the actor's movement, controlled by the discipline of music, he found the connection between time and space. In light Appia saw the living medium which could bring into a single emotional plane the perpendicular scenery, the horizontal floor and the moving actor. "Only light and music," he wrote, "can express 'the inner nature of all appearance!' "

Basic to Appia's complex theoretical and technical explorations was the concept of a single artist controlling the interaction of light, music and movement. Ideally, he pointed out in *L'Oeuvre d'art vivante*, the author-director is this artist. "It is a sacrilege," he wrote, "to specialize these two functions." In modern theatre, however, the traditional "artist of the theatre" did not seem able to exercise both functions. "There is only one way to emerge from this blind alley," Appia asserted in his *Staging Wagnerian Drama*, "and that is to entrust the entire interpretation of the drama to a single person."

In *Die Musik und die Inscenierung* (1895) Appia assigned that interpretation to the director. "The man we call director today," he wrote, "whose job consists in merely arranging completed stage sets, will, in poetic drama, play the role of a despotic drillmaster who will have to understand how much preliminary study stage setting requires, utilize every element of scenic production in order to create an artistic synthesis, reanimate everything under his control at the expense of the actor, who must eventually be dominated. Whatever he does will to a great extent depend upon his individual taste; he must work both as an experimenter and as a poet, play with his scenic materials but at the same time be careful not to create a purely personal formula. . . . He will be very like the leader of an orchestra; his effect will be a similarly magnetic one."

Appia was not the first to insist on the need for a director, but he was the first to bind him to the aesthetic program for a living theatre. Yet it was not his fortune to be the recognized herald of a new era. The synthetic ideal and the new synthesizing artist were popularized by a less rigorous thinker but more effective propagandist.

Gordon Craig was the evangelist of the "new movement." In 1905 he sounded the clarion call in *The Art of the Theatre*. Here Craig declared: "The art of the theatre is neither acting nor the play, it is not scene nor dance, but it consists of all the elements of which these things are composed: action, which is the very spirit of acting; words, which are the body of the play; line and color, which are the very heart of the scenes; rhythm, which is the very essence of dance." Only an "artist of the theatre" could master "actions, words, lines, color, and rhythm." By his mastery this artist "would restore the art of the theatre to its home by means of his own creative genius." In Craig's manifesto the director became the alchemist of theatre.

In his magical laboratory the artist of the theatre would unite performance and audience by rhythmic incantation. Craig said: "The theatre was for the people, and always for the people. The poets would make theatre for the select dilettanti. They would put difficult psychological thoughts before the public expressed in difficult words, and would make for this public something which was impossible for them to understand, and unnecessary for them to know; whereas the theatre must show them sights, show them life, show them beauty, and not speak in difficult sentences." In place of sentences made difficult by the absence of common values, Craig offered patterns of light, color and movement. "The theatre of the future will be a theatre of visions, not a theatre of sermons nor a theatre of epigrams ... an art which says less yet shows more than all; an art which is simple for all to understand it feelingly; an art which springs from movement, movement which is the very symbol of life."

Because his cry voiced the malaise of all theatre workers, Craig's manifestoes, though intensely personal, became the common language of an international movement. His own productions were few and never completely successful. His romantic nocturnal sketches were basically impractical as scenic designs. Even the manifestoes were contradictory and often illogical. Craig himself was not oblivious to the pitfalls of his neurotic perfectionism. A caption to a design called

SELF-PORTRAIT (1919). WOODCUT BY GORDON CRAIG. (FROM *Edward Gordon Craig* BY JANET LEEPER.)

"Wapping Old Stairs" reads: "Quite an impossible scene; that is to say, impossible to realize on a stage. But I wanted to know for once what it felt like to be mounting up impossible ladders and beckoning to people to come up after me." Few were able or wanted to climb "impossible ladders," but the challenge to make the climb had to be taken up. Stanislavsky invited Craig to the Moscow Art Theatre; Brahm let him work at the Lessing Theatre; Reinhardt learned from him; Copeau drew sustenance from him. The theatrical world was shaken by an ineffectual dreamer.

Craig more than anyone else insisted that the rediscovery of the art of theatre must grow out of research and experimentation, unhampered by the limitations of the commercial stage. He propagandized for a school, for "new lives—new habits—a new order of work." In 1913 he himself founded a school at the Arena Goldoni in Florence. For one fateful year the master and some thirty students lived in an atmosphere of "new sights and sounds . . . to breed . . . new feelings, new thoughts . . . and open eyes." "After that," Craig exclaimed, "it only remains for the dramatic spirit to honor us by appearing in our midst." The outbreak of World War I closed Craig's school. But the fruitful impetus rather than the actual accomplishment, in this as in most of his work, was what mattered. Research, study, experimentation in a new fresh atmosphere became the ideal.

In directorial procedure Craig exemplified a new emotional approach. In 1926 when he went to Denmark to stage Ibsen's *The Pretenders* for Johannes Poulsen, he explained his working methods: "In preparing a production I proceed in an illogical manner and try to perceive things feelingly, rather than thinkingly. . . . I reach out and touch a play with my left hand, as it were, and try to receive the thing through my senses, and then make some note with my right hand which will record what it is I have felt. Though I have found that I have often had to revise the first impression . . . I continue to employ this method because I have so often found that this sensitive way of touching a piece—when it is a real piece—is more illuminating to me than to stop and begin thinking it over at once. Thinking comes afterwards. Thinking is for practical purposes. I think out a method of making clear to the spectator what I have felt and seen."

Craig's subjective method is evident, for example, in his conversations with Stanislavsky concerning the character of Ophelia in his interpretation of *Hamlet* for the Moscow Art Theatre. Craig insisted that Ophelia was "an insignificant creature." To Stanislavsky's question "Why then was Hamlet in love with her?" Craig replied: "He was in love with his own imagination, with an imaginary woman." "I'm afraid then," Stanislavsky countered, "we shall have to explain it to the audience during one of the intervals." Otto Brahm, in examining one of Craig's designs for *Venice Preserved*, asked: "Where is the door?" He received the characteristic reply: "There is no door; there is a way in and out."

Hamlet: "Lights, lights, lights." (1927) Woodcut by Gordon Craig. (From *Edward Gordon Craig* by Janet Leeper.)

Although both Craig and Appia were in quest of integrated, living theatre, their primary impact was on the scenic arts. The designs of both men, rather than their theoretical justifications, set a generation dreaming. Scenic illusion has always been the easiest theatrical component to shape to new purposes. The synthetic movement, which produced no new plays and no new actors, reduced itself to a scenic reform in which suggestive simplicity covered with a "veil of light or darkness" the clumsy literalism of the naturalist's "tasteless parlor." Expressionism, like naturalism, became a technique of staging. It could be used, as Sheldon Cheney once complained, by an astute commercial manager who was unaware of and indifferent to the aesthetic values of which the staging was to be the mere outer form.

Neither naturalism nor expressionism succeeded in the perhaps impossible task of imposing a single point of view—either objective or subjective—on the theatre of an age whose distinguishing quality was its multiplicity of views. The failure of these partial perspectives led to an eclectic theatre in which the director was the sole creator of significant form. In the "theatrical" theatres of Jacques Copeau, Max Reinhardt and Vsevolod Meyerhold the director reached the acme of his powers.

Both as practicing director and as theorist, the ascetic Jacques Copeau revealed in their finest and most dedicated form all the preoccupations of the artist of the theatre. In founding the Vieux Colombier in 1913 Copeau wanted to bring together "under the direction of one man, a troupe of young, disinterested, and enthusiastic players" whose ambition was to *serve* the art to which they had devoted themselves. The creative director was essential for the unity of which Copeau so frequently spoke. In a letter to Louis Jouvet, his co-worker and *régisseur* (stage manager), Copeau wrote: "I would put all the books under lock and key, to forbid you to use them (that bothers you, eh?).... The science of the past, it is I who will absorb it, who will direct it, who will clarify it and who will transmit it to you little by little, all fresh, all new, pell-mell with the personal godsend of my unpublished science. No substitution. A creation. Life."

Copeau's unpublished science involved more than the synthesis of theatrical arts. "Nothing is easier," he wrote, "than to relate artistically the dimension, the decoration, the lighting, etc., of the stage to the character and requirements of each play we produce." But he declared: "That is not my ambition.... It will never bring about a renovation or transformation of the scenic *life*."

What Copeau sought was "a certain emancipation" which involved first of all a clear understanding of the director-author relationship in modern theatre. "It is true," he wrote, "that creating a dramatic work in words and actually mounting it on the stage with live actors are but two phases of one and the same intellectual operation." Aeschylus, Shakespeare and Molière illustrate this single artistic creativity. But Copeau revealed that "in our day the playwright is usually a master who has let slip the instrument of his mastery." He must therefore turn to the director, who is a specialist in methods of interpretation.

Since Copeau saw the poet alone as "the true origin and life of all drama as Aeschylus was of Greek drama," he insisted that "the director must capture the spirit of the primitive unity of drama and incorporate its rhythm in his work." He described the virtues of the director as "sincerity and modesty, maturity, reflection, eclecticism; he does not invent ideas, he recovers them. His role is to translate the author, to read the text, to feel the inspiration of it, to possess it as a musician reads notes and sings them at the first sight."

Unlike some of his peers, Copeau did not deny the playwright's text, substituting for it pure stage technique. Although this led to the accusation that he was excessively literary, Copeau's attachment to the play was not at all literary. He saw the play itself in a new theatrical light. What Appia found in the precise definitions of musical nota- tion, Copeau found in plays themselves, which, he said, contained "time-spans—movements and rhythms—comparable to those in music, and as in music, capable of engendering space." He discovered a "stage economy that corresponds to dramatic economy; a performing style engendered by a literary style."

Copeau believed that the physical structure of the theatre could "heighten and enhance the intellectual structure of a play." This led him to evolve a stage which has been called the first presentational playhouse in the modern world. By using a permanent architectural background and a small platform—*un tréteau nu*—as his playing space, he felt that "the *décor* was replaced by a device which by itself, by its presence, was already action, which materialized the form of the action." This functional playing area was brought into direct contact with the audience by the removal of footlights and proscenium.

To achieve all these objectives was no easy task. Although Copeau's productions were more beautiful and more meaningful than others on the French stage, Copeau himself never felt satisfied. He considered his work only the first step in what he called "our conscientious researches." "Theatre cannot remain living unless it remains an *atelier*," he insisted. In the prospectus of the Vieux Colombier school Copeau endorsed Craig's belief that only out of new training and new conditions of work would a new scenic life appear. In the syllabus for the school he offered unity of doctrine, unity of direction, unity of teaching, based in part on music and in part on the old rhythms and forms of the antique theatre. To Copeau such research was more

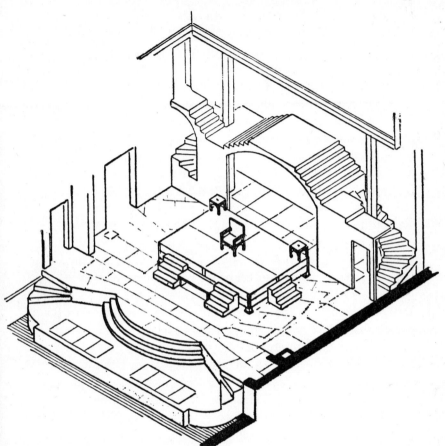

COPEAU'S STAGE AT THE VIEUX COLOMBIER. DRAWING BY LOUIS JOUVET.
(FROM *Twentieth Century Stage Decoration* BY W. R. FUERST
AND SAMUEL J. HUME.)

important than successful production. He therefore allowed the Vieux
Colombier to disintegrate while he went off with a small group of
devoted disciples, *les Copiaux,* to continue his lifelong quest for theatrical renovation.

While Copeau sought the "idea of a theatre" in dramatic rhythm
and in a permanent architectural stage, his renowned contemporary

Max Reinhardt took the other path open to the modern director. Surrendering to the multifarious conflicting preoccupations of modern man, Reinhardt never regarded the form of theatre as set. In his long years of productivity he used techniques which, culled from all stages of history, ran the gamut of theatrical invention.

No characteristic of Reinhardt more astounded the theatrical world than the rich diversity of his productions. No one style, no one method of decoration or interpretation, no one point of view animated his many theatres. In one of his few published utterances Reinhardt defended his catholicity: "It would be a theory as barbaric as it is incompatible with the principles of theatrical art, to measure with the same yardstick, to press into the same mold, the wonderful wealth of the world's literature. The mere suggestion of such an attempt is an example of pedantic scholasticism. There is no one form of theatre which is the only true artistic form." For Reinhardt "all depends on realizing the specific atmosphere of the play, and on making the play live." How did Reinhardt make his plays live in the absence of some accepted idea of what the theatre is and does, in the absence of a point of view shared by dramatist, director and audience?

The slogan "The theatre belongs to the theatre" epitomizes Reinhardt's accomplishment. He offered audiences theatre for theatre's sake. Like modern poets and painters, Reinhardt wanted to exploit the intrinsic qualities of his medium. He was able to achieve any and every theatrical effect by carefully organizing and arranging his materials—play, actors, mass movement, music, light, stage space, and auditorium.

The great Reinhardt *Regiebuch* contains his dexterous use of the theatrical medium. In it, wrote Arthur Kahane, his literary adviser and spokesman, Reinhardt gives "physical form to the text, describing in the most minute detail and in a continuous series all situations, positions, and expressions. Thus by the very reality of his technical means, he remodels and reworks the entire drama, provides lyric paraphrases, scenic directions, and hints for the actor. When this book is finished, the first picture of the entire work stands ready before his eyes; also the entire plan for the ensuing preparations, for the dramaturgy, for the music, for the distribution and studying of the parts." Reinhardt's

Regiebuch represents "a complete, detailed paraphrase of the play in the stage manager's language."

Rehearsals, Reinhardt told Morton Eustis, were a "period of adjustment" in which all participants in the production were, "in some manner, adapted to his own conception of the play," a conception recorded in the *Regiebuch*. Reinhardt came to rehearsals with his corps of

NOTATION FROM FIRST PAGE OF REINHARDT'S *Regiebuch* FOR *Danton's Death*. (BY COURTESY OF WILLIAM W. MELNITZ.)

régisseurs "all laden with books," as R. Ben Ari described it on the basis of his experience as a Reinhardt actor, and he molded the performance in the light of the detailed notes of his master plan.

In the elaborate Reinhardt workshop the dramatist's text was no longer the primary material. It had become merely one of many theatrical ingredients. In *Sumurun* and *The Miracle* he dispensed with words completely. Reinhardt's influence on most writers was bad, observed Richard Beer-Hofmann, for they depended on Reinhardt to fill in what their meager imaginations could not supply. Reinhardt rather liked incomplete, imperfect plays, said Beer-Hofmann, "for he found therein the opportunity to do what he wished in the depth of his heart to do, and did: Be a poet or at least collaborate in the creation of poetry."

For the actor the Reinhardt touch was a hypnotic one. "He tortures us, he drives us forward, he resolves every doubt," said Gertrude Eysoldt. According to Morton Eustis, at early rehearsals Reinhardt treated his actors "almost as if they were puppets, controlling every movement and gesture, the slightest change in intonation, impressing the stamp of his personality on them collectively and individually until they [were] molded into his own conception of the roles."

Lacking a sanctioned image of what theatre is and does, Reinhardt made the theatre his world and the world his theatre. In Berlin, London and New York, theatres were turned into Gothic cathedrals for *The Miracle*, and at Salzburg he turned the cathedral into a theatre for *Jedermann*. To him, Kahane wrote, the theatre was not "the willing servant of literature, satisfied with producing preconceived scenes in as correct and intelligible a manner as possible." It was "a thing in itself, following its own laws, its own path, a *theatrum mundi*." To him every new production was a new world which he created with "its own lights and shadows, its own beauty and ugliness, its heaven and its hell."

Nothing suggests so forcibly the relationship of the modern director to his antique predecessors as this panegyric to the Reinhardtian theatre. Here was the rediscovery of theatre, but revolutionary changes in society had robbed the rediscovery of significant meaning. In the past, theatre had been a world with its Heaven and its Hell, but it was a microcosm, a mirror of the real world, not a purely theatrical concoction whose references to the larger world were tenuous and vapid.

Reinhardt actually tried to reproduce the antique theatre in his Grosses Schauspielhaus, hoping that this "Theatre of the Five Thousand" could contain modern life as once the great arena had contained the Greek community. "Under the influence of these mighty spaces, these big, severe lines," Kahane explained, "all that is small and petty

INTERIOR VIEW OF THE GROSSES SCHAUSPIELHAUS.

disappears, and it becomes a matter of course to appeal to the hearts of great audiences with the strongest and deepest elements. The petty and unimportant—elements that are not eternal in us—cease to have effect. The theatre can only express the great eternal elemental passions and the problems of humanity. In it spectators cease to be mere spectators; they become the people; their emotions are simple and primitive, but great and powerful, as becomes the eternal human race."

Without a traditional way of life, without a myth, without a ritual attitude to sustain it this theatre was doomed to failure. What successes it did have in its brief existence under Reinhardt were the successes of a director who played on very generalized emotions through the theatrical devices of light, color, mass movement and music. Huntly Carter asked of Reinhardt's production of *Oedipus*: "If Reinhardt is not giving us Greek drama, what is he giving us? The reply is Reinhardtism—an essence of drama of his own distilling."

The personal distillation of the director was the modern substitute for the whole complex of social and theatrical factors that had once made theatre the great collective art. Reinhardt illustrates this process in its baroque, Wagnerian aspect. Vsevolod Meyerhold illustrates it in its constructivist, Marxian aspect.

Different as their theatres were, Reinhardt and Meyerhold have much in common. Both, for example, began as actors under great naturalist directors—Reinhardt under Brahm, Meyerhold under Stanislavsky. Both experimented with expressionist drama; both went on to attempt a new social integration—Reinhardt in the Theatre of the Five Thousand, Meyerhold in the Theatre of the Revolution.

Meyerhold's revolt early in the century against the naturalism of Stanislavsky inevitably led him to follow the director's métier. In place of naturalism's "morbid human curiosity," Meyerhold wanted symbolic expression of life. Since there were no conventional or traditional symbols available, Meyerhold, as *régisseur*, had to invent them. In place of naturalism's attempt to reproduce reality of detail Meyerhold wanted to "point the irony of a situation." Since there was no accepted framework in which to place theatrical situations, Meyerhold had to impose his own point of view. Instead of naturalism's "intelligent reader" Meyerhold wanted actors who could convey ideas technically. Since there was no frankly *theatrical* technique Meyerhold had to invent it and teach it to his actors. For well over a quarter of a century—through the Revolution and the first decades of the Soviets—Meyerhold tried to create a modern equivalent of the vital, symbolic, *theatrical* theatres of the past.

Meyerhold's directorial art, like the acting of the old Italian comedians he admired, was an improvised one. He prepared no *Regiebuch*. He told Harold Clurman: "I am able to keep everything quite clearly in my head. Anyhow, I am likely to stage a scene one way and days later come to rehearsal and change the staging completely. For me every rehearsal is a sketch." Each improvised effect, however, was dictated by an exacting sense of form. Meyerhold conceived production in terms of musical analogies. *The Inspector-General*, for example, was planned along the lines of a sonata. Each new improvisation was then a variation on a theme. Norris Houghton, in *Moscow Rehearsals*, remarks: "One line may become the motivation for five minutes of cadenzas which the virtuosity of Meyerhold will have invented, before the theme—that is, the text of the play—is continued."

Here is Meyerhold talking to the actors at the first rehearsal of a proposed program of three Chekhov one-acters—*The Proposal*, *The Bear* and *The Jubilee*—as recorded by Houghton: "Two things are essential for a play's production, as I have often told you. First, we must find the thought of the author; then we must reveal that thought in a theatrical form. This form I call a *jeu de théâtre* and around it I shall build the performance. Molière was a master of *jeux de théâtre*: a central idea and the use of incidents, comments, mockery, jokes—anything to put it over. In this production I am going to use the technique of the traditional vaudeville as the *jeu*. Let me explain what it is to be. In these three plays of Chekhov I have found that there are thirty-eight times when characters either faint, say they are going to faint, turn pale, clutch their hearts, or call for a glass of water; so I am going to take this idea of fainting and use it as a sort of leitmotif for the performance. Everything will contribute to this *jeu*."

Both the play and the actors were mere raw material for Meyerhold's art. The text took a position subordinate to his *jeu*, his creative business. One Russian commentator suggested that Meyerhold's production of *The Inspector-General* "should be called Meyerhold's mental associations apropos *The Inspector-General*." In rehearsing scenes from this most famous of his productions Meyerhold kept his brigade of *régisseurs* busy recording business for a character who had no lines at all in Gogol's text. On the programs of his theatre Meyerhold's name appeared as "author of the spectacle."

To realize his conception of a play Meyerhold used his actors as a sculptor uses clay. The actor's objective was to be pliable in order to become the living embodiment of Meyerhold's ideas. In his school they were prepared for this task. There each day's work began with practice in "bio-mechanics," stage movement, that gave Meyerhold's actors "the trained body, the well-functioning nervous system, correct reflexes, vivacity and exactness of reaction, the control of one's body." All that Meyerhold wanted of actors in addition to this training was "a certain talent for music and a certain amount of intelligence."

VSEVOLOD MEYERHOLD. CARICATURE BY KUKRINIKSI.

Since Meyerhold was the sole creative artist in his theatre, the work of art was the rehearsal, not the performance. At rehearsals one could see "a full production as well as a fascinating performance," observed a young Russian director, Yuri Zavadsky. The actual performance, Zavadsky suggested, was like "great music wheezed out on a barrel-organ. . . . Each repeated presentation of a production more and more 'forgets' its creator, Meyerhold."

What makes Meyerhold so fascinating a figure in the directorial history we have been sketching is the fact that out of his own creativity he had rediscovered the use of symbols and the vigorous theatricality that had once made theatre the great public art. Then unique social circumstances gave him unrestricted opportunity to experiment. Liberated by the Russian Revolution from the demands of established taste, Meyerhold was authorized to evolve a significant dramatic form for a new audience in a "new" society. He was the logical choice to inaugurate a "theatrical October" in emulation of the "political October." In the early days of the Soviets, theatre again became an art at the center of the life of its time, and Meyerhold, as the artist of the Revolution, rallied actor and audience around collective sentiments. Messages from the fighting front interrupted the performance that prefigured in theatrical symbols the new social life.

Despite seemingly propitious circumstances, Meyerhold's continued search for vital theatrical conventions never culminated in a persisting idea of theatre. The "Picasso of theatre," as Louis Lozowick calls him, Meyerhold experimented with endless inventiveness. "His whole career," Norris Houghton suggests, "seems to have been a search for a style which would completely satisfy him. He has never found the perfect form." Meyerhold was seemingly in a race with his own brilliant eclecticism, and the audience could not keep up the pace. A more stabilized society self-consciously turned to the past for its tradition, and after twenty years of theatrical *jeux* the innovator was stripped of his theatre and faced with the insupportable charge of "distorting the classics." The proletarian theatre, of which he was at first the sole prophet, rejected him. His art remains the lonely, brilliant creation of the visionary director.

The great directors stand pre-eminent because of the grandeur of their vision or the magnitude of their accomplishment, but many others contributed significant ideas and practices to make the modern theatre the theatre of the director. In Russia, for example, Vladimir Nemirovich-Danchenko, co-founder with Stanislavsky of the Moscow Art Theatre, was more than the partner with the "literary veto" who brought the plays of Chekhov to the theatre. He was a practicing director who, for example, handled more rehearsals of the initial Art Theatre production of *The Sea Gull* than Stanislavsky himself. In his autobiography, *My Life in the Russian Theatre*, Nemirovich-Danchenko defined the *régisseur* as "a triple-faced character: 1. The *régisseur*-interpreter, who instructs *how* to play, so that it is possible to call him the *régisseur*-actor or the *régisseur*-pedagogue. 2. The *régisseur*-mirror, reflecting the individual qualities of the actor. 3. The *régisseur*-organizer of the entire production. The public," continued Nemiro-vich-Danchenko, "knows only the third, because he alone is visible in everything; in the *mise en scènes,* in the designs, in the sounds, in the

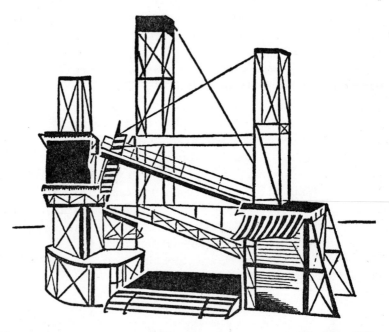

Constructivist setting for Tairov's production of *The Man Who Was Thursday* (1923). (From *New Theatres for Old* by Mordecai Gorelik.)

lighting, in the harmony of the crowd scenes. The *régisseur*-interpreter and the *régisseur*-mirror, however, are invisible. They have sunk themselves into the actor."

Alexander Tairov stood outside the Art Theatre company, although his actress-wife, Alice Koonen, came from its ranks. At his Kamerny Theatre, Tairov experimented with projects for a "theatre unbound" in which heroic gesture and formalized rhythm would replace the facsimile naturalism of Stanislavsky. So personal and autocratic was his fascinating theatre, however, that unlike the other Russian pioneers, Tairov had no artistic progeny.

From the polar giants, Stanislavsky and Meyerhold, however, came a young director who tried to mediate between the latter's theatricality and the former's "truth of inner experience." Eugene Vakhtangov, one of Stanislavsky's best pupils, projected a new theatre which, built on the accomplishments of his precursors, would yet be suited to the needs of the socialist society. He proposed a theatrical collective in place of the autocratic director for a collectivist society. It was his disciples, among them Boris E. Zakhava, who translated Vakhtangov's ideals into a theatrical structure. At the Vakhtangov Theatre they practiced a directorial procedure consonant with socialistic ideals, but one which might be used by individualistic groups. The theatre collective would decide what plays were to be produced, and then would assign to one of their several directors the play most suited to his special talents. Before actual production work was begun, the chosen director would submit to the collective a formal, standardized report on his plans for the play. Actor and author, if possible, discussed with the director his ideas, and then either accepted or rejected them. If accepted or acceptably revised, the plans would then first be put into operation. Yet even at this point the director's control did not become absolute, for rehearsals began with round-table discussions by the actors on interpretation of roles. They contributed their ideas to those outlined by the director. Only then, scene by scene, section by section, did the play assume its theatrical form under the supervision of the director but with the co-operation and consultation of the whole theatre.

One of Meyerhold's pupils, Nikolai Okhlopkov, also tried to synthesize the Meyerhold and Stanislavsky approaches in the light of new social needs. In the arena of his Realistic Theatre he sought an emotional union in which "actor and spectator must clasp hands in fraternity." Okhlopkov stated his aims in the following words: "Thus we assert the realism of the theatre through theatrical means, appealing to the imagination of the spectator and at the same time providing it with a powerful stimulus. Thus the audience co-operates with the actors in every performance, so that the actor applauds the audience as well as the audience the actor."

In Germany it was not only Brahm and Reinhardt who prepared the way for later directors, but also early innovators like Georg Fuchs. At his Kuenstler Theater in Munich, Fuchs, like Appia and Craig, invoked rhythm as the primal element capable of reviving the ritualistic theatre of communal exaltation. He constructed a "relief stage," a shallow platform that thrust the actors forward to the audience, as his solution to the international quest for closer union between stage and auditorium.

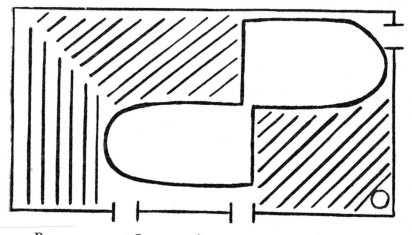

PLAYING AREA OF OKHLOPKOV'S ARENA STAGING OF *Aristocrats*.

During the twenties Leopold Jessner seemed a successor to Reinhardt in his forceful theatricality. But Jessner distinguished his art from what he called the "impressionism" of Reinhardt as well as from the realism of the Meininger-Brahm tradition. Jessner offered a concentrated, intense theatre of symbols in place of the detailed, formless verisimilitude of the realists or the subtle illusion of Reinhardt. He felt that theatre, the unique amalgam of many arts, expressed with special urgency the whole modern search for fresh means of artistic expression. He insisted that new forms in theatre could be created only by the will of the *régisseur*, who had the right to rearrange each text in accordance with his theatrical interpretation.

The actual practice of the theatre of symbols is suggested in Jessner's commentary on his most famous production, *Richard III*, in which all the major action was played on an enormous stairway (the *Jessner-treppen*) that occupied the whole center of the stage: "Gloucester's coronation takes place on this staircase, which is entirely covered in red, the color of blood. On the highest step the newly crowned King stands. At his feet the courtiers gather, not any more the historical presentation of the courtiers of that time, but symbols of a uniform society, numbed by nepotism, all in blood-red gowns. The following battle scenes are also enacted on this staircase, symbolized by the rhythm of countless drums behind the stage. This is not to give the illusion of an actual battle, but to show its dynamic tension. Even the costumes are symbolic. The party of Richmond, the army which fights for truth, is clothed in white. The warriors of Richard, who shed blood for blood's sake, are dressed in red. This significant performance found the strongest expression of its inner laws in the scene of the breakdown. Richard III sways down the same red stairs on which he stood in the zenith of his glory, a king, now half undressed, torn, confused, already insane, and at the bottom he is killed by the white warriors."

At the great Volksbuehne, whose artistic roots went back to Brahm, Juergen Fehling and Erwin Piscator carried on the process of directorial innovation. Fehling made his mark there with his startling production of Ernst Toller's expressionistic *Masse-Mensch*, and through the twenties Fehling continued to serve theatre with an art that, in the words of Julius Bab, was "clarified and strengthened through expressionism until only the spiritual [stood] out." Erwin Piscator challenged Volksbuehne audiences from 1924 to 1927 with his daring exploitation of unusual stage devices—conveyor belts, slides, charts—in the cause of a political idea. Later in the United States he continued experimentation to achieve a "new reality" and "new objectivity" in theatre.

Bertolt Brecht, playwright-poet-director, transformed a political ideology into a new theatre aesthetic. The Epic Theatre, largely his creation as director and theorist, is one of the few current efforts to evolve a distinctively modern idea of a theatre. In his *A Little Organum for the Theatre* Brecht poses the basic question: "What is the productive attitude toward nature and society which we children of a scientific age can accept with pleasure in our theatre?" Brecht recognizes the great social change which has made the old theatrical unity impossible. He insists that "society has no common mouthpiece as long as it is split into struggling classes. For art to be unpartisan means only that it belongs to the ruling party." Brecht calls for a point of

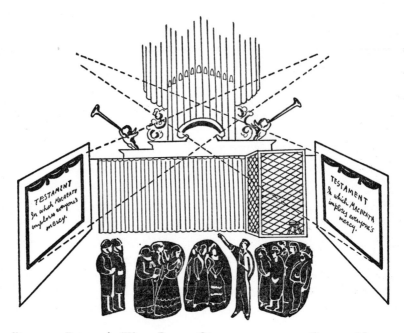

BERTOLT BRECHT'S *Three-Penny Opera* DESIGNED BY CASPAR NEHER. SKETCH BY MORDECAI GORELIK AFTER A PHOTOGRAPH.

view that is chosen "outside the theatre." He invokes alienation in place of empathy since his objective is to "astonish" the audience into a realization that "society is susceptible of change."

As a practicing director Brecht works with his personal version of a *Regiebuch*, the *Modell*, in which the form of a particular play is crystallized by interpretive comment and a minute photographic record. Brecht uses all the varied theatrical arts to achieve his new purpose.

"Let us call in all the sister arts but not in order to produce a composite art work (*Gesamtkunstwerk*) in which they all surrender and lose themselves. They should, together with the art of acting, promote the common task each in his own way. Their intercourse with each other consists in reciprocal alienation."

In France, Antoine and Copeau provided the basic training for succeeding theatrical generations. Firmin Gémier, a director who sought inspiration in antiquity and the Middle Ages, was one of Antoine's early co-workers. He attacked the purely literary view of drama, seeking "to create an atmosphere where each assisting celebrant communes with his neighbors and the author in a sort of social religion." The phrases of the great playwrights, he asserted, "are like caskets which one must open so that their soul is liberated and displays itself in action. That is why the text does not entirely contain them. They absolutely demand the stage and *mise en scène*."

Gaston Baty, who worked with Gémier, also revolted against *Sire le Mot*. He countered the criticism that he treated great dramatic works only as "pretexts" for his imagination by saying: "A text cannot say everything. It can go only as far as all words can go. Beyond them begins another zone, a zone of mystery, of silence, which one calls the atmosphere, the *ambiance*, the climate, as you wish. It is that which it is the work of the director to express."

Georges Pitoëff, who worked with Baty, Louis Jouvet and Charles Dullin as a theatrical *Cartel des Quatre*, wanted to project on his stage what he called "*une autre vérité*," the impalpable essence of things. "With realism," as he notes, "it was sufficient to copy life exactly. With what can the new *mise en scène* be compared? With imaginary truth? That is not easy. It is necessary to have confidence, to believe and not to know. It is almost in the domain of religion." His productions were therefore schematized and abstract rather than detailed and realistic.

Dullin, Jouvet and Jean-Louis Barrault owe their inspiration primarily to Copeau, as does Michel Saint-Denis, who has been working in England. Dullin tried to achieve at his Atelier what Copeau had sought at the Vieux Colombier, to create "a living organism having its function in modern society, responsive to the preoccupations, the enthusiasms of everyone." His theatre was a school in which playwrights and actors learned, in the words of his pupil Barrault, a "method" rather than a "métier."

Jouvet, who had been Copeau's stage manager, preserved in his own Théâtre Athénée the artistic taste and poetic distinction of his mentor. But Jouvet came to feel that the search for laws of theatre and of directing, to which Copeau had devoted his efforts, was of little avail. On the publication of Copeau's *mise en scène* for *Les Fourberies de Scapin* Jouvet declared: "The art of the director is an art of adjusting to

JEAN-LOUIS BARRAULT IN *Baptiste*. DRAWING BY MAYO.

contingencies. It isn't a profession, it is a state. One is a director as one is a lover. The varieties are infinite."

Barrault, now the leading French director, stems from Copeau via Dullin and Etienne Decroux, master of mime. His graceful and eclectic art has brought new life to the classical tradition of the Comédie-Française and has given a receptive stage to his contemporaries. Barrault has stated the aims of his company in these words: ". . . from the classics we seek nourishment, through the study of gesture and speech we hope to perfect our technique, by periodic excursions into the unknown we hope to enrich ourselves, and all in *the service of modern authors."* The spirit of Copeau's quest still echoes in the pages of Barrault's *Reflections on the Theatre*, but one feels, as Harold Clurman observed in a review of this book, that Copeau's "comprehensive feeling for theatre as a craft and a cultural instrument" has given place to the more immediate problems of tasteful staging of individual plays.

In England and the United States the director has never assumed the completely dominant position of his European counterpart. In England the actor-producer tradition has lived on nobly from Henry Irving to John Gielgud and Laurence Olivier, who have enriched it by the social and artistic spirit that informed their early years at the Old Vic. Tyrone Guthrie, who was also associated with the vigorous endeavors of the Old Vic, now endows productions throughout the world with his refined artistry. It is interesting to note that the only Englishman, apart from Gordon Craig, of course, who stands alongside the early directors is Harley Granville-Barker. He not only set new scenic standards in his productions but also proposed an "exemplary theatre" that would stimulate a reorientation of theatrical life, a mission in part accomplished by the Old Vic.

American directors, in our typical American spirit, have been essentially pragmatic. They have perfected the technical "know-how" absorbed from the European innovators and from indigenous craftsmen like Belasco and Steele MacKaye. Only in the little-theatre movement of the twenties was there widespread interest in the "craft and the cultural instrument." Maurice Browne, who worked at the Chicago Little Theatre, in his essay "The New Rhythmic Drama" offered Americans a new perspective. The seminal ideas and practices of Craig and Reinhardt could be felt in the artistry of Robert Edmond Jones and Norman Bel Geddes. On Broadway, Arthur Hopkins, in using Jones as his collaborating artist, sought to realize his own desire to "make the stage speak with one voice."

The ferment of the thirties added a striking social dimension to the primarily artistic revival of the twenties. The Federal Theatre, for example, in its manifold activities revitalized the theatrical community. Early in the great depression the directors of the Group Theatre—Harold Clurman, Lee Strasberg, Cheryl Crawford—wanted "to say something" with their plays and wanted their productions to be informed by a consistent theatrical technique. They achieved a common artistic point of view with a permanent company trained in the use of the Stanislavsky method. But they soon saw that true unity of production was, in Clurman's words, "antecedent to the formation of the theatre group as such. It [was] a unity of background, of feeling, of thought, of need, among a group of people that [had] formed itself consciously or unconsciously from the undifferentiated masses."

OPERATING ROOM IN THE GROUP THEATRE PRODUCTION OF
Men in White.

In their manifesto "What the Group Theatre Wants" the central concern of the epoch of the director was voiced once again: "In the end, however, the development of playwrights, actors, repertory and the rest are important only as they lead to the creation of a tradition of common values, an active consciousness of a common way of looking at and dealing with life. A theatre in our country today should aim to create an Audience. When an audience feels that it is really at one with a theatre; when audience and theatre-people feel that they are both the answer to one another, and that both may act as leader to one another, there we have the Theatre in its truest form. To create such a Theatre is our real purpose."

It was out of the impulse to create such a theatre that the director originally came into being. The absence of shared values and a casual rather than a consecrated audience meant that integrated theatre could not spontaneously emerge. Missing from our depersonalized society were the collective experiences basic to the theatres that we take as our ideal. The director as a single creative force tried to fabricate the conditions necessary for "Theatre in its truest form." Within the proscenium frame or in the reconstructed arena, he forced the varied theatre arts to blend harmoniously. By his artistic omnipotence he made it possible for the stage to reflect the kaleidoscopic images of modern life. The great directors thus achieved their aspirations on the microcosm of the stage. But they were frustrated by the realm beyond the footlights in their basic intention of restoring the communal idea of theatre. To make these two worlds one remains the challenge of the theatre of tomorrow.

H.K.C.

Part II

VISION AND
METHOD

ဇာ

A NOTE ON TERMINOLOGY

THE person we call the director in the United States, in England is called the producer, in Germany and Russia the *régisseur*. In France, however, *régisseur* refers to the stage manager, while the director is known as the *metteur en scène*.

In the selections which follow, the term *mise en scène* is used interchangeably for staging and production as a whole.

GEORGE II,

DUKE OF SAXE-MEININGEN

(1826-1914)

Pictorial Motion

I N COMPOSING a stage effect, it is important to keep the middle of the picture from being congruent with the middle of the stage. If one follows the geometric principle of the golden mean, the stage divides into two even parts, which is likely to lead to monotony in the distribution and grouping. Assimilation in the total picture becomes more or less symmetrical, creating a wooden, stiff and boring impression.

(The charm of Japanese art can be largely attributed to their avoidance of symmetry. *"L'ennui naquit un jour de l'uniformité,"* Boileau remarked about art in general. In the graphic arts, the uniformity the French esthetes call "the mother of boredom" is symmetry.)

The exception proves the rule; the grouping of the principal figure— or the principal mass of figures—in the center can work out if the neighboring figures or groups are placed on the side at more or less regular intervals. It can create a happy artistic effect, particularly if a powerfully exalted mood is desired. (One is reminded of the Sistine Chapel. There the picture is one of leisurely rest.) But the stage must always depict movement, the continuous unfolding of a story. That is why this method is to be generally avoided, as it creates a lifeless effect and holds up the action.

It rarely works to have a figure dead center. Scenery and other objects are to be placed whenever possible on the sides, of course at a certain distance from the wings, and so as to be visible to the audience.

Quoted by Max Grube: *Geschichte der Meininger*. Stuttgart: Deutsche Verlags-Anstalt, 1926, 51–58.

The actor must never stand dead center, directly in front of the prompter, but always slightly to the left or right of his box.

The middle foreground of the stage, about the width of the prompter's box, from the footlights to the background, should be considered by the actor merely as a passageway from right to left or vice versa; otherwise he has no business there.

Likewise, two actors should avoid standing in similar relation to the prompter's box.

One should give special attention, also, to the relative position of the actor and the scenery. That relation must be correct.

Directors are frequently remiss in not paying enough attention to the actor's relation to the scenery—the trees, buildings, etc., which are painted in perspective. It is of course impossible to be free of all error, since every time a live actor—whose physical proportions are unchanging—takes a step backward, he appears proportionately bigger with respect to the painted sets. But such errors can be kept down to a minimum, and flagrant violations can be avoided.

Thus, when going toward a set depicting a receding street or any other background perspective, the actor should not walk so close that the physical disproportion becomes conspicuous. He should not—as so often is the case—stand directly in front of a painted house, where the door reaches as high as his hips, where without extending himself he can look into the second-story windows, and where, when he raises his arm, he can touch the chimney.

Set pieces toward which the actor must walk should always have at least approximately the correct dimensions relative to the human beings on stage. That is why, for example, the temple in Goethe's *Iphigenie auf Tauris* should be placed 'way downstage so that the pillars, which can extend almost to the top of the flies, tower over the human figures. It is not a question of allowing the audience to get a full view of the temple from top to bottom. It is enough if they can see a part of the colonnade, the end of a joist, and a section of the roof, whereas the rest—the crown of the pediment—can be concealed in the foliage of the trees in the flies.

Similarly, the balcony in *Romeo and Juliet* is usually situated much too low. The fact that Juliet may be a little too high up if the balcony is built at about the proper height is less of a drawback than the conventional way of setting the scene. Usually, when the balcony is rather low, the audience is disturbed at the thought that Romeo, even if he is not an especially good athlete, has only to make one leap to reach his "unattainable" beloved and hold her in his arms.

Actors should never lean against painted pieces of scenery (pillars and the like). If they move about freely, they cannot help touching the painted piece, thus causing it to shake and destroying the stage illusion; if they move about very carefully so as not to disturb the canvas flat, their stage business conveys a feeling of constraint and they perform in an obviously self-conscious manner.

Set pieces on which the actor can lean or sit (such as doorposts, tree trunks, and the like) must be made of resistant materials, and they must be plastic objects. As a matter of fact, this is usually the case in all our better modern theatres today.

When both painted and sculptured pieces are used on the stage, the director should see to it that the different materials employed do not achieve two different effects which are disturbing to the audience. Transitions from natural or artificial flowers to painted ones, for example, must be made with unusual smoothness, so that the one can hardly be distinguished from the other.

It is completely unartistic, even absurd, when, for example, the one rose that has to be plucked from a rosebush is a palpable flower (whether real or artificial) whereas all the rest are painted roses; or when, in the workshop of the *Violin-Maker of Cremona*, one sees a half-dozen violins painted on the back flat together with their shadows and there, right in the midst of them, is the real violin with its real shadow. In addition to everything else, this honest-to-goodness violin seems out of proportion alongside the painted violins and appears to be too large, more like a viola than a violin.

It is a mistake to try to harmonize walk-ons with what is painted in perspective on the flats at the rear of the stage. In the scene of the building of Zwing-Uri in Schiller's *Wilhelm Tell*, for example, youngsters made up and dressed like building workers will not give the impression of adults simply because they are 'way upstage. All the motions and gestures of children are quite different from those of grownups. Moreover, the blurring of contours and the softening of colors, which nature achieves by means of distance and which painting can reproduce, cannot be achieved by live persons moving about on the stage. Living beings are much more sharply defined than painted objects. Hence what the audience sees are not adults reduced in size by the perspective of distance but tiny gnomelike creatures, children made up to look like old men.

Strips of canvas, carefully cut, painted blue, and running diagonally above the stage—in stage parlance, "ozones"—should never be used. In landscape sets, you should always use trees with a broad expanse of branches that arch above the stage picture and set it in relief. Usually, these arched effects can also be used for city, street, or market scenes. Often too the action permits one to string garlands of flowers or flags, pennants, and streamers above streets and squares. If that is not feasible and the sky must appear above the stage, painted clouds in the flies are always preferable to blue strips. Monotonous-looking, ugly blue "ozones" should not be found in any reputable scene designer's storeroom.

Generally, the first rehearsals of a new play with crowd scenes and a large cast make the director's hair stand on end. He almost doubts the possibility of bringing to life and molding this rigid, inflexible mass. It helps him a great deal in this task to have the scenery unchanged from the beginning. Changing the sets, rehanging certain parts of the scenery, moving the furniture during the rehearsals slows up everything, gets on the director's nerves, bores his co-workers and puts them to sleep.

In costume plays, weapons, helmets, arms, swords, etc., must be used as soon as possible, so that the actor is not encumbered by the unusual handling of heavy armor during the performance.

With these plays it is obligatory that the actors rehearse in costume even before the dress rehearsal, which only differs from the opening night by the exclusion of the public. He should wear either his own costume, or if it is not yet ready, or has to be saved, one distinctly similar in cut. The actors must have, for many rehearsals before the dress rehearsal, the same headgear, coats, trains, etc., or at least costumes like the ones they will wear at the performance. The performance should not present the actor with any unforeseen or surprising situation. The spectator must be given the opportunity of becoming accustomed to the unusual apparel of the past. The actor should not, by his appearance or gestures, give the impression of wearing some costume the wardrobe mistress has just handed him; one must not be reminded of a costume ball or a carnival.

Carriage and gestures are influenced by changing from modern clothes to those of the past. Our perfectly familiar way of standing with heels together, which is the accepted one for the military at a halt, and which civilians also use in greeting superior and notable people, looks out of place in older costumes—from the ancient Greek period to the Renaissance—and is completely wrong. This position, heel to heel, seems to have been introduced along with the step of the minuet. A peasant leader cannot stand like an *Abbé galant* from the time of wigs, or with clicked heels, like a lieutenant in a modern drawing room.

The natural, correct and visually satisfying posture in costume from the days of pigtails on, is feet apart and placed one in front of the other.

The general rule is: all parallels on the stage are to be avoided as much as possible. This applies to costume plays in certain ways as well.

Spears, halberds, lances, javelins, etc., should never be carried pointing in the same direction as the modern guns and bayonets of our infantry and cavalry. There should be a certain freedom in the holding of old weapons; they should not be held at even intervals or point in the same direction. Here, they should be made to crowd each other, there be further apart, not perpendicular but at an angle and intersecting.

Any helmet, not antique, worn by an actor must be pulled down over the forehead until only the muscle above the eyebrows is visible. The popular way of wearing it on the back of the head and neck is tenor-style and does not belong in the theatre. Our costumed heroes and lovers are undoubtedly afraid of disturbing their ringlets by pulling a helmet on correctly. But we can't be affected by that!

The use of parallels is particularly bad in relating the position of one actor with another. Since the parallel position of a single person, facing the footlights squarely, is bad; so two or three actors of approximately the same height doing likewise will give a most disagreeable impression.

Nor should an actor move in a parallel line. For example, an actor moving from forward right to left forward should, by imperceptible and subtle means, break the straight line, not the best on the stage, by moving on a diagonal.

If three or more actors play a scene together, they should never be placed in a straight line. They must stand at angles to each other. The space between the individual actors must always be uneven. Regular intervals create a sense of boredom and lifelessness like figures on a chessboard.

It is always an advantage to have an actor touch a piece of furniture or some other near-by object naturally. That enhances the impression of reality.

Should the stage have different levels—steps, an uneven floor strewn with rocks, and the like—the actor must remember to give his posture a rhythmical, living line. He must never stand with both feet on the same step. He should, if there is a stone close by, stand with one foot on it. Should he be walking down stairs and for some reason—such as having to speak a line or notice some object—be obliged to stop, one foot should always be placed lower than the other. By this device, his entire appearance takes on freedom and ease. "One foot off the ground," should be the director's theme song in such cases.

The handling of crowds on the stage requires a special preparation.

Hardly any theatre exists that can afford to use its own personnel as walk-ons. With the exception of the chorus and the so-called supers, among whom there frequently exist some well-trained actors who feel at home on the stage and can act, a considerable crowd has to be used, for whom these rehearsals and performances are only a side line, and who must be paid each time. Among this fluctuating crowd whom the director does not know, occasionally are found a few usable people who can take direction, understand what is said to them and are not too clumsy in rehearsals. Naturally, one also finds a completely unusable element, with whom nothing can be done, who are awkward and ridiculous and who sometimes even follow their own inspiration, want to act their way and cause great disruption. It is the first job of the director to sort out of this crowd, and as soon as possible, the talented from the untalented, separating the goats from the sheep. The doubtful and naïve ones must only serve as padding.

The walk-ons should then be divided into small groups and trained separately.

Each group is then led by an experienced actor or member of the chorus, who acts as "cover" and stands in front of them on the stage. It is in a way the responsibility of this leader to see to it that the group entrusted to him follows orders. He is responsible to the director in seeing that the positions, gestures, etc., are taken at the right moment.

The leader is given cues and certain general directions from the script such as "noise, tumult, murmurs, cries, etc." These are then translated into words by the director and must be learned by heart. These interpolations should naturally be dealt with in various ways and should never be handled in unison.

The job of these leaders is not an easy one. It is a pity and sometimes an artistic error that these "actors" of the group consider their responsibility inferior and unworthy of a real artist. They rid themselves of the job wherever possible, or brush it off and at the performance make obvious their lack of enthusiasm.

At Meiningen, various artists without exception are used as leaders of walk-ons. The amazing effectiveness of first-night performances at Meiningen can be largely attributed to the lively participation of the crowds. This is in contrast to the awkward, wooden apathy of the supers to which we had accustomed ourselves and which makes such a disastrous impression.

The ugly and erroneous positions of individual actors in relation to each other are particularly disturbing in crowd scenes. The chief charm of groups is in the line of the heads. Just as a similarity of posture is to be avoided, so a regularity of height in actors standing near each other is, wherever possible, to be shunned. When it can be done, individuals should stand on different levels. Some can kneel, some stand near by, some bending, some upright. It is effective to have those looking at one person or situation form an uneven semicircle whenever it can be done.

Care must be taken that the actors nearest to the public and seen most by the spectators stand so that their shoulders are in various relations to the footlights. One should remind a walk-on to change his position as soon as he notices himself standing like his neighbor. In a good picture, one finds few figures in the same position or facing the same way. One has to repeat this order to the actors and supers at nearly every rehearsal, as it is continuously forgotten.

Special reminders must be given the supers not to stare at the audience. They do this naturally, since for many of them acting is a new and unusual experience, and their aroused curiosity makes them look around the dark auditorium.

Disturbing events like the removal of dead or wounded people should be "covered," meaning kept as much as possible from the audience's sight. This must not be done by means of a thick impenetrable wall of people, which looks self-conscious and ridiculous. The "cover" must be rather flexible so that one sees enough and not too much of what is taking place and can understand what it is all about.

When the impression of a great crowd is desired, one should place the groups so that the people on the sides are lost in the shadows of the wings. No one in the audience can be permitted to see where the grouping stops. The grouping must give the illusion that other crowds are also forming behind the scene.

ANDRÉ ANTOINE

(1858-1943)

Behind the Fourth Wall

IRST of all, what is directing? One of the most authoritative men of our time, Monsieur Porel, speaking at the International Theatre Congress in 1900, has defined our art in terms that are so precise and well chosen that I feel it a duty and a pleasure to quote his comments:

Without directing, without this respectful and precise science, this powerful and subtle art, many plays would not have come down to us; many comedies would not be understood; many plays would not enjoy success.

To grasp clearly the author's idea in a manuscript, to explain it patiently and accurately to the hesitant actors, to see the play develop and take shape from minute to minute. To watch over the production down to its slightest details, its stage business, even its silences, which are sometimes as eloquent as the written script. To place the bewildered or awkward supernumeraries where they belong and to train them, to bring together in one cast obscure actors and stars. To harmonize all these voices, all these gestures, all these various movements, all these dissimilar things—in order to achieve the right interpretation of the work entrusted to you.

Then, having accomplished this and having methodically done all your preliminary studying in the calm of your library, to take charge of the material side of production. To supervise patiently and accurately the carpenters, scene-painters, costumers, upholsterers, and electricians.

Then when this second part of the job is finished, to fuse it with the first by making the cast perform with real furniture and props. Finally, to view the finished production at arm's length, as a whole. To take into account the tastes and habits of the audience in just the right proportions, to omit anything that may be needlessly dangerous, to cut

André Antoine: "Causerie sur la mise en scène," *La Revue de Paris*, Vol. 10, April 1, 1903, 596–612.

anything that is too long, to eliminate errors of details that are inevitable in any work that is done quickly.

To listen to advice from interested parties, to weigh it in the mind, to decide when to follow and when to reject their advice. Finally, with a quickening of the heart, to open one's hand, give the signal, let the work appear before so many assembled people! It is an admirable profession, is it not? One of the most curious, one of the most fascinating, one of the most subtle in the world!

I shall certainly not make any effort to find a clearer or more artistic formula. In my opinion, modern directing must perform the same function in the theatre as descriptions in a novel. Directing should—as, in fact, is generally the case today—not only fit the action in its proper framework but also determine its true character and create its atmosphere.

This is an important task—and one that is completely new—for which our classical French theatre has done little to prepare us. The result is that, despite the wealth of effort expended these past twenty years, we have not yet formulated any principles, laid down any foundations, established any teaching methods, trained any personnel.

A few independent-minded innovators in the theatre—Montigny, Perrin, and Porel—have shown initiative, under the stress of the growing needs of contemporary stage production. They have begun to break the old molds; but the results have been slow to appear. These results have been paralyzed by throwbacks to classicism in the individuals themselves as well as in the people under them.

Taught by them and under their direct influence, we have been able, for other reasons, to continue the work that was initiated. In my own case, I was influenced by the new needs and new conditions in the freer and more living works submitted to me by my associates in the Théâtre Libre.

I entered the theatre quite late—when I was close to thirty. I was rejected by the Conservatoire to which I had instinctively applied in order to draw inspiration from such masters as Got and Coquelin, whose genius dazzled me. To compensate for my lack of experience, I was fortunate enough not to be weighed down by old traditions or hampered by routine methods. I learned about the theatre by following logic and common sense—as must have been the case in bygone days, when the theatre first developed.

For a long time—some fifteen years—during my spare time as a white-collar employee with a passionate curiosity about things of the theatre, I realized that the actor's "profession" and the complacency of audiences had stifled all simplicity, life, and naturalness—in the matter of directing as well as acting.

Experience is the best teacher. Since everyone around me—playwrights and actors—was new, without preconceived notions or falsified traditions, we did our best in what we felt was the truest, clearest manner. Thus experience and practice preceded theory.

Here I must reiterate: directing is an art that has just been born. Nothing—absolutely nothing—prior to the past century with its theatre of intrigue and situation, led to its flowering.

Without going back to the earliest examples of our dramatic literature—ceremonies that arose from the church and remained solemn events held in the open air—we may say that the classical French theatre did not, for several centuries, need "staging," in the sense in which we use the term.

A simple backdrop was enough to denote a palace, a public square, or a drawing room.

As far as the actor was concerned, often he received a court costume from the king or one of the high nobility (thus, Richelieu gave Bellecoeur a knight's costume in which to create the role of the Cid); and the actor's sole ambition was to appear in a splendid costume before a chosen audience and to recite his part rather than to play it or live it. . . .

Nevertheless, drama continued to evolve. A theatre of intrigue and material situations appeared, a theatre which took into account the social status and daily life of its characters. Unity of place was violated. Figaro leaped through windows and Count Almaviva broke down doors. Hugo published his preface to *Cromwell* and the great Alexandre Dumas joined with him. The Middle Ages replaced antiquity. Tragic episodes and heroic combats were no longer the themes of the stage: Hernani fenced, Saint-Mégrin looked up at the stars before going to see the Duchesse de Guise, and Ruy Blas pushed pieces of furniture in front of the doors of his low-ceilinged room before dying in peace. Géronte, Célimène, and Sganarelle gave way to Marguerite Gautier, Giboyer, and Poirier. Actors ate on the stage, slept there, sat down on their bed to dream—as did Chatterton. Directing was born and thenceforth became a faithful servant of dramatic production.

Acting itself, always lagging, began to change. Frédéric no longer acted in the style of Talma, although he was just as great; and the romantic "white plume"—in reality, a striving for truth, for life—made audiences forget rhetorical declamation of tragedy.

But if you bear in mind Porel's outline of the work that is necessary in producing a play, you can just imagine what ceaseless efforts and what tireless patience are needed in order to achieve truth and life!

Apparently, the audience has no idea of the labor that goes into a play it has just applauded. In the theatre, after the fifth or sixth performance, many persons imagine that the physical arrangement of the scenes and the movements of the characters are left to chance or to the initiative of the actors.

The better the play is acted and the more lifelike it seems, the more convinced is the naïve spectator of this supposition. He has no idea of the slow and complicated work of rehearsals. . . .

Let us begin now at the beginning. The producer, after assigning the actors their parts, gives the script to the director. From that point on, the latter is in charge.

I have purposely made a sharp distinction between these two: the producer and the director. Generally speaking, our producers assume these two functions. But they are quite distinct and require talents that are almost always incompatible.

To be a producer, first of all, is a profession. To be a director—or *metteur en scène*—is an art.

In our time, the profession of producer demands above all the qualities of a manager, a businessman; if, in addition, our producer has a little boldness and, by chance, the desire to hunt for interesting works, if through experience he acquires that special flair for "hits," then he will not find the day long enough for his many tasks.

On the other hand, the director or *metteur en scène* must remain free of any financial worries or calculations. Many producers, taken up with the problems I have just mentioned, have a director on their pay-roll—almost always a veteran actor or one who has not had much success. They use him to sketch out the staging, to do the preliminary work which they probably consider of little interest. They are wrong. They fail to realize that these first hours are crucial: later, when they step into the picture, it is too late. The play has already taken shape and is in a definite mold. Would a painter give someone else the job of drawing the sketch for a picture he wanted to paint?

In other theatres—at the Comédie-Française, for example—one of the actors in the cast, the most "talented" or the most famous, is given the task of conducting rehearsals. This is likewise a bad method: a talented actor is not necessarily endowed with the qualities that make him a good director. Many great artists are often unfit for that job; their personal temperament and the creative instinct which is their forte deprive them of one of the essential faculties of a true director: a view of the whole. No matter how hard he tries, an actor sees only his own part; and if he is the director, unconsciously but nonetheless surely he will increase the scope and importance of that part—to the detriment of all the others. A mediocre actor who is not in the cast is always superior, on the other side of the footlights, to the noted artist playing on the stage.

The difficulty lies in finding artistic men of the theatre who are will-ing to confine themselves to this exciting but obscure work. In some countries, where the value of this teamwork has been more quickly recognized than here in France, the director's name appears on the playbill.

Remember that such a man must have the actors in the palm of his hand and that actors, in Molière's words, are "strange animals to drive." To obtain the maximum from them—not only in effort but also in results—one must know them and live with them. Methods of work and ways of acting differ with each artist, according to his tempera-ment or character. It is a little world all its own, a nervous and im-pressionable world, which has to be now coaxed and now scolded.

Many actors, through negligence or especially because of shyness, use every possible excuse to try to get out of working, as a thoroughbred sometimes refuses to jump over a hurdle. It is quite an art and also a pleasure to persuade them—for they are almost always the most gifted and the most interesting actors.

Others, touchy and vain, must be guided, advised, and convinced without their being aware of it.

In short, directing is a career by itself—an amusing but subtle kind of diplomacy. Then too, when you realize that the director must also understand the author, feel his work, transcribe it, transpose it, and interpret to every one of the actors the part assigned to him, you will understand why I am so keen to see this special kind of career develop in our country, why I am so desirous of developing this personnel which we do not now have. Great producers are not those who have made millions but those I have mentioned above. I prefer to call them great directors, for they have molded artists, developed talents, and created new modes of expression.

The first time I had to direct a play, I saw clearly that the work was divided into two distinct parts: one was quite tangible, that is, finding the right *décor* for the action and the proper way of grouping the characters; the other was impalpable, that is, the interpretation and flow of the dialogue.

First of all, therefore, I found it useful, in fact, indispensable, carefully to create the setting and the environment, without worrying at all about the events that were to occur on the stage. For it is the environment that determines the movements of the characters, not the movements of the characters that determine the environment.

This simple sentence does not seem to express anything very new; yet that is the whole secret of the impression of newness which came from the initial efforts of the Théâtre Libre.

Since our theatre has the bad habit of assigning the actors to their first places in an empty theatre on a bare stage, before the sets are built, we are constantly thrown back on the four or five classic "positions," more or less elaborated according to the director's taste or the scene designer's talent, but always identically the same.

For a stage set to be original, striking, and authentic, it should first be built in accordance with something seen—whether a landscape or an interior. If it is an interior, it should be built with its four sides, its four walls, without worrying about the fourth wall, which will later disappear so as to enable the audience to see what is going on.

Next, the logical exits should be taken care of, with due regard for architectural accuracy; and, outside the set proper, the halls and rooms connecting with these exits should be plainly indicated and sketched. Those rooms that will only be partly seen, when a door opens slightly, should be furnished on paper. In short, the whole house—and not just the part in which the action takes place—should be sketched.

Once this work is done, can you see how easy and interesting it is, after examining the landscape or an interior from every one of its angles, to choose the exact point at which we shall have to cut in order to remove the famous fourth wall, while retaining a set that is most authentic in character and best suited to the action?

It is very simple, is it not? Well, we do not always proceed in that manner—either through negligence, or lack of time, or because we press into service old sets that have been used in other plays. Yet it is only too true that you can never stage a play well in an old set.

Once we have sketched the four-sided plan, according to the method outlined above, it may be that the whole apartment is not absolutely necessary for the action. In modern life, in our living rooms, bedrooms, and studies, the floor plan as well as the nature of our occupations causes us unconsciously to live and work in certain places rather than in others. In winter, we are more apt to gather around a fireplace or a stove; in summer, on the contrary, we are drawn toward the sunlit windows, and we instinctively go there to read or breathe.

You will understand how important these considerations gradually become when you have to build your set. The Germans and the English do not hesitate: they combine, cut, and ingeniously break up space, so as to present in the central portion of the stage picture nothing but the fireplace, window, desk, or corner they need.

These settings—so picturesque, so alive, with such novel and intimate charm—are sadly neglected in France because our scene designers are still influenced, in spite of everything, by the traditional heritage of our classical theatre. They feel that the eye will not tolerate a lack of symmetry.

Their hidebound timidity is all the more inexcusable in that our architects, within the small land areas at their disposal, have built modern houses with unusual designs and broken lines; and to the scene designer these can be an inexhaustible source of picturesqueness and variety.

I shall deliberately pass over the actual building of our set. A detailed study of the various questions involved would lead us too far afield: the use of different woods, of iron, of cloth or paper, and of woodwork in relief, which the English frequently utilize.

Yet I must confess that several experiments I have made have failed to give any appreciable results. Thus, genuine wallpaper, upholstered fabrics, leather, woodwork paneling, expensive and perishable cardboards do not alter the general look of the set much; and frequently, since they light up badly, they simply look as though they were painted.

Nevertheless, ceilings in relief and visible beams give a sense of solidity and weight which was unknown in the make-believe painting of the old stage sets. It is also of considerable practical value, both for the actor's ease of mind and the authenticity of the set, to fashion complete doorframes and window frames. . . .

Now our set is built, with its four bare walls. Before rehearsing his actors on the stage, our director must walk across it many times and conjure up all the action which is to take place on it. He must also furnish it sensibly and logically, decorating it with all the familiar objects which the inhabitants of the place use, even outside the action of the play itself, in the time-lapses between acts.

This operation, conducted painstakingly and lovingly, gives life to the set. The pieces of furniture are placed where they belong, still without any attention being paid to the audience; and later, when the fourth wall disappears, they will give the most picturesque effects.

Much progress, however, remains to be made. For a long time our scene designers painted beds, tables, and fireplaces in perspective; but, yielding to the insistent desire for real-life things which audiences have shown these past ten years, our present-day designers have displayed an excess of zeal. They have provided far too many pieces of furniture and made them just as real as could be; but they have failed to realize that these pieces of furniture are never in the proper proportions to the set, and that flawless staging would require furniture built in perspective.

Moreover, we have to struggle against two of the basic improbabilities of our modern stage settings: the height of the set, which we cannot lower without risking the danger that spectators in the upper balconies will not see part of the play, and the width of the frame. There used to be a third difficulty, which fortunately is fast disappearing from all our theatres: the deadly proscenium arch! Soon it will be nothing but a sad memory, and the nightmare of scene designers.

In using furniture, we must devise ways of eliminating that peculiar impression of emptiness which comes from frameworks that are too wide. In this field, at least, we have made much progress with the means at hand. Memories of the classical theatre no longer paralyze us; we have gone far beyond the single-table set in *Tartuffe*.

The question of painted props has also been successfully solved. Today, an object painted on a flat disturbs and distracts the eye of even the most inexperienced theatregoer. Occasionally, it still happens that some of our scene designers surreptitiously slip vines, simulated flowers, or shrubbery into a landscape or outdoor set. But directors are on guard against such practices. How often have geraniums or creeping vines been eliminated from an attractive set just as soon as they were discovered!

In our interior sets, we must not be afraid of an abundance of little objects, of a wide variety of small props. Nothing makes an interior look more lived in. These are the imponderables which give a sense of intimacy and lend authentic character to the environment the director seeks to re-create.

Among so many objects, and with the complicated furnishings of our modern interiors, the performers' acting becomes, without their realizing it and almost in spite of themselves, more human, more intense, and more alive in attitudes and gestures.

And now the lights!

Here there is always a lively controversy, which still makes the ghost of Sarcey shudder. Most of our directors still favor the crude, glaring light of footlights and spotlights—except for a few night effects obviously called for in the script.

Nevertheless, our lighting equipment is markedly improving every day. We have come a long way from the sorry-looking candles, tapers, oil lamps and gaslights—in this field we have made steady, uninterrupted progress.

For light is the life of the theatre, the good fairy of the *décor*, the soul of the staging. Light alone, intelligently handled, gives atmosphere and color to a set, depth and perspective. Light acts physically on the audience: its magic accentuates, underlines, and marvelously accompanies the intimate meaning of a dramatic work. To get excellent results from light, you must not be afraid to use and spread it unevenly.

The audience, even though it is thrilled by a beautiful stage set skillfully lighted, is not yet at the point where it can forego discerning clearly the face and the slightest gestures of a favorite actor. We know your aversion for those carefully prepared effects in half darkness; yet far from spoiling your impression, these effects really safeguard it, without your suspecting it. So we directors must stand our ground and make no concessions in that respect. One day we shall be right: the broad public will finally realize or feel that, to create a stage picture, values and harmonies are needed which we cannot obtain without sacrificing certain parts. The audience will realize that it gains thereby a deeper and more artistic general impression. . . .

Now the second part of our work begins. We can now bring on the characters: their home is ready, full of life and brightness.

But here, in the guise of traditions, we are going to encounter all the routines, all the resistances, the whole crippling heritage of the past. They have given us statues—and we need living, moving human beings. We have to make characters live their daily lives—and we get men and women who have been taught that in the theatre, as contrasted with real life, one must never speak while walking. So they insist on speaking out at the audience, just as they did two hundred and fifty years ago; they get out of character to comment on or emphasize what the playwright has put in their mouth. They have been taught (in that same old pompous style!) that they must have the proper inflection, declaim according to the rules, recite their lines elegantly so as not to sound vulgar and familiar. They have learned to play up effects of detail, even though these have no interest or meaning in the over-all picture, and they strive with all their might to win applause from the audience by using every device and trick of the trade.

To interpret the character they are supposed to portray, they have only two instruments at their disposal: voice and face. The rest of their body does not participate in the action. They wear gloves and are always superbly groomed; and, since they no longer have the elaborate or majestic costumes of a former age, they wear rings or a flower in their buttonhole.

Rigorously trained in the primitive and rudimentary movements of our classical theatre, ruined forever by scenes of "furies" and "dreams," they ignore the complexity, the variety, the nuances, the life of modern dialogue—its turns of phrase, its subtle intonations, its overtones, its eloquent silences.

That is a true picture of almost all our beginners after they have finished their course in dramatic art. Every year we see dozens of them graduate and bury themselves in some small town, loaded down with this outmoded baggage which will plague them for the rest of their career.

The best of our acting personnel (I am not, of course, speaking of the Comédie-Française, whose artists are trained solely, and rightfully so, to interpret the classics) are recruited from among actors who have risen in the ranks. They have developed themselves, by contact with audiences and in the serious work of laborious rehearsals. They may stammer, as did Dupuis, Réjane, or Huguenet; but they do not "recite." They live their parts; and they are the marvelous interpreters of our contemporary drama.

These actors know:

That movement is the actor's most intense means of expression;

That their whole physical make-up is part of the character they represent, and that at certain moments in the action their hands, their back, and their feet can be more expressive than any oral ranting;

That every time the actor is revealed beneath the character, the dramatic continuity is broken;

And that by emphasizing a word, they often destroy its effect.

They know too that every scene in a play has a movement all its own, subordinated in turn to the general movement of the play; and that

nothing must disturb a group effect—neither a glance at the prompter
nor any attempt at individual "mugging."

Finally, they make their characters come alive before our eyes; they
faithfully depict for us every aspect of their characters, both the material as well as the spiritual.

The high-flown style, that everlasting curse of all the arts, which has
always been opposed to truth and life, is no longer here to plague us;
and the theatre of manners, the comedies of character, and the social
plays of our time have found their true interpreters in these actors.

The stilted teachings of the Conservatoire, indiscriminately incul-
cated in whole generations of young people whose ambition is a single
theatre that will not use one out of ten of them, have victimized an
untold number of beginners. Such institutions falsify and level temperaments: they take all the young talents of which the modern theatre
has such an urgent need and stamp them haphazardly in the mold of
their classical heroes.

There are many other things I should have liked to discuss: crowds,
their means of expression, their shouts, the way they are grouped. . . .
But I shall have to refrain. This "chat" has already lasted too long.

I should have liked to express all my admiration for the classical
theatre and the amazement I feel when I see that many are seriously
considering the possibility of rejuvenating it by modernizing the staging of classical plays.[1] I, on the contrary, if ever I have the honor to
direct in a state theatre, should like to turn back and restore our masterpieces within the true framework they require: that of their own time.
I should like to see Racine played with the court costumes of that
period, in simple and harmonious sets, without any external trappings
that might lessen the impact of Racine's genius.

Since Nero speaks of sometimes panting at the feet of Julia, since
Orestes sighs, I should like to redesign for them those majestic costumes which go so well with their frenzies and their passionate loves.

Any attempt at local color or historical accuracy in such masterpieces appears to me futile: in the eyes of a contemporary of Pericles,

---

[1] This apparent reluctance to modernize the classics is probably due to the fact
that Antoine was seeking the directorship of the Odéon at the time these remarks
were published.

Lekain or Talma would have seemed as little a Greek as Baron. I firmly believe that we change the meaning of those marvelous tragedies when we try to "situate" them—either in the country or the period in which they arose. I cannot conceive of the exquisite temple of the Winged Victory sacrilegiously torn out of the context of the splendid landscape it dominates; and I wish that I could have seen the "Night Watch" in the smoke-filled hall in which it was hung. I am sure that it shone more resplendently there than it does now, mounted beneath a red velvet canopy in the Amsterdam Museum.

Those of us who have not had the great good fortune to be called and trained to interpret and preserve the theatrical art of the past are satisfied to serve, with all that is in us, the theatre of today. We must simply strive to do our best by experimenting as much as possible.

If we discover something really solid and lasting, we shall have added to the common heritage. *La Parisienne*—with a husband who talks about his rent, his children's pants, and a job as tax collector—must not be directed and played like *Le Misanthrope*. Yet it is—I hope and I believe—no less a masterpiece in the history of the theatre, a glorious link in the endless golden chain.

OTTO BRAHM

(1856-1912)

Style and Substance

THE form in which Sophocles' *Antigone* is now given in the German theatre dates back to the 1840's. Frederick William IV gave the initial impulse; Tieck, Felix Mendelssohn, and Böckh directed and backed the production. Played first in the little theatre of the New Palace in Potsdam, the piece then went to the Royal Theatre and Opera House in Berlin, and from there to other German theatres.

The production at the Deutsches Theater departs in several respects from the tradition established in the 1840's. This involves distinctly different problems: the division into scenes, the chorus, and the performance style as a whole. These changes have proved popular, and many have approved of them; but others—the conservative-minded—have felt that these innovations go "too far." Personally I must confess that, on the contrary, the changes do not strike me as sufficiently radical; I feel that they do not go far enough.

Anyone who has closely followed the productions of the Deutsches Theater will quickly realize that this presentation of *Antigone* is based on the same artistic conception as that of all its previous play productions. This conception is, in a word, realism; and since the *Antigone* of the 1840's was based on an opposing conception, the divergence was bound to arise.

The tragedy, in Tieck's adaptation, was presented on a straight-line, rectangular, elevated space—supposed to correspond to the ancient Greek stage; it was played across the entire stage, beneath a colonnade. The Deutsches Theater, seeking to eliminate all stiffness and woodenness from its productions of modern drama, has also broken with this

---

Otto Brahm: *Kritische Schriften ueber Drama und Theater*. Berlin: S. Fischer, 1913, 86–93.

symmetrical pattern. It has learned from the Meininger to broaden or narrow its stage artistically; to make it living and livable. Thus, sharp corners have been softened; the wings have been arranged with deliberate asymmetry; the downstage playing area is connected with a second playing area upstage by means of steps. Every device has been used to achieve fullness of life. The sets for *Antigone* flout academic rules: the square in front of the Royal Palace of Thebes is, as Sophocles describes it, really an "open square," not one carefully measured off by a precise gauge; the height and width of the stage are not exactly symmetrical, and space has been left free downstage and on the sides. Trees grow, tapestries decorate the palace walls, and the over-all impression given is: here human beings can live and feel at home. The older setting, however, gave the impression: here we have good acoustics, here actors can recite their lines well.

A second change concerns the chorus. This is not grouped across the entire stage but off to one side; not just around the altar but with free play of movement. Here too it is obvious that practical considerations involving the smallness of the theatre have played their part. Mendelssohn's music, however, has been retained, even though that was perhaps the most questionable feature of the older production. I do not mean the musical composition as such but its relationship to the Sophoclean spirit: here there is a disparity that always disturbs me. The fact that Maestro Böckh has finally approved of this arrangement does not set my mind at rest. Sophocles called for a speaking chorus; in the Mendelssohn music choruses are sung. And the music has something bright and gay which contradicts the basic theme of the tragedy; at times (as, for example, in "The foolhardy one atones for his foolhardy word") it sounds even operatic and frequently recurs in that same vein.

But are all our innovations, as conceived or executed, valid? Are they in keeping with the spirit of ancient Greece? Is the performance on the stage of the Deutsches Theater "genuinely" classical? That is the big question that is being asked. It is a big question indeed, for in the answer to it lies the meaning of the tragedy as performed in our theatre.

We call those creations classics if they achieve a never-ending, immediate effect across the centuries. They survive the ravages of time. This does not mean, however, that they always have identical meaning for the various generations. Shakespeare's impact on his century was different from his impact on our present-day audiences. Just because he lives, he too changes, along with human beings. As we have often seen, artistic impressions from earlier periods evolve in us and with us (without there being any renewed contact with the themes treated); just as works of art rise or fall in our opinion, simply as a result of the passage of time, so too the creations of the great masters develop, as does humanity itself. But what is true of all the arts is especially true of the dramatic art; it strives to make an immediate impression on receptive but naïve audiences, who come to the theatre without any complicated pretensions at literary culture. And what truer, more genuine, more striking impression can it make than if it is imbued with the same spirit as that which dominates its contemporary world? Dramatic art can only be modern—whether it presents Shakespeare or Schiller, Sophocles or Kleist. Today the realistic style is valid for all; only within this style can the nuances between previous periods and our own be skillfully brought out.

Purely practical, not theoretical, considerations lead us to this point of view. What is valid for us in the works of the classics—in *Antigone*, for example? We see that our deepest impressions are not the same as those of the ancient Greeks. *Antigone* is the nearest to us of all the Greek tragedies because within ourselves we find the same conflict as that which permeates the play: the conflict between the rights of the individual and the rights of the community, between individual emotions and reasons of state. In *Antigone* we see two equally justified attitudes opposing each other, both of them charged with passion, both high-minded and exclusive. Antigone's defiant reverence clashes with Creon's unbending rule; and the excess of her zeal proves tragic to both. But we do not see the tragedy as the Greeks did: to them, Antigone and Creon were not heroes of equal stature. Their sympathies belonged to Antigone; Creon was only the foil, the figure needed as a contrast to the protagonist. He was not a significant character in his own right. A glance at the other two plays in the trilogy confirms this: in *Oedipus Rex* and *Oedipus at Colonus*, Creon is not the powerful ruler. He is the intriguer "with spiteful mouth"; the man with "ever-nimble tongue, cunningly contriving to give everything the appearance of truth." In these plays he is nothing in and of himself; he is merely Oedipus' foil, as he was that of Antigone. To Greek audiences he could not be considered of equal rank because he was played by "the third actor," whereas Antigone's role was taken by the first actor (the *protagonist*). And just as a modern actor, playing the part of an underling, for example, can never hope to win applause from the naïver members of the audience, with the gallery gods ever ready to hiss him because of the role he portrays, so contrariwise Greek audiences were prejudiced in advance against the *tritagonist* ("the third actor") as soon as he appeared on stage to play his role.

To us the basic theme of the tragedy is quite a different one. The climax of the tragedy affects us in a wholly un-Greek way, when we witness the change of mood wrought in Creon by Tiresias the seer and view sympathetically the ruler's collapse. This transformation was what alienated Greek audiences most: in fact, only the third actor was allowed to portray such changes. In his *Technique of the Drama*, a book of finely reasoned comments which has helped shape my own thinking on the matter, Gustav Freytag writes: "The Greeks were very sensitive to vacillations of the will. The greatness of their heroes lay above all in their steadfastness. The first actor would have found it difficult to portray a character who, in any major situation, allowed himself to be dominated by other persons in the play." But we, in our Deutsches Theater production, are deeply moved when Creon, shattered by the terrible words of the seer, goes to pieces and cries out: "Woe! Woe!" at the prospect of the downfall of his dynasty.

The powerful realistic coloring of the production reinforces this impression. And we offer still another simple observation in support of our frankly modern style of presentation. To present the classics in a classical manner—is that really possible? As far as the Greek theatre is concerned, the question is easily answered: no one wants to transfer the mask and buskin of the antique stage to our contemporary scene. But can we really present Shakespeare in the style of his actors; can we enjoy a Hamlet as Burbage played him? Today we do not even see our own German dramatists—Goethe and Schiller, for example—the way their contemporaries and the next generation after that saw them.

We hear them, not in the accents of Esslair and Emil Devrient, but in those of Sonnenthal and Kainz. The former were modern in their day, the latter modern in our day; and when Frau Crelinger and Frau Jachmann played Antigone with sweeping gestures and resounding voice, they were not acting in the Greek style, as they thought, but in the style of their time—only at that time the Weimar style prevailed, and today's theatre calls for the realistic style. But reactionaries in the theatre, intent on clinging to the outworn, get bogged down in hollow conventions and so miss the truth of life.

In that sense the *Antigone* production of the Deutsches Theater offered too little, not too much, realism. The movements of Antigone and Ismene still showed the influence of the Weimar school of acting: at times the actresses flung their arms out wide, at times they assumed rigid poses, like "frozen statues." Incidentally, it is wrong to think of these gestures as antique: as a matter of fact, stage rules forbade the Greek players to bring their arms higher than their face; and to fling them into the air was considered inexpressive. At the beginning of the play, moreover, Fräulein Gessner and Fräulein Jürgens were permitted to use Teschendorff's well-known painting as a model for their positions—in other words, a picture which certainly cannot be said to convey a genuine conception of the ancient world. It is not by these conventional gestures that Fräulein Gessner achieves her effect; it is by a very personal acting style in which, half unconsciously, her dynamic stage personality comes alive. When she wrings her hands in woe; when, summoned by Creon, she tosses her head high; when, as death approaches, her body begins suddenly to shudder—all this shows that she is completely in the part. This actress's body is more eloquent than her voice: in the latter she still has much to learn, in the way in which she builds her speeches as well as in an intelligent use of her rich organ. At the present time, she often forces her voice; and if we criticize it, it is not because it is a question of *Antigone* but because it is unaesthetic in any play. Nor has Herr Pohl as Creon mastered his diction; he falls easily into a fatal singsong. He lingers over certain individual words without any rhyme or reason and pauses at every verse ending, as if facing a barrier. He does not have the breath for the part—in the narrow as well as the broad sense of the term—and he does not convey the ruler's sense of power. But in the climax he is superb; here he becomes impassioned, he shows real feeling, and the result is excellent acting.

Herr Höcker played the Watchman with commendable art. The man's garrulousness and peasant slyness, his crude joy when he is out of danger, and his philistine show of sympathy at the sacrifice—all these traits rang true. His performance and Kainz's fiery Haemon offer the best examples of what the Deutsches Theater can do; they also show that modern realism in presentation and the style of classical drama are not mutually exclusive.

DAVID BELASCO

(1859-1931)

Creating Atmosphere

ET us assume that a play has been brought into acceptable form in its manuscript and I have made up my mind to produce it. My first step in the practical work of production is to study out the scenes, which must be constructed as carefully as the play itself, for a skillfully devised scene is always of vital assistance to an episode. In this preliminary work I seldom follow the stage directions on the printed page, either of my own plays or those of other dramatists. I prefer to plan the scenes myself with reference to stage values.

I consider where a window or door, a balcony or a fireplace, will be most effective. The feeling of the scene is always a great factor in determining its arrangement, for symbolism to a certain extent enters the production of every play. For instance, sunlit scenes imply happiness, moonlit scenes give a suggestion of romance, while tragedy or sorrow should be played in gloom. It is never advisable to stage comedy scenes, which depend for their interest upon the wittiness of the dialogue, in exterior settings, for the surroundings suggest too great an expanse; if acted in an interior setting the lines become immeasurably more effective.

Such details as these must be carefully thought out, and as I become more familiar with the lines and episodes the scenes gradually form themselves. Then I make a rough sketch, taking into account the necessary arrangement of furniture or other properties and considering how the characters can be maneuvered to best advantage.

When I have settled these matters approximately, I send for my scenic artist. With him seated in front, I take the empty stage and, as

David Belasco: *The Theatre Through Its Stage Door*. Edited by Louis V. Defoe. New York: Harper and Brothers, 1919, 53–89, 165–167, 189–195, *passim*.

far as possible, try to act the whole play, making every entrance and exit and indicating my ideas of the groupings of the characters and their surroundings. This process, which would probably seem farcical to a casual onlooker, will consume perhaps four or five evenings, for not one detail can be left to chance or put aside until I am satisfied that it cannot be improved.

During this process one must treat the play as a human being; it must laugh at certain points, at others it must be sad; lovers must come together in certain lights; and all its changing moods must be blended harmoniously. For the completed play is impressive and fulfills its purpose only to the extent that it carries an audience back to its own experiences. If my productions have had an appealing quality, it is because I have kept this important fact constantly in mind and have tried, while concealing the mechanism of my scenes, to tug at the hearts of my audiences.

Having explained in detail my ideas and turned over a manuscript to him, the scenic artist proceeds to make a drawing of the scenes, following my crude sketches, and thus we reach a definite starting point. In due course of time—it may be a week or a month—the scenic artist will have constructed the actual scene models which are set up in the perfectly equipped miniature theatre of my studio. But changes are always suggesting themselves, and often these models, which are about four feet long, have to be taken apart and reconstructed several times.

It is time now to begin to consider what to me is the all-important factor in a dramatic production—the lighting of the scenes. With my electrician I again go over the play in detail, very much according to the method I have previously followed with my scenic artist. When he has thoroughly grasped my ideas and become quite familiar with the play itself, we begin our experiments, using the miniature theatre and evolving our colors by transmitting white light through gelatin or silk of various hues. Night after night we experiment together to obtain color or atmospheric effects, aiming always to make them aid the interpretation of the scenes.

Lights are to drama what music is to the lyrics of a song. No other factor that enters into the production of a play is so effective in conveying its moods and feeling. They are as essential to every work of dramatic art as blood is to life. The greatest part of my success in the theatre I attribute to my feeling for colors, translated into effects of light. Sometimes these effects have been imitated by other producers with considerable success, but I do not fear such encroachments. It may be possible for others to copy my colors, but no one can get my feeling for them. . . .

If, as I conceive it, the purpose of the theatre be to hold the mirror up to nature, I know of no better place to obtain the effects of nature than to go to nature itself. To fulfill this purpose with integrity, to surround the mimic life of the characters in drama with the natural aspects of life, to seek in light and color the same interpretative relation to spoken dialogue that music bears to the words of a song, is, I contend, the real art, the true art of the theatre. He who goes direct to nature for the effects he introduces on the stage can never be wrong. It is upon this creed that I base my faith in realism in dramatic art.

The lighting effects on my stages have been secured only after years of experiment and at an expense which many other producers would consider ridiculous. Sometimes I have spent five thousand dollars attempting to reproduce the delicate hues of a sunset and then have thrown the scene away altogether. I recall that when I produced *The Girl of the Golden West*, I experimented three months to secure exactly the soft, changing colors of a California sunset over the Sierra Nevadas, and then turned to another method. It was a good sunset, but it was not Californian.

These experiments have always been the most interesting part of my work as a producer, although they have also been the most perplexing and sometimes the most baffling. It is no easy matter, for instance, to indicate the difference between the moon and stars of a Japanese night and the fanciful moon and stars of fairyland. But there is, nevertheless, a difference which an audience must be made to feel, without detecting the mechanism, just as one is conscious of heat, yet does not see it, on entering a warm room. . . .

The scene models having been approved and the very important matter of the lighting being well under way, it is time now to begin the building of the actual scenes. I turn my carpenters over to my scenic artist, who furnishes to them the plans. They then construct

the scenery in my own shops, for I never have such work done by contract. I will allow nothing to be built out of canvas stretched on
frames. Everything must be real. I have seen plays in which thrones
creaked on which monarchs sat, and palace walls flapped when persons touched them. Nothing so destructive to illusion or so ludicrous
can happen on my stage. . . .

I generally prefer to leave the costuming until after the first week of
rehearsals, when I am reasonably sure of my actors, unless it happens
to be a costume play which I am producing. If it demands other than
modern clothes, I write a full description for the characters, deciding
whether their hair shall be smooth or shaggy and whether they shall or
shall not wear beards, and then call a costume designer into consultation. All this is very necessary in a costume play, in order to preserve
the color harmonies of my scenes. If, on the other hand, it be a modern
play that I am producing, I send my actors, when the proper time
comes, to the various shops to be fitted for their clothing.

. . . In order to keep in my own complete control this important
detail of a dramatic production, I provide all the clothing worn by the
people in my companies. It is the ordinary practice, in the case of fancy
costumes, for the producer to supply them, but so-called modern clothing is expected to be furnished by the actors themselves. But I have
found it advisable to regulate every detail which enters into productions on my stage, and the advantage I gain by such caution greatly
outweighs the expense. . . .

When I produced *The Darling of the Gods* I sent to Japan for the
costumes of my principal actors, as well as for the other paraphernalia
of its scenes. When I presented *Du Barry* I sent a commissioner to
France, where he purchased the rich fabrics and had them dyed to reproduce exactly the dresses and styles of the Court of Louis XV, as
shown by portraits painted during that period.

The problem of obtaining appropriate costumes, however, varies
with every play. I have dumfounded a tramp by asking him to exchange a coat on his back for a new one. Sometimes a poor girl of the
street has attracted my attention because she was like a character I had
in mind. I have sent for her and bought her dress, hat, shoes, and
stockings. My wardrobe people have rummaged for weeks through

pawnshops and second-hand stores to find a vest or some other article of apparel appropriate to an eccentric character in one of my plays. From fashionable dressmakers and tailors have come bills that would stagger a rich society woman.

While all these various details of the production are moving along, I am hunting everywhere for my cast. In fact, I have been on the look-out for actors and actresses suitable to the various characters from the moment I made up my mind to accept the play. Applicants for parts come to my office in swarms, but generally they are members of the profession who are too familiarly known to the public, since I prefer, as far as possible, to develop my own actors. I ransack the varieties and the cheap stock companies, and I both go to see the people and have them come to see me. If I happen to be producing a play for a star, the organization of the company is somewhat simplified, but in any event I always choose my players with the greatest care. In making my selections I would much prefer to have an actor resemble the character he is to represent than have him depend upon disguise and the assumption of manners, for my motto as a producer has been to keep as close to nature as possible.

I have been dealing, up to this point, with what, to a theatre audience, are the impersonal factors in the evolution of a play on my stage. Until my company is fully organized its members, of course, remain scattered. In due course of time—I usually allot about six weeks to rehearsals of a play which does not offer unusual difficulties—notices are sent out for the people to assemble. When they arrive at the theatre I always make it a practice to be on hand to receive them. I want them to feel from the outset an intimate relationship to me and to one another. Some have already played together in the same companies; some know one another only by reputations, and some are strangers. I introduce them to one another and treat them as guests in my drawing room, rather than as employees on my stage. After a few moments spent in general conversation I then invite them to accompany me to the reading room, where they find a long, well-lighted table surrounded by comfortable chairs.

When we are all seated—I at the head of the table with the scene models beside me—I invariably give a few preliminary instructions. First of all I caution the members of the company not to discuss the play outside my theatre. I impress upon them that the ultimate result of our efforts will depend upon the spirit of co-operation which each brings to it and that the success of the whole is more important to me than any of its parts. I urge that they must not judge the value of their characters by the number of lines allotted to them to speak, but rather by the artistry which the characters permit. Above all, I ask them not to be selfish, but to assist one another because, after all, they are only the component parts of a single picture.

My sermon preached and reiterated, I then read the play from beginning to end, without interruptions or comments. This ceremony finished, the individual parts are distributed by the prompter. . . .

Talk about stage fright! The suffering of actors at a first public performance is nothing compared to what they undergo when, with no one but myself present, they first read their parts from the manuscript. Each character is closely analyzed as we proceed. Invariably our discussions bring out more of the psychology of the roles than the author ever dreamed his play contained. When the reading is finished we indulge in a little general conversation—the pleasant social relationship of the members of a theatrical company is always important—and then the rehearsal is adjourned until the following morning. . . .

When I am satisfied that the members of the company have in their minds a clear conception of the play and its characters—up to this point they have been only reading and listening, not acting—I make it a rule to turn them over to my stage director, who supervises them during the first rehearsal on the stage. He, in the meantime, has been studying the play and listening to the readings, and knows, roughly at least, what I am aiming to accomplish. I have always found it better to keep out of sight during the first experiments in the real acting, for when I am present the actors stand still and depend upon me for directions.

I always caution the stage director to let them give him everything, that he must give them nothing. In this way they rely upon their own initiative and, so to speak, squeeze themselves dry. Their invention

seems to grow when they know they can do as they please. With this
confidence gained, I take control of the play again and we go at it in
earnest.

Now the period of hardest work has been reached. I have kept my
people on the stage twenty hours at a stretch, making some of them
read a single line perhaps fifty times, experimenting with little subtleties of intonation or gesture, and going over bits of business again and
again. Infinite patience is needed to make others understand the soul
of a character as the author or producer conceives it, and such patience,
coupled with the knack of communicating his own ideas, must be possessed by every successful producer.

I have never resorted to bullying in order to make my actors do as I
wish; I have always found that the best results can be gained by appealing subtly to their imagination. I can convey more to them by a
look or a gesture than by a long harangue or a scolding.

Peculiarities in the actors are also disclosed by these experiments.
Some may be able to speak their lines more effectively while seated
than while standing; some play better on the right side of the stage
than on the left, or vice versa; one arrives at his best results deliberately,
another by nervous energy; I have even known actors whose work
varied according to whether they directly faced the audience or presented their profiles to it. Experience has taught me not to direct my
players arbitrarily, but to be guided by what they can best do. Their
peculiarities are the results of temperament and personality, which the
intelligent stage director should always attempt to preserve. I try to
correct mannerisms when they are bad, for bad mannerisms are as
destructive to good acting as weeds to a garden; but when mannerisms
are indexes of personality they have a distinct value. . . .

All these idiosyncrasies in my actors I try to preserve, when they are
not so pronounced that they seem to be affectations. I direct them so
that such personal peculiarities will be put to effective uses. This is one
of the reasons why I always work with the company before me. Of late
there has sprung up a practice of organizing several companies—in
some instances half a dozen—and sending them on tour in plays which
happen to have met with unusual popularity in New York. There is a
great commercial advantage in such a policy, for it permits the profits

of a successful play to be quickly gathered and it simplifies the work of the producer, because invariably the secondary companies attempt no more than to imitate the methods of the original organization. For this reason bad art must inevitably result. Therefore I am opposed to it. I have never directed a second company; if I did, I fear I would change all the business of the play, and possibly make alterations in the play itself. I would discover immediately that what one set of players could do most effectively in a certain manner, another set would have to do in a wholly different way, dependent upon the temperament, personality, and technical equipment of each. When actors attempt only to imitate a model, they become automatons and the artistic finish of both the play and its performance is consequently sacrificed.

So we go over the speeches time after time, generally spending a week or ten days on each act. During this period I have insisted that my actors avoid trying to memorize their roles until their conception of them is fully formed and they are actually molded into the characters. Otherwise, with every word glibly at their tongues' ends, they will presently begin to talk like parrots. Furthermore, they are always unconsciously studying and memorizing while rehearsing. . . .

During all the time that rehearsals have been in progress—and perhaps for many weeks or even months before the first reading—other preparations for the production have been going on. Carpenters have been building the scenery in my shop, artists have been painting it at their studios, electricians have been making the paraphernalia for the lighting effects, property men have been manufacturing or buying the various objects needed in their department, and costumers and wigmakers have been at work. All these adjuncts to the play have been timed to be ready when they are needed. At last comes the order to put them together. Then for three or four days my stage resembles a house in process of being furnished. Confusion reigns supreme with carpenters putting on doorknobs, decorators hanging draperies, workmen laying carpets and rugs, and furniture men taking measurements.

Everything has been selected by me in advance. My explorations in search of stage equipment are really the most interesting parts of my work. I attend auction sales and haunt antique shops, hunting for the things I want. I rummage in stores in the richest as well as in the poorest sections of New York. Many of the properties must be especially made, and it has even happened that I have been compelled to send agents abroad to find exactly the things I need. . . .

When I produced *The Easiest Way* I found myself in a dilemma. I planned one of its scenes to be an exact counterpart of a little hall bedroom in a cheap theatrical boardinghouse in New York. We tried to build the scene in my shops, but, somehow, we could not make it look shabby enough. So I went to the meanest theatrical lodginghouse I could find in the Tenderloin district and bought the entire interior of one of its most dilapidated rooms—patched furniture, threadbare carpet, tarnished and broken gas fixtures, tumbledown cupboards, dingy doors and window casings, and even the faded paper on the walls. The landlady regarded me with amazement when I offered to replace them with new furnishings.

While the scenery and properties are being put together I lurk around with my notebook in hand, studying the stage, watching for defects in color harmonies, and endeavoring to make every scene conform to the characteristics of the people who are supposed to inhabit them. However great the precaution I may have observed, I generally decide to make many more changes. Then, when the stage is furnished to my satisfaction, I bring my company up from the reading room and introduce them to the scenes and surroundings in which they are to live in the play.

There is a vast difference between rehearsing a company on an empty stage and in the fully equipped settings of a play. The change involves retracing many steps which have already been taken, and undoing many things which seemingly have been done well; but I have been unable to discover a way to avoid it. Now we have the actual width and depth of the stage to guide us and we are able to time with mathematical exactness entrances and exits and the movements of the actors from one place to another. When the characters are put into the permanent scenes, the stage director must also consider them from a somewhat different point of view. The players must be adapted to the scene, not the scene to the players, for the effort should always be to lose the identity of the scene and intensify the identity of the characters. I have always been a strong advocate of stage settings which stimulate the imagination of my audiences and at the same time adorn my plays, but first, last, and always I try not to attract the eye when attention should be fixed upon the dialogue. . . .

At last, when every little imperfection in the interpretations of the characters has been detected and perfected, I set apart one perform-ance at which I try not to consider the acting, but the play itself. I am on the lookout for repetitions in the dialogue that may have escaped me, unduly emphatic speeches and climaxes that have not been con-sistently approached. I keep a stenographer beside me taking down notes and suggestions, for I try not to interrupt the performance or in-terfere with the inspiration of the players. These final changes made, the company are bidden to become letter-perfect in their roles as they are now developed. This task of unlearning and learning again is one of the hardest that an actor is called upon to perform. It needs a trained mind to do it quickly and successfully. . . .

At about this time, if all the costumes are ready, I hold what I call my "dress parade." I have my actors dress exactly as they are to be seen in the play, with every detail of clothing—shoes, gloves, neckties, wigs, beards, and cosmetics complete—and march them back and forth across the stage. It frequently happens that changes will be advisable in the appearance of some of them, and the time to decide such mat-ters is now. I supply every detail of the wardrobe which actors wear on my stage, whether I am producing a costume drama or a modern comedy. In every respect the production and all that pertains to it must be in perfect harmony. I take pains to caution the players to "make up" with reference to the predominating tone of the lighting of the stage. In my own theatres the dressing rooms are equipped with rows of electric bulbs of every hue, so that the actors may gauge the exact effect of the pigments which they put on their faces. But when, occasionally, I have produced plays in other houses than my own, this important precaution has not been possible, and sometimes it has led to grave defects in the appearance of some of the characters. . . .

The dress parade over, and the time for the dress rehearsals being at hand, I give my attention to a curtain rehearsal. One who is not famil-iar with the little touches, apart from the play itself, which aid the general effect of a dramatic production may not realize how important it is to have the curtain work in harmony with the feeling of the scene upon which it rises and falls. I have sometimes experimented with a curtain fifty times, raising or lowering it rapidly, slowly, or at medium speed. The curtain men must be taught to feel the climaxes as keenly as the actors and to work in unison with them. This is a good time, also, if the play has a musical accompaniment, to rehearse the score with my orchestra leader and musicians, and weld them into parts of the completed whole.

We are ready for the final dress rehearsals now. The production, which has been developing day by day for six weeks or more, has become as complete and its performance is as spontaneous as if it were being given before a crowded audience.

The stage is ordered cleared, the actors are sent to their dressing rooms to get themselves ready, and I take my place, with my scenic artists and others attached to my staff, in the front of the empty theatre. The people are likely to be more nervous than on a real opening night, for they are conscious that they are to be subjected to concentrated criticism from which there is no appeal. In a crowded theatre they are sure of pleasing at least a part of the audience; it is a different affair when they are trying to meet the approval of only one person. The introductory music, if there be music, is played, up goes the curtain, and the performance begins.

I try not to interrupt if it can possibly be avoided, preferring to reserve my criticisms until the end. But if indefensible mistakes occur—if, for instance, a character on leaving a drawing room forgets his hat or stick or gloves—I am cruel enough in my comments to make sure that the blunder will never occur again. It is too late now for praising, coaxing, or cajoling. I go on the principle that the good things will take care of themselves, but that not a single flaw must be left undetected. The dress rehearsal ended, I commend the company when I can, reprove them when I must, and generally discuss tempo, deportment, and elocution—everything, in fact, that suggests itself to me. Then the curtain is lowered, the scene is "struck," and we go over the play again and again until, so far as I can judge, nothing more remains to be done. . . .

Any play worth producing at all is entitled to the most perfect interpretation that can be secured for it. Any means that aids the audience's grasp and understanding of it, or that appeals to the aesthetic sense, is useful and legitimate in the theatre—provided the stage director never loses sight of the fact that, when all is said and done, the play itself is the main thing, that the actors are always the chief instruments through which the story is to be told, and that the scene is only a background against which the dramatist's work is being projected.

If for however brief a time scenery, accessories, or any of the details of the environment, no matter how clever they be in themselves, distract the audience's attention from the play proper or cease to be other than mere assisting agencies, their value is destroyed and they become more a hindrance than an aid and, consequently, an inartistic blunder. One must remember that in nature the glory and beauty of the stars are never obliterated by the background of the sky. . . .

But all these adjuncts of lighting, color, and costumes, however useful they may be, and however pleasing to an audience, really mark the danger point of a dramatic production. No other worker in the American theatre has given so much time and energy to perfecting them as I; nevertheless, I count them as valuable only when they are held subordinate to the play and the acting. The stage always accomplishes more through the ability of its actors than through the genius of its scenic artists and electrical experts. And if the theatre in this country now is in a state of decline, it is because too much attention is being paid to stage decoration, important as it is when held in its proper place, and too little to the work of the players.

It is at once significant and deplorable that our scenic artists study continually, our actors seldom. And it is a fact that, except in the rarest cases, the more indifferent the quality of the acting the more elaborate is likely to be the surroundings in which it is found. If the artistic success of a play depended principally upon its scenery and decorations, anyone who could afford to engage a good painter might become a dramatic producer almost overnight. And if this be the end sought by dramatic art, then we have had no past theatre. Shakespeare would doubtless have utilized every accessory and aid known to our modern stage, yet the greatness of his dramatic genius was established without them.

Only when the stage director is resolved that the play shall stand first in importance in a theatre production can he safely employ the countless pictorial aids which contribute to its effect and its appeal. Only when he relies upon his actors as the chief means of its interpretation should he venture upon those other agencies which help to bring it into closer relation with life and nature.

In short, to paraphrase Hamlet's words, the play must always be the thing, whether to stir the aesthetic impulse of the public or to catch the conscience of the king.

ADOLPHE APPIA

(1862-1928)

Light and Space

FOR some years now dramatic art has been in a process of change. Naturalism on the one hand, Wagnerianism on the other, have violently displaced the old landmarks. Certain things which, twenty years ago, were not "of the theatre" (to use an absurdly hallowed expression) have almost become commonplace. This has resulted in some confusion: we no longer know to which type a given play belongs; and the fondness we have for foreign productions fails to give us guidance.

This would not, however, create serious difficulties if our stages adapted themselves to every new effort. Unfortunately, this is not the case. The author with his manuscript—or the composer with his score—may be in agreement with the actors; but once on the stage, in the blaze of the footlights, the new idea slips back into its old framework—and our directors ruthlessly cut anything that goes beyond that.

Many assert that it cannot be otherwise, that the conventions of scene design are rigid, etc. I say just the opposite. And in the following pages I have tried to formulate the basic elements of staging which, instead of paralyzing and stifling dramatic art, will not only be faithful to it but will also be a source of inexhaustible suggestion for the playwright and his interpreters.

I trust that the reader will bear with me during this difficult résumé.

Our modern staging is entirely the slave of painting—the painting of sets—which purports to give us the illusion of reality. But this illusion is itself an illusion, because the physical presence of the actor contradicts it. In fact, the principle of the illusion achieved by painting on

Adolphe Appia: "Comment reformer notre mise en scène," *La Revue (Revue des Revues)* Vol. L, No. ii, June 1, 1904, 342-349.

vertical pieces of canvas ("flats") and that of the illusion achieved by
the plastic, living body of the actor are in contradiction. So it is not by
developing in isolation the play of these two kinds of illusions—as is
done on all our stages—that we shall obtain an integrated and artistic
performance.

Let us therefore examine modern stagecraft from these two points of
view in turn.

It is impossible to set up on our stages real trees, real houses, etc.;
besides, that would hardly be desirable. Hence we feel that we must
imitate reality as faithfully as possible. But to render things plastically
is difficult, often impossible, and in any case very expensive. That
forces us, it would seem, to reduce the number of things represented.
Our directors, however, are of a different mind. They consider that the
stage set must represent anything they want it to; consequently, what
cannot be rendered plastically must be painted. Undoubtedly, painting allows one to show the audience a countless number of things.
Thus it seems to give to staging a much-sought freedom; so our
directors stop right there. But the basic principle of painting is to
reduce everything to a flat surface. How then can it fill a three-dimen-
sional space—the stage? Without any attempt to solve the problem,
the directors have decided to cut up the painting and to set up these
"cut-outs" on the floor of the stage. It means therefore giving up any
attempt to paint the lower part of the stage picture: if it is a landscape,
for example, the top will be a dome of forest scenery; to the right and
left there will be trees; at the rear there will be a horizon and a sky—and
at the bottom, the floor of the stage! This painting, which was supposed to represent everything, is forced from the very outset to
renounce representing the ground; because the illusory forms it depicts
must be presented to us vertically, and *there is no possible relationship*
between the vertical flats of the set and the stage floor (or the more or
less horizontal canvas covering it). That is why our scene designers
cushion the base of the flats.

So the ground cannot be reproduced by painting. But that is precisely where the actor moves! Our directors have forgotten the actor:
they want to produce a *Hamlet* without Hamlet! Are they willing to
sacrifice a bit of the dead painting in favor of the living, moving body

of the actor? Never! They would rather give up the theatre! But since
it is nonetheless necessary to take into account this quite living body,
painting consents to place itself here and there at the actor's disposi-
tion. At times it even grows generous, although by so doing it looks
quite ridiculous; at other times, however, when it has refused to yield a
single inch, it is the actor who becomes ridiculous. The antagonism is
complete.

We have begun with painting. Now let us see what direction the
problem would take if we began with the actor, with the plastic, moving human body, seen solely from the point of view of its effect on the
stage—as we have done with the stage setting.

An object becomes plastic for our eyes only by the light that strikes
it—and its plasticity cannot be artistically produced except by an
artistic use of light. That is self-evident. So much for form. The
movement of the human body requires obstacles in order to express
itself; all artists know that the beauty of the body's movements depends
on the variety of the points of support afforded by the ground and
other objects. The actor's mobility cannot therefore be improved
artistically except by an integrated relationship with other objects and
the ground.

Hence the two basic conditions for an artistic presentation of the
human body on the stage are: lighting that brings out its plasticity,
and a harmonizing with the setting which brings out its attitudes and
movements. Here we are a long way from painting indeed!

Dominated by painted sets, the *décor* sacrifices the actor and, more
than that, as we have seen, a good deal of its pictorial effect, since it
must cut up the painting. This is contrary to the essential principle of
the art of painting. Moreover, the stage floor cannot share in the illusion offered by the flats. But what would happen if we subordinated
it to the actor!

First of all, we would make lighting free again! As a matter of fact,
under the domination of the painted set, the lighting is completely
absorbed by the *décor*. The things represented on the flats must be
seen: so lights are lit and shadows are painted. . . . Alas! It is from this
kind of lighting that the actor must take what he can get! Under such
conditions it cannot be a question either of true lighting or of any

plastic effect whatever! Lighting in itself is an element the effects of which are limitless; once it is freed, it becomes for us what the palette is for the painter. All the color combinations become possible. By simple or complex searchlights, stationary or moving, by partial obstruction, by different degrees of transparency, etc., we can achieve infinite modulations. Lighting thus gives us a means of externalizing in some way most of the colors and forms that painting freezes on the canvas and of distributing them dynamically in space. The actor no longer walks *in front of* painted lights and shadows; he is immersed in an atmosphere *that is destined for him.* Artists will be quick to grasp the scope of such a reform.[1]

Now comes the crucial point: the plasticity in the *décor* necessary for the actor's harmony of attitudes and movements. Painting has gained the upper hand on our stages, replacing everything that could not be realized plastically, and it has done this with the sole aim of giving the illusion of reality.

But are the images it piles up thus on the vertical flats indispensable? Not at all: there is not one play that needs even a hundredth part of them. For note this well: these images are not living, they are *indicated* on the canvas like a kind of hieroglyphic language. They *signify* only the things they purport to represent—and all the more so because they cannot enter into real, organic contact with the actor.

The plasticity required by the actor aims at an entirely different effect: the human body does not seek to produce the illusion of reality *since it is itself reality!* What it demands of the *décor* is simply to set in relief this reality. This results inevitably in a shift in the aim of the stage set: in the one case it is the real appearance of *objects* that is sought; in the other, it is the highest possible degree of reality of the human body.

Since these two principles are technically opposed, it is a question of choosing one or the other. Is it to be the accumulation of dead images

---

[1] A well-known artist in Paris, Mariano Fortuny, has invented a completely new system of lighting, based on the properties of *reflected* light. The results have been extraordinarily successful—and this far-reaching invention will bring about a radical transformation in staging in all the theatres . . . in favor of lighting.

and decorative richness on the vertical flats, or is it to be the spectacle of the human being in all its plastic and mobile manifestations?

Can there be any possible hesitation in our answer? Let us ask ourselves what we are looking for in the theatre. We have beautiful painting elsewhere, and fortunately not cut up. Photography allows us to sit in our armchair and view the whole world; literature evokes the most fascinating pictures in our imagination; and very few people are so devoid of feeling that they are not able from time to time to contemplate a beautiful sight in nature. We come to the theatre in order to witness a dramatic *action*. It is the presence of the characters on the stage that motivates this action; without the characters there is no action. So it is the actor who is the essential factor in staging; it is he whom we come to *see*, it is from him that we expect the emotion, and it is for this emotion that we have come. Hence it is above all a question of basing our staging on the actor's presence. To do this, we must free staging of everything that is in contradiction with the actor's presence.

This, then, is the way we must frankly pose the technical problem.

Some may object that this problem has at times been rather successfully solved on several of our Paris stages—at the Théâtre Antoine, for example, or elsewhere. No doubt; but why has this always happened with the same type of plays and settings? How would those directors go about staging *Troilus and Cressida* or *The Tempest, The Ring of the Nibelung* or *Parsifal*? (At the Grand Guignol Theatre, they are adept at showing us a concierge's lodging; but what happens, for example, when they want to depict a garden?)

Our staging has two distinct sources: opera and the spoken drama. Up to now, with very few exceptions, opera singers have been considered glorified machines for singing, and the painted set has been the outstanding feature of the spectacle. Hence its impressive development. The evolution of the spoken play has been different: the actor of necessity comes first, since without him there is no play; and if the director occasionally feels that he has to borrow some of the trappings of opera, he does so prudently and without losing sight of the actor. (Let the reader compare in his memory the decorative effect of such a lavish play production as *Theodora* with that of any opera.) Yet the principle of stage illusion remains the same for the spoken play as for the opera, and it is that principle which is the most seriously violated. Besides, dramatists are well acquainted with two or three combinations in which modern staging can achieve a little illusion despite the presence of the actor; and so they never venture beyond them.

During the last few years, however, things have changed. With the Wagnerian music-dramas, opera has come closer to the spoken play, and the latter (apart from the plays of naturalism) has sought to overcome its former limitations, to come nearer to the music-drama. Then, strangely enough, it turns out that our staging no longer fits the needs of either the one or the other! The ostentatious display that opera makes of painting no longer has anything to do with a Wagner score (the Wagnerian directors, at Bayreuth and elsewhere, do not yet seem to realize this); and the monotony of the settings in the spoken drama no longer satisfies the sharpened insight of the dramatists. Everyone feels the need of a reform, but the power of inertia keeps us in the same old rut.

In such a situation theories are useful, but they do not lead far. We must come directly to grips with stage design and, little by little, transform it.

The simplest method perhaps would be to take one of our plays exactly as it is, *already completely set*, and to see what could be done with its staging if it were based on the principle elaborated above. Of course we would have to choose carefully a play written especially for modern staging, or an opera that adapts itself perfectly to it. The *décors* in our traditional theatres are of no help to us. On the contrary, we must choose a dramatic work whose requirements obviously do not jibe with our present-day means: a play by Maeterlinck, or some other play of the same type, or even a Wagnerian music-drama. The latter is preferable because music, by definitely delimiting the duration and intensity of the emotion, can be a valuable guide. Besides, the sacrifice of illusion would be less conspicuous in a Wagnerian music-drama than in a spoken play. We shall then see everything in the fixed set which runs counter to our efforts; we shall be forced to make concessions that are quite revealing. The question of lighting will concern us first of all: on this point we will have an example of the tyranny of painted flats; and we shall understand—no longer theoretically but in a thoroughly concrete manner—the immense harm still being done to the actor and, by him, to the dramatist.

No doubt that would only be a modest effort; but it is extremely difficult to accomplish such a reform all at once, because it is as much a question of reforming the audience's taste as it is of transforming our staging. Moreover, the results of material and technical work *on ground that is already familiar* are perhaps surer than those arising from a radical reform.

Take, for example, the second act of *Siegfried*. How are we to represent a forest on the stage? First of all, let us be clear as to the following: is it *a forest* with characters, or rather *characters* in a forest? We are at the theatre to witness a dramatic action. Something takes place in this forest which apparently cannot be expressed by painting. Here then is our point of departure: So and So does this and that, says this and that, in a forest. To design our set we do not have to try to visualize a forest; but we must depict in detailed and logical sequence everything that takes place in this forest. Hence perfect knowledge of the score is indispensable, and the director's source of inspiration is thus completely different: his eyes must remain *riveted on the characters*. Then if he thinks of the forest, it will be as a kind of special atmosphere surrounding and hovering above the actors—an atmosphere which he can grasp only *in its relation* to the living, moving actors from whom he must not avert his eyes. At no point in his conception, therefore, will the stage picture remain a lifeless arrangement of painting; it will always be alive. In that way the staging becomes the creation of a stage picture in its time-flow. Instead of starting with a painted set ordered by somebody or other from somebody else, with the actor then getting along as best he can with shoddy props, we start with the actor. It is his art we wish to high-light and for which we are ready to sacrifice everything. It will be: Siegfried here and Siegfried there—and never: the tree for Siegfried, the road for Siegfried. I repeat: we no longer seek to give the illusion of *a forest* but that of *a man* in the atmosphere of a forest. Reality here is a man, alongside whom no other illusion matters. Everything this man touches must be part of his destiny—everything else must help create the appropriate atmosphere around him. And if we look away from Siegfried for a moment and raise our eyes, the stage picture does not of necessity have to give us an illusion: the way it is arranged has *only* Siegfried in mind; and when a slight rustling of the trees in the forest attracts Siegfried's attention, we the spectators *will look at Siegfried* bathed in the moving lights and shadows; we will not look at parts of the *décor* set in motion by backstage manipulation.

Scenic illusion is the living presence of the actor.

The setting for this act, as it is now presented to us on stages throughout the world, fails woefully to live up to our conditions. We must simplify it a great deal, give up lighting the painted flats as is now the rule, institute a complete reform in the arrangement of the stage floor and, above all, provide for our lighting by installing a wealth of electrical equipment regulated in great detail. The footlights—that astonishing monstrosity—will hardly be used. Let us add that most of this work of re-creation will be with the characters, and the production will not be finally set until after several rehearsals with the orchestra (indispensable conditions which may now seem exorbitant yet are elementary!).

An attempt along these lines cannot fail to teach us the course to follow in transforming our rigid and conventional staging into living, flexible, and artistic material, suitable for any dramatic creation whatever. We shall even be surprised that we have so long neglected so important a branch of art and have consigned it, as unworthy of our personal attention, to men who are not artists.

As far as staging is concerned, our aesthetic feeling is still in a state of paralysis. A person who would not tolerate in his own apartment an object that was not of the most exquisite taste, finds it quite natural to buy a high-priced seat in a hall that is ugly and built in defiance of good sense, and to sit there for a couple of hours watching a play alongside which the worst chromos from an antique dealer are delicate works of art.

Methods of staging, like methods in the other arts, are based on forms, light, and colors. These three elements are at our disposal; consequently we can use them in the theatre, as elsewhere, in an artistic manner. Up to now it was felt that staging should achieve the highest possible degree of illusion—and it is this principle (an unaesthetic principle if ever there was one!) that has paralyzed our efforts. I have endeavored to show in these pages that the art of scene design must be based on the only *reality* worthy of the theatre: the human body. We have seen the first and elementary consequences of this reform.

The subject is a difficult and complex one, particularly in view of the misunderstandings surrounding it and the bad habits we have formed from frequenting present-day plays. To be thoroughly convincing, I would have to develop this idea a good deal further. I would have to discuss the brand-new task that is incumbent on the actor; the influence that a flexible and artistic scene design would inevitably exert on the dramatist; the stylizing power of music on a stage production; the changes that will be required in building new stages, new theatres, etc. It is impossible for me to do that here;[2] but perhaps the reader will have found in my aesthetic desire something approaching his own. In that case, it will be easy for him to continue this work by himself.

---

[2] I have published a complete study of the subject in Germany with the publishing house of Bruckmann in Munich. The volume, illustrated with sketches, is called: *Die Musik und die Inscenierung.*

GORDON CRAIG

(b. 1872)

The Artist of the Theatre

STAGE-DIRECTOR: You have now been over the theatre with me, and have seen its general construction, together with the stage, the machinery for manipulating the scenes, the apparatus for lighting, and the hundred other things, and have also heard what I have had to say of the theatre as a machine; let us rest here in the auditorium, and talk awhile of the theatre and of its art. Tell me, do you know what is the Art of the Theatre?

PLAYGOER: To me it seems that Acting is the Art of the Theatre.

STAGE-DIRECTOR: Is a part, then, equal to a whole?

PLAYGOER: No, of course not. Do you, then, mean that the Play is the Art of the Theatre?

STAGE-DIRECTOR: A play is a work of literature, is it not? Tell me, then, how one art can possibly be another?

PLAYGOER: Well, then, if you tell me that the Art of the Theatre is neither the acting nor the play, then I must come to the conclusion that it is the scenery and the dancing. Yet I cannot think you will tell me this is so.

STAGE-DIRECTOR: No; the Art of the Theatre is neither acting nor the play, it is not scene nor dance, but it consists of all the elements of which these things are composed: action, which is the very spirit of acting; words, which are the body of the play; line and color, which are the very heart of the scene; rhythm, which is the very essence of dance.

Edward Gordon Craig: *The Art of the Theatre*. London: T. N. Foulis, 1905.

PLAYGOER: Action, words, line, color, rhythm! And which of these is all-important to the art?

STAGE-DIRECTOR: One is no more important than the other, no more than one color is more important to a painter than another, or one note more important than another to a musician. In one respect, perhaps, action is the most valuable part. Action bears the same relation to the Art of the Theatre as drawing does to painting, and melody does to music. The Art of the Theatre has sprung from action-movement-dance. . . .

The reason why you are not given a work of art on the stage is not because the public does not want it, not because there are not excellent craftsmen in the theatre who could prepare it for you, but because the theatre lacks the artist—the artist of the theatre, mind you, not the painter, poet, musician. The many excellent craftsmen are, all of them, more or less helpless to change the situation. They are forced to supply what the managers of the theatre demand, but they do so most willingly. The advent of the artist in the theatre world will change all this. He will slowly but surely gather around him these better craftsmen of whom I speak, and together they will give new life to the art of the theatre.

PLAYGOER: But for the others?

STAGE-DIRECTOR: The others? The modern theatre is full of these others, these untrained and untalented craftsmen. But I will say one thing for them. I believe they are unconscious of their inability. It is not ignorance on their part, it is innocence. Yet if these same men once realized that they were craftsmen, and would train as such—I do not speak only of the stage-carpenters, electricians, wigmakers, costumers, scene-painters, and actors (indeed, these are in many ways the best and most willing craftsmen)—I speak chiefly of the stage-director. If the stage-director was to technically train himself for his task of interpreting the plays of the dramatist—in time, and by a gradual development he would again recover the ground lost to the theatre, and finally would restore the Art of the Theatre to its home by means of his own creative genius.

PLAYGOER: Then you place the stage-director before the actors?

STAGE-DIRECTOR: Yes; the relation of the stage-director to the actor is precisely the same as that of the conductor to his orchestra, or of the publisher to his printer.

PLAYGOER: And you consider that the stage-director is a craftsman and not an artist?

STAGE-DIRECTOR: When he interprets the plays of the dramatist by means of his actors, his scene-painters, and his other craftsmen, then he is a craftsman—a master craftsman; when he will have mastered the uses of actions, words, line, color, and rhythm, then he may become an artist. Then we shall no longer need the assistance of the playwright—for our art will then be self-reliant.

PLAYGOER: Is your belief in a Renaissance of the art based on your belief in the Renaissance of the stage-director?

STAGE-DIRECTOR: Yes, certainly, most certainly. Did you for an instant think that I have a contempt for the stage-director? Rather have I a contempt for any man who fails in the whole duty of the stage-director.

PLAYGOER: What are his duties?

STAGE-DIRECTOR: What is his craft? I will tell you. His work as interpreter of the play of the dramatist is something like this: he takes the copy of the play from the hands of the dramatist and promises faithfully to interpret it as indicated in the text (remember I am speaking only of the very best of stage-directors). He then reads the play, and during the first reading the entire color, tone, movement, and rhythm that the work must assume comes clearly before him. As for the stage directions, descriptions of scenes, etc., with which the author may interlard his copy, these are not to be considered by him, for if he is master of his craft he can learn nothing from them.

PLAYGOER: I do not quite understand you. Do you mean that when a playwright has taken the trouble to describe the scene in which his men and women are to move and talk, that the stage-director is to take no notice of such directions—in fact, to disregard them?

STAGE-DIRECTOR: It makes no difference whether he regards or disregards them. What he must see to is that he makes his action and scene match the verse or the prose, the beauty of it, the sense of it. Whatever picture the dramatist may wish us to know of, he will

describe his scene during the progress of the conversation between the
characters. Take, for instance, the first scene in *Hamlet*. It begins:

> Ber. Who's there?
> Fran. Nay, answer me; stand and unfold yourself.
> Ber. Long live the king!
> Fran. Bernardo?
> Ber. He.
> Fran. You come most carefully upon your hour.
> Ber. 'Tis now struck twelve; get thee to bed, Francisco.
> Fran. For this relief much thanks, 'tis bitter cold,
>   And I am sick at heart.
> Ber. Have you had quiet guard?
> Fran. Not a mouse stirring.
> Ber. Well, good night.
>   If you do meet Horatio and Marcellus,
>   The rivals of my watch, bid them make haste.

That is enough to guide the stage-director. He gathers from it that it
is twelve o'clock at night, that it is in the open air, that the guard of
some castle is being changed, that it is very cold, very quiet, and very
dark. Any additional "stage directions" by the dramatist are trivialities.

PLAYGOER: Then you do not think that an author should write any
stage directions whatever, and you seem to consider it an offense on his
part if he does so?

STAGE-DIRECTOR: Well, is it not an offense to the men of the
theatre?

PLAYGOER: In what way?

STAGE-DIRECTOR: First tell me the greatest offense an actor can give
to a dramatist.

PLAYGOER: To play his part badly?

STAGE-DIRECTOR: No, that may merely prove the actor to be a bad
craftsman.

PLAYGOER: Tell me, then.

STAGE-DIRECTOR: The greatest offense an actor can give to a dramatist is to cut out words or lines in his play, or to insert what is known as
a "gag." It is an offense to poach on what is the sole property of the

playwright. It is not usual to "gag" in Shakespeare, and when it is done it does not go uncensured.

PLAYGOER: But what has this to do with the stage directions of the playwright, and in what way does the playwright offend the theatre when he dictates these stage directions?

STAGE-DIRECTOR: He offends in that he poaches on their preserves. If to gag or cut the poet's lines is an offense, so is it an offense to tamper with the art of the stage-director.

PLAYGOER: Then is all the stage direction of the world's plays worthless?

STAGE-DIRECTOR: Not to the reader, but to the stage-director, and to the actor—yes.

PLAYGOER: But Shakespeare——

STAGE-DIRECTOR: Shakespeare seldom directs the stage-director. . . . Would you like to hear what scene directions Shakespeare actually wrote for *Romeo and Juliet?* He wrote: "*Actus primus. Scaena prima.*" And not another word as to act or scene throughout the whole play. And now for *King Lear.*

PLAYGOER: No, it is enough. I see now. Evidently Shakespeare relied upon the intelligence of the stage-men to complete their scene from his indication. . . . But is this the same in regard to the actions? Does not Shakespeare place some descriptions through *Hamlet,* such as "Hamlet leaps into Ophelia's grave," "Laertes grapples with him," and later, "The attendants part them, and they come out of the grave"?

STAGE-DIRECTOR: No, not one word. All the stage directions, from the first to the last, are the tame inventions of sundry editors, Mr. Malone, Mr. Capell, Theobald and others, and they have committed an indiscretion in tampering with the play, for which we, the men of the theatre, have to suffer.

PLAYGOER: How is that?

STAGE-DIRECTOR: Why, supposing any of us reading Shakespeare shall see in our mind's eye some other combination of movements contrary to the "instructions" of these gentlemen, and suppose we represent our ideas on the stage, we are instantly taken to task by some knowing one, who accuses us of altering the directions of Shakespeare—nay more, of altering his very intentions.

PLAYGOER: But do not the "knowing ones," as you call them, know that Shakespeare wrote no stage directions?

STAGE-DIRECTOR: One can only guess that to be the case, to judge from their indiscreet criticisms. Anyhow, what I wanted to show you was that our greatest modern poet realized that to add stage directions was first of all unnecessary, and secondly, tasteless. We can therefore be sure that Shakespeare at any rate realized what was the work of the theatre craftsman—the stage-director, and that it was part of the stage-director's task to invent the scenes in which the play was to be set.

PLAYGOER: Yes, and you were telling me what each part consisted of.

STAGE-DIRECTOR: Quite so. And now that we have disposed of the error that the author's directions are of any use, we can continue to speak of the way the stage-director sets to work to interpret faithfully the play of the dramatist. I have said that he swears to follow the text faithfully, and that his first work is to read the play through and get the great impression; and in reading, as I have said, begins to see the whole color, rhythm, action of the thing. He then puts the play aside for some time, and in his mind's eye mixes his palette (to use a painter's expression) with the colors which the impression of the play has called up. Therefore, on sitting down a second time to read through the play, he is surrounded by an atmosphere which he proposes to test. At the end of the second reading he will find that his more definite impressions have received clear and unmistakable corroboration, and that some of his impressions which were less positive have disappeared. He will then make a note of these. It is possible that he will even now commence to suggest, in line and color, some of the scenes and ideas which are filling his head, but this is more likely to be delayed until he has re-read the play at least a dozen times.

PLAYGOER: But I thought the stage-director always left that part of the play—the scene designing—to the scene painter?

STAGE-DIRECTOR: So he does, generally. First blunder of the modern theatre.

PLAYGOER: How is it a blunder?

STAGE-DIRECTOR: This way: A has written a play which B promises to interpret faithfully. In so delicate a matter as the interpretation of so elusive a thing as the spirit of a play, which, do you think, will be the surest way to preserve the unity of that spirit? Will it be best if *B* does all the work by himself? Or will it do to give the work into the hands of *C*, *D*, and *E*, each of whom see or think differently to *B* or *A*?

PLAYGOER: Of course the former would be best. But is it possible for one man to do the work of three men?

STAGE-DIRECTOR: That is the only way the work can be done, if unity, the one thing vital to a work of art, is to be obtained.

PLAYGOER: So, then, the stage-director does not call in a scene painter and ask him to design a scene, but he designs one himself?

STAGE-DIRECTOR: Certainly. And remember he does not merely sit down and draw a pretty or historically accurate design, with enough doors and windows in picturesque places, but he first of all chooses certain colors which seem to him to be in harmony with the spirit of the play, rejecting other colors as out of tune. He then weaves into a pattern certain objects—an arch, a fountain, a balcony, a bed—using the chosen object as the center of his design. Then he adds to this all the objects which are mentioned in the play, and which are necessary to be seen. To these he adds, one by one, each character which appears in the play, and gradually each movement of each character, and each costume. He is as likely as not to make several mistakes in his pattern. If so, he must, as it were, unpick the design, and rectify the blunder even if he has to go right back to the beginning and start the pattern all over again—or he may even have to begin a new pattern. At any rate, slowly, harmoniously, must the whole design develop, so that the eye of the beholder shall be satisfied. While this pattern for the eye is being devised, the designer is being guided as much by the sound of the verse or prose as by the sense or spirit. And shortly all is prepared, and the actual work can be commenced.

PLAYGOER: What actual work? It seems to me that the stage-director has already been doing a good deal of what may be called actual work.

STAGE-DIRECTOR: Well, perhaps; but the difficulties have but commenced. By the actual work I mean the work which needs skilled labor, such as the actual painting of the huge spaces of canvas for the scenes, and the actual making of the costumes.

PLAYGOER: You are not going to tell me that the stage-director actually paints his own scenes and cuts his own costumes, and sews them together?

STAGE-DIRECTOR: No, I will not say that he does so in every case and for every play, but he must have done so at one time or another during his apprenticeship, or must have closely studied all the technical points of these complicated crafts. Then will he be able to guide the skilled craftsmen in their different departments. And when the actual making of the scenes and costumes has commenced, the parts are distributed to the different actors, who learn the words before a single rehearsal takes place. (This, as you may guess, is not the custom, but it is what should be seen to by a stage-director such as I describe.) Meantime, the scenes and costumes are almost ready. I will not tell you the amount of interesting but laborious work it entails to prepare the play up to this point. But even when once the scenes are placed upon the stage, and the costumes upon the actors, the difficulty of the work is still great.

PLAYGOER: The stage-director's work is not finished then?

STAGE-DIRECTOR: Finished! What do you mean?

PLAYGOER: Well, I thought now that the scenes and costumes were all seen to, the actors and actresses would do the rest.

STAGE-DIRECTOR: No, the stage-director's most interesting work is now beginning. His scene is set and his characters are clothed. He has, in short, a kind of dream picture in front of him. He clears the stage of all but the one, two, or more characters who are to commence the play, and he begins the scheme of lighting these figures and the scene.

PLAYGOER: What, is not this branch left to the discretion of the master electrician and his men?

STAGE-DIRECTOR: The doing of it is left to them, but the manner of doing it is the business of the stage-director. Being, as I have said, a man of some intelligence and training, he has devised a special way of lighting his scene for this play, just as he has devised a special way of painting the scene and costuming the figures. If the word "harmony" held no significance for him, he would of course leave it to the first comer.

PLAYGOER: Then do you actually mean that he has made so close a study of nature that he can direct his electricians how to make it appear as if the sun were shining at such and such an altitude, or as if the moonlight were flooding the interior of the room with such and such an intensity?

STAGE-DIRECTOR: No, I should not like to suggest that, because the reproduction of nature's lights is not what my stage-director ever attempts. Neither should he attempt such an impossibility. Not to *reproduce* nature, but to *suggest* some of her most beautiful and most living ways—that is what my stage-director shall attempt. The other thing proclaims an overbearing assumption of omnipotence. A stage-director may well aim to be an artist, but it ill becomes him to attempt celestial honors. This attitude he can avoid by never trying to imprison or copy nature, for nature will be neither imprisoned nor allow any man to copy her with any success.

PLAYGOER: Then in what way does he set to work? What guides him in his task of lighting the scene and costumes which we are speaking about?

STAGE-DIRECTOR: What guides him? Why, the scene and the costumes, and the verse and the prose, and the sense of the play. All these things, as I told you, have now been brought into harmony, the one with the other—all goes smoothly—what simpler, then, that it should so continue, and that the director should be the only one to know how to preserve this harmony which he has commenced to create? . . .

We have passed in review the different tasks of the stage-director— scene, costume, lighting—and we have come to the most interesting part, that of the manipulation of the figures in all their movements and speeches. You expressed astonishment that the acting—that is to say, the speaking and actions of the actors—was not left to the actors to arrange for themselves. But consider for an instant the nature of this work. Would you have that which has already grown into a certain unified pattern, suddenly spoiled by the addition of something accidental?

PLAYGOER: How do you mean? I understand what you suggest, but will you not show me more exactly how the actor can spoil the pattern?

STAGE-DIRECTOR: *Unconsciously* spoil it, mind you! I do not for an instant mean that it is his wish to be out of harmony with his surroundings, but he does so through innocence. Some actors have the right instincts in this matter, and some have none whatever. But even those whose instincts are most keen cannot remain in the pattern, cannot be harmonious, without following the directions of the stage-director.

PLAYGOER: Then you do not even permit the leading actor and actress to move and act as their instincts and reason dictate?

STAGE-DIRECTOR: No, rather must they be the very first to follow the direction of the stage-director, so often do they become the very center of the pattern—the very heart of the emotional design.

PLAYGOER: And is that understood and appreciated by them?

STAGE-DIRECTOR: Yes, but only when they realize and appreciate at the same time that the play, and the right and just interpretation of the play, is the all-important thing in the modern theatre. Let me illustrate this point to you. The play to be presented is *Romeo and Juliet*. We have studied the play, prepared scene and costume, lighted both, and now our rehearsals for the actors commence. The first movement of the great crowd of unruly citizens of Verona, fighting, swearing, killing each other, appalls us. It horrifies us that in this white little city of roses and song and love there should dwell this amazing and detestable hate which is ready to burst out at the very church doors, or in the middle of the May festival, or under the windows of the house of a newly born girl. Quickly following on this picture, and even while we remember the ugliness which larded both faces of Capulet and Montague, there comes strolling down the road the son of Montague, our Romeo, who is soon to be lover and the loved of his Juliet. Therefore, whoever is chosen to move and speak as Romeo must move and speak as part and parcel of the design—this design which I have already pointed out to you as having a definite form. He must move across our sight in a certain way, passing to a certain point, in a certain light, his head at a certain angle, his eyes, his feet, his whole body in tune with the play, and not (as is often the case) in tune with his own thoughts only, and these out of harmony with the play. For his thoughts (beautiful as they may chance to be) may not match the spirit or the pattern which has been so carefully prepared by the director.

PLAYGOER: Would you have the stage-director control the movements of whoever might be impersonating the character of Romeo, even if he were a fine actor?

STAGE-DIRECTOR: Most certainly; and the finer the actor the finer his intelligence and taste, and therefore the more easily controlled. In fact, I am speaking in particular of a theatre wherein all the actors are men of refinement and the director a man of peculiar accomplishments.

PLAYGOER: But are you not asking these intelligent actors almost to become puppets?

STAGE-DIRECTOR: A sensitive question! which one would expect from an actor who felt uncertain about his powers. A puppet is at present only a doll, delightful enough for a puppet show. But for a theatre we need more than a doll. Yet that is the feeling which some actors have about their relationship with the stage-director. They feel they are having their strings pulled, and resent it, and show they feel hurt—insulted.

PLAYGOER: I can understand that.

STAGE-DIRECTOR: And cannot you also understand that they should be willing to be controlled? Consider for a moment the relationship of the men on a ship, and you will understand what I consider to be the relationship of men in a theatre. . . . It will not be difficult for you to understand that a theatre in which so many hundred persons are engaged at work is in many respects like a ship, and demands like management. And it will not be difficult for you to see how the slightest sign of disobedience would be disastrous. Mutiny has been well anticipated in the navy, but not in the theatre. The navy has taken care to define, in clear and unmistakable voice, that the captain of the vessel is the king, and a despotic ruler into the bargain. Mutiny on a ship is dealt with by a court-martial, and is put down by very severe punishment, by imprisonment, or by dismissal from the service.

PLAYGOER: But you are not going to suggest such a possibility for the theatre?

STAGE-DIRECTOR: The theatre, unlike the ship, is not made for purposes of war, and so for some unaccountable reason discipline is not held to be of such vital importance, whereas it is of as much importance as in any branch of service. But what I wish to show you is that until discipline is understood in a theatre to be willing and reliant obedience to the director or captain no supreme achievement can be accomplished.

PLAYGOER: But are not the actors, scene-men, and the rest all willing workers?

STAGE-DIRECTOR: Why, my dear friend, there never were such glorious-natured people as these men and women of the theatre. They are enthusiastically willing, but sometimes their judgment is at fault, and they become as willing to be unruly as to be obedient, and as willing to lower the standard as to raise it. As for nailing the flag to the mast—this is seldom dreamed of—for *compromise* and the vicious doctrine of compromise with the enemy is preached by the officers of the theatrical navy. Our enemies are vulgar display, the lower public opinion, and ignorance. To these our "officers" wish us to knuckle under. What the theatre people have not yet quite comprehended is *the value of a high standard and the value of a director who abides by it.*

PLAYGOER: And that director, why should he not be an actor or a scene-painter?

STAGE-DIRECTOR: Do you pick your leader from the ranks, exalt him to be captain, and then let him handle the guns and the ropes? No; the director of a theatre must be a man apart from any of the crafts. He must be a man who knows but no longer handles the ropes.

PLAYGOER: But I believe it is a fact that many well-known leaders in the theatre have been actors and stage-directors at the same time.

STAGE-DIRECTOR: Yes, that is so. But you will not find it easy to assure me that no mutiny was heard of under their rule. Right away from all this question of positions there is the question of the art, the work. If an actor assumes the management of the stage, and if he is a better actor than his fellows, a natural instinct will lead him to make himself the center of everything. He will feel that unless he does so the work will appear thin and unsatisfying. He will pay less heed to the play than he will to his own part, and he will, in fact, gradually cease to look upon the work as a whole. And this is not good for the work. This is not the way a work of art is to be produced in the theatre.

PLAYGOER: But might it not be possible to find a great actor who would be so great an artist that as director he would never do as you say, but who would always handle himself as actor, just the same as he handles the rest of the material?

STAGE-DIRECTOR: All things are possible, but firstly, it is against the nature of an actor to do as you suggest; secondly, it is against the nature of the stage-director to perform; and thirdly, it is against all nature that a man can be in two places at once. Now, the place of the actor is on the stage, in a certain position ready by means of his brains to give suggestions of certain emotions, surrounded by certain scenes and people; and it is the place of the stage-director to be in front of this, that he may view it as a whole. So that you see even if we found our perfect actor who was our perfect stage-director, he could not be in two places at the same time. Of course we have sometimes seen the conductor of a small orchestra playing the part of the first violin, but not from choice, and not to a satisfactory issue; neither is it the practice in large orchestras.

PLAYGOER: I understand, then, that you would allow no one to rule on the stage except the stage-director?

STAGE-DIRECTOR: The nature of the work permits nothing else.

PLAYGOER: Not even the playwright?

STAGE-DIRECTOR: Only when the playwright has practiced and studied the crafts of acting, scene-painting, costume, lighting, and dance, not otherwise. But playwrights, who have not been cradled in the theatre, generally know little of these crafts. Goethe, whose love for the theatre remained ever fresh and beautiful, was in many ways one of the greatest of stage-directors. But, when he linked himself to the Weimar theatre, he forgot to do what the great musician who followed him remembered. Goethe permitted an authority in the theatre higher than himself, that is to say, the owner of the theatre. Wagner was careful to possess himself of his theatre, and become a sort of feudal baron in his castle.

PLAYGOER: Was Goethe's failure as a theatre director due to this fact?

STAGE-DIRECTOR: Obviously, for had Goethe held the keys of the doors that impudent little poodle would never have got as far as its dressing-room; the leading lady would never have made the theatre and herself immortally ridiculous; and Weimar would have been saved the tradition of having perpetrated the most shocking blunder which ever occurred inside a theatre.

PLAYGOER: The traditions of most theatres certainly do not seem to show that the artist is held in much respect on the stage.

STAGE-DIRECTOR: Well, it would be easy to say a number of hard things about the theatre and its ignorance of art. But one does not hit a thing which is down, unless, perhaps, with the hope that the shock may cause it to leap to its feet again. And our Western theatre is very much down. The East still boasts a theatre. Ours here in the West is on its last legs. But I look for a Renaissance.

PLAYGOER: How will that come?

STAGE-DIRECTOR: Through the advent of a man who shall contain in him all the qualities which go to make up a master of the theatre, and through the reform of the theatre as an instrument. When that is accomplished, when the theatre has become a masterpiece of mechanism, when it has invented a technique, it will without any effort develop a *creative art* of its own. But the whole question of the development of the craft into a self-reliant and creative art would take too long to go thoroughly into at present. There are already some theatre men at work on the building of the theatres; some are reforming the acting, some the scenery. And all of this must be of some small value. But the very first thing to be realized is that little or no result can come from the reforming of a single craft of the theatre without at the same time, in the same theatre, reforming all the other crafts. *The whole Renaissance of the Art of the Theatre depends upon the extent that this is realized.* The Art of the Theatre, as I have already told you, is divided up into so many crafts: acting, scene, costume, lighting, carpentering, singing, dancing, etc., that it must be realized at the commencement that ENTIRE, not PART reform is needed; and it must be realized that *one* part, one craft, has a *direct* bearing upon each of the other crafts in the theatre, and that no result can come from fitful, uneven reform, but only from a systematic progression. Therefore, the reform of the Art of the Theatre is possible to those men alone who have studied and practiced all the crafts of the theatre.

PLAYGOER: That is to say, your ideal stage-director.

STAGE-DIRECTOR: Yes. You will remember that at the commencement of our conversation I told you my belief in the Renaissance of the Art of the Theatre was based in my belief in the Renaissance of the stage-director, and that when he had understood the right use of actors, scene, costume, lighting, and dance, and by means of these had mastered the crafts of interpretation, he would then gradually acquire the mastery of action, line, color, rhythm, and words, this last strength developing out of all the rest. . . . Then I said the Art of the Theatre would have won back its rights, and its work would stand self-reliant as a creative art, and no longer as an interpretive craft.

PLAYGOER: Yes, and at the time I did not quite understand what you meant, and though I can now understand your drift, I do not quite in my mind's eye see the stage without its poet.

STAGE-DIRECTOR: What? Shall anything be lacking when the poet shall no longer write for the theatre?

PLAYGOER: The play will be lacking.

STAGE-DIRECTOR: Are you sure of that?

PLAYGOER: Well, the play will certainly not exist if the poet or playwright is not there to write it.

STAGE-DIRECTOR: There will not be any play in the sense in which you use the word.

PLAYGOER: But you propose to present something to the audience, and I presume before you are able to present them with that something you must have it in your possession.

STAGE-DIRECTOR: Certainly; you could not have made a surer remark. Where you are at fault is to take for granted, as if it were a law for the Medes and Persians, that that *something* must be made of words.

PLAYGOER: Well, what is this something which is not words, but for presentation to the audience?

STAGE-DIRECTOR: First tell me, is not an idea something?

PLAYGOER: Yes, but it lacks form.

STAGE-DIRECTOR: Well, but is it not permissible to give an idea whatever form the artist chooses?

PLAYGOER: Yes.

STAGE-DIRECTOR: And is it an unpardonable crime for the theatrical artist to use some different material to the poet's?

PLAYGOER: No.

STAGE-DIRECTOR: Then we are permitted to attempt to give form to an idea in whatever material we can find or invent, provided it is not a material which should be put to a better use?

PLAYGOER: Yes.

STAGE-DIRECTOR: Very good; follow what I have to say for the next few minutes, and then go home and think about it for a while. Since you have granted all I asked you to permit, I am now going to tell you out of what material an artist of the theatre of the future will create his masterpieces. Out of ACTION, SCENE, and VOICE. Is it not very simple?

And when I say *action*, I mean both gesture and dancing, the prose and poetry of action.

When I say *scene*, I mean all which comes before the eye, such as the lighting, costume, as well as the scenery.

When I say *voice*, I mean the spoken word or the word which is sung, in contradiction to the word which is read, for the word written to be spoken and the word written to be read are two entirely different things.

And now, though I have but repeated what I told you at the beginning of our conversation, I am delighted to see that you no longer look so puzzled.

VSEVOLOD MEYERHOLD

(b. 1873)

Theatricality

W HEN I spoke of the methods open to the stage director who sought to reconstruct the characteristic stages of model theatrical epochs, when I discussed the two methods at the disposal of the director who contemplated the production of a play from an old theatre, I failed to mention one possible exception. In the production of a play from the old theatre, it is not at all necessary to subordinate the staging to *methods of archaeology*. In the matter of reconstruction the stage director need have no worry over the faithful reproduction of the architectural features on the antique stage. The production of a genuinely old play may be done in *free composition* in the spirit of primitive stages but on one indispensable condition: to take from the old stage the *essence* of those architectural features which would be most appropriate to the spirit of the work in production.

In order to produce, for example, *Don Juan* by Molière, it would be a mistake to attempt an exact replica of any contemporary stage of Molière's time: Palais Royal or Petit-Bourbon.

If we probe into the spirit of Molière's work we will discover that he strove to expand the framework of the contemporary stage which had been more suitable to the pathos of Corneille than to plays which had evolved out of elements of folk art.

The academic theatre of the Renaissance which failed to utilize the possibilities inherent in the forward thrust of the forestage, set apart at a respectable distance from each other the actor and the public. The

Vsevolod Meyerhold: *O Teatre*. Petrograd: 1913, 121–128. The staging of *Don Juan* discussed here is a description of Meyerhold's production at the Alexandrinsky Theatre, St. Petersburg, in 1910.

first rows of seats were pushed back not only to the center of the orchestra but further still to the wall opposite the stage.

Could Molière acquiesce in this separation of actor and audience? Could Molière's overflowing gaiety find full release in such circumstances? Could the full breadth of his bold and true strokes be seen to advantage? Could the author, hurt by the suppression of *Tartuffe*, hurl his denunciatory soliloquies across that stage? Were not the columns in the wings a hindrance to the free gestures and gymnastic movements of Molière's actors?

Molière was the first theatrical master under *Le Roi Soleil* who strove to carry the action forward from the depth and the center of the stage to the *proscenium*, to its very edge.

Both the stage of antiquity and the popular stage of Shakespeare's time required no illusory sets like ours. Nor was the actor a source of stage illusion. With his gestures, facial expression, plastic movements, the actor was the *sole* vehicle for the realization of the dramatist's idea.

This was also the case in medieval Japan. In the Nō plays with their exquisite ceremonial, in which action, dialogue, song were rigidly stylized, in which the chorus performed a role similar to that of the Greek chorus, in which the wild fury of the music tended to transport the public into a world of hallucination, the stage director placed the actors so close to the edge of the platform that their dances, movements, gesticulation, mimicry, poses were in full view.

Speaking of the production of *Don Juan* it was not by accident that I mentioned the methods of the old Japanese theatre.

From descriptions of Japanese theatrical performances approximately contemporaneous with Molière's predominance on the French stage, we learn that special attendants, so-called Corumbo in black cloaks, like priestly cassocks, would prompt the actors in view of the audience. Whenever the costume of a female character (played by a male) fell into disarray in a moment of high exaltation, Corumbo would hasten to arrange his train into beautiful folds and put his hair dress in order. It was part of his duty to pick up objects which the actors had dropped or forgotten on the stage. After a scene of battle he would remove from the stage lost headgear, weapons, cloaks. When a hero died Corumbo would throw a black cloth over the corpse under the cover of which the actor disappeared from the stage. When action required total darkness Corumbo would kneel down at the feet of the hero and throw light on his face by a candle attached to a long rod.

The Japanese have preserved to this day the mannerisms of the actors dating back to the creators of Japanese drama, Onono-Otsu (1513-1581), Satsumo-Joun (b. 1595) and the Shakespeare of Japan, Chikamatsu-Monzaimon.

Is not there something analogous in the present attempts of the Comédie-Française to revive the methods of Molière's comedians?

In the extreme west of Europe (France, Italy, Spain, England) as in the extreme east of Asia (Japan) within the limits of one epoch (second half of the XVI and the whole of the XVII centuries) the theatre resounded with the tinkling bells of pure theatricality.

Is it not clear why each device on every stage of that brilliant theatrical epoch was adopted precisely on the wonderful platform called the proscenium?

And, what about the proscenium?

Like a circus arena pressed on all sides by a circle of spectators, the proscenium is brought close to the public so that not a single gesture, not a single act, not a single facial expression shall be lost in the dust of the wings. And mark well how resourcefully planned are these gestures, actions, postures, expressions. Indeed—could the pompous affectations, the lack of plasticity in bodily movement be suffered by a public placed as close to the actor as was made necessary by the proscenium of the old English, Spanish, Italian, Japanese stages.

This proscenium so skillfully employed by Molière was the best insurance against the aridity of Corneillian methods which had been nursed in the Court of Louis XIV.

Furthermore—how notable have been the gains for Molière's work when performed on the proscenium although created in the wholly unfavorable climate of the contemporary stage! How spontaneously alive are the grotesque figures of Molière moving unhampered on the protruding forestage! The atmosphere of this space is not cramped by columns, while the light flooding this dustless atmosphere plays only on the lithe figures of the actors. Everything around seems especially made to increase the play of light both from the candles on the stage and the candles in the auditorium which throughout the performance is never darkened.

While rejecting the obligatory use of detail typical only of the stage of Louis XIV (curtain with cutout for head of announcer) could the stage director ignore the entourage associated with the style of the time which reared the theatre of Molière?

There are plays like *Antigone* by Sophocles or *Woe from Wit* by Griboyedov which can be appreciated by a modern spectator through the prism of his own time. *Antigone* and *Woe from Wit* might even be performed in modern dress. The hymn to liberty in the former; the conflict of two generations in the latter play are expressed with such clear and insistent emphasis that their message can be transmitted in any environment.

There are on the other hand plays whose cardinal idea will be fully appreciated by a modern spectator only if in addition to grasping the fine subtleties of the plot he will be made aware of that elusive climate which in a bygone age surrounded the actors, the theatre and the audience. There are plays which cannot be comprehended otherwise than if they are presented in a way intended to arouse in the spectator a receptivity to the action on the stage by setting it in a milieu analogous to the one that surrounded the audience of a specific past. Such a play is *Don Juan* by Molière. The public will only then appreciate the full subtlety of this charming comedy if it enters at once into a rapport with the smallest facets of the epoch in which the work was created. That is why the director who would undertake to stage *Don Juan* must first of all fill the stage and the auditorium with such an atmosphere that the dramatic action could not be grasped otherwise than through the prism of that atmosphere.

If one reads *Don Juan* by Molière without knowing the epoch which created his genius, how boring it appears! How indifferently the plot is developed compared with, say, the plot of *Don Juan* by Byron, not to speak of *El Burlador de Sevilla* by Tirso de Molina. When we read *Woe from Wit* by Griboyedov chords of our own time seem to be echoed from every page, and this makes the play especially significant for the contemporary public. When, however, we read the lengthy monologues of Elvire (Act I) or the long soliloquy of Don Juan, flaying hypocrisy (Act V), our attention flags. In order to make the modern spectator listen to these perorations without getting bored, in order to make him follow a whole series of dialogues without finding them remote, it is necessary to remind him insistently throughout the play of all those thousands of looms of the Lyonnaise manufactories which supplied the silk for the monstrously large Court of Louis XIV, of the Hôtel des Gobelins, that veritable city of painters, sculptors, jewelers, cabinet-makers, of the furniture built under the superintendence of the outstanding artist Le Brun, of all those craftsmen who made mirrors and lace according to the Venetian models, stockings according to the English, cloth according to the Dutch, tin and copper according to the Germans.

Hundreds of wax candles in three chandeliers above and two candelabra on the proscenium. Blackamoors inundating the stage with intoxicating perfumes, which flow drop by drop from a crystal flask onto a red-hot plate. Blackamoors flitting over the stage to pick up a lace handkerchief dropped by Don Juan or offer a chair to a tired actor. Blackamoors tying the laces on the shoes of Don Juan as he argues with Sganarelle. Blackamoors passing lanterns to the actors when the stage is in semidarkness. Blackamoors removing from the stage the cloaks and sabers after the desperate fight between Don Juan and the brigands. Blackamoors crawling under the table when the statue of the Commander appears. Blackamoors ringing a silver bell to summon the audience and in the absence of a curtain, announcing intermissions— all these are not stage tricks for the diversion of snobs; all this is in support of the main idea: to reveal as behind an incense-laden veil the perfumed and gilded realm of Versailles.

And the more resplendent the costumes and accessories (even if the architecture of the stage is extremely simple) the greater the contrast between Molière's temperament as comedian and the solemn affection of Versailles.

Was it the vagabondage over the provinces that put such a sharp stamp of forthrightness on the character of Molière? Or life in jerry-built stroller's stalls? Perhaps the struggle against hunger? Or was his defiant tone born amid the love-making actresses who cast the poet into such gloom and disappointment? In any case, after a period of friendly relations with Molière, Louis XIV seems to have found ample reason for growing cool.

The discord between *Le Roi Soleil* whose image is suggested in the lavish decorations on the proscenium, the discord between the King and the poet who in this pompous atmosphere makes Sganarelle complain of a stomach-ache (contrast of precious background versus Molière's mordant grotesques)—would not this discord now fuse into such a harmony that the spectator will inevitably fall under the spell of Molière's theatre? And would any detail of this creative genius be lost upon the spectator?

Don Juan is being performed without a curtain. There was none in the theatres of Palais Royal or of Petit-Bourbon.

But why remove the curtain? The spectator is usually indifferent in front of a curtain however well painted by whatever gifted artist. The spectator who came to see what is behind the curtain awaits its rise with apathy. And when it is up, how long will it be before he absorbs the full enchantment of the atmosphere surrounding the players. It is quite otherwise when the stage is open from beginning to end, when the extras with their own peculiar pantomime prepare the stage in sight of the audience. Long before the actor appears on the boards the spectator has already inhaled deeply the air of an epoch. And then that which in the reading of the play seemed superfluous or boring is now seen in a totally different light.

And it is unnecessary to darken the stage either during intermission or in the course of the performance. Bright light infects with a festive mood those who come to the theatre. The actor noting a smile on the lips of the spectator begins to enjoy his own sight as in a mirror. The actor who wears the mask of Don Juan will win the hearts not only of the masked Mathurine and Charlotte but also of the owners of those beautiful eyes whose sparkle he will detect in the auditorium as an answer to the smile in his own role.

GEORGE BERNARD SHAW

(1856-1950)

The Art of Rehearsal

My Dear McNulty,

As to stage technique, there are several stage techniques; and people may be very clever in one or more of them without being good at them all, and may even—especially in acting—know bits of them and not the rest. The beginning and end of the business from the author's point of view is the art of making the audience believe that real things are happening to real people. But the actor, male or female, may want the audience to believe that it is witnessing a magnificent display of acting by a great artist; and when the attempt to do this fails, the effect is disastrous, because then there is neither play nor great acting: the play is not credible nor the acting fascinating. To your star actor the play does not exist except as a mounting block. That is why comparatively humble actors, who do not dare to think they can succeed apart from the play, often give much better representations than star casts.

Many star actors have surprisingly little of what I call positive skill, and an amazing power of suggestion. You can safely write a play in which the audience is assured that the heroine is the most wonderful creature on earth, full of exquisite thoughts, and noble in character to the utmost degree, though, when it comes to the point, you find yourself unable to invent a single speech or action that would surprise you from your aunt. No matter: a star actress at £250 a week will do all that for you. She will utter your twaddle with such an air, and look such unutterable things between the lines, and dress so beautifully and

George Bernard Shaw: *The Art of Rehearsal; a Private Letter to an Irish Colleague in Response to a Request for Advice and Information.* New York: Samuel French, 1928. Copyright, 1928, by Bernard Shaw. By permission of the Public Trustee and The Society of Authors.

move so enigmatically and enchantingly, that the imagination of the audience will supply more than Shakespeare could have written.

This art of suggestion has been developed to an abnormal degree by the emptiness of the mechanical "well-made play" of the French school. And you may be tempted to say, "If this woman is so wonderful when she is making bricks without straw, what heights would she not reach if I were to give her straw in abundance?" But if you did you would be rudely disillusioned. You would have to say to the actress: "Mere suggestion is no use here. I don't ask you to suggest anything: I give you the actual things to do and say. I don't want you to look as if you could say wonderful things if you uttered your thoughts: I give you both the thoughts and the words; and you must get them across the footlights." On these conditions your star might be dreadfully at a loss. She might complain of having too many words. She would certainly try hard to get in her old suggestive business between the lines; to escape from the play; to substitute a personal performance of her own for the character you wanted to make the audience believe her to be; and thus your trouble with her would be in direct proportion to her charm as a fashionable leading lady.

The success of the Dublin Abbey Street Theatre was due to the fact that when it began none of the Company was worth twopence a week for ordinary fashionable purposes, though some of them can now hold a London audience in the hollow of their hands. They were held down by Yeats and Lady Gregory ruthlessly to my formula of making the audience believe that real things were happening to real people. They were taught no tricks, because Yeats and Lady Gregory didn't know any, having found out experimentally only what any two people of high intelligence and fine taste could find out by sticking to the point of securing a good representation.

Now as to your daily business in the theatre. It will be more laborious than you expect. If before you begin rehearsing you sit down to the manuscript of your play and work out all the stage business; so that you know where every speech is to be spoken as well as what it is to convey, and where the chairs are to be and where they are to be taken to, and where the actors are to put their hats or anything else they are to take in their hands in the course of the play, and when they are to rise and when they are to sit, and if you arrange all this so as to get the maximum of effect out of every word, and thus make the actors feel that they are speaking at the utmost possible advantage—or at worst that they cannot improve on your business, however little they may like it—and if you take care that they never distract attention from one another; that when they call to one another they are at a due distance; and that, when the audience is looking at one side of the stage and somebody cuts in on the other, some trick (which you must contrive) calls the attention of the audience to the new point of view or hearing, etc., then you will at the first rehearsal get a command of the production that nothing will shake afterwards. There will be no time wasted in fumbling for positions, and trying back and disputing.

When you have put your actors through an act for the first time in this way, go through it again to settle the business firmly in their memory. Be on the stage, handling your people and prompting them with the appropriate tones, as they will, of course, be rather in the dark as to what it is all about, except what they may have gathered from your reading of the play to them before rehearsal. Don't let them learn their parts until the end of the first week of rehearsal: nothing is a greater nuisance to an actor who is trying to remember his lines when he should be settling his positions and getting the hang of the play with his book in his hand.

One or two acts twice over is enough for each preliminary rehearsal. When you have reached the end of the first stage, then call "perfect" rehearsals (that is, without books). At these you must leave the stage and sit in the auditorium with a big notebook; *and from that time forth never interrupt a scene, nor allow anyone else to interrupt it or try back.* When anything goes wrong, or any improvement occurs to you, make a note; and at the end of the act go on the stage and explain your notes to the actors. Don't criticize. If a thing is wrong and you don't know exactly how to set it right, say nothing. Wait until you find out the right thing to do, or until the actor does. It discourages and maddens an actor to be told merely that you are dissatisfied. If you cannot help him, let him alone. Tell him what to do if you know: if not, hold your tongue until it comes to you or to him, as it probably will if you wait.

Remember that when the "perfect" rehearsals begin, the whole affair will collapse in apparent and most disappointing back-slidings for at least a week as far as the long parts are concerned, because in the first agony of trying to remember the words everything else will be lost. You must remember that at this stage the actor, being under a heavy strain, is fearfully irritable. But after another week the words will come automatically; and the play will get under way again.

Remember (particularly during the irritable stage) that you must not tell an actor too much at once. Not more than two or three important things can be borne at one rehearsal; and *don't* mention trifles, such as slips in business or in words, in a heart-broken desperate way, as if the world were crumbling in ruins. Don't mention anything that doesn't really matter. Be prepared for the same mistake being repeated time after time, and your directions being forgotten until you have given them three or four days running.

If you get angry and complain that you have repeatedly called attention, etc., like a schoolmaster, you will destroy the whole atmosphere in which art breathes, and make a scene which is not in the play, and a very disagreeable and invariably unsuccessful scene at that. Your chief artistic activity will be to prevent the actors taking their tone and speech from one another, instead of from their own parts, and thus destroying the continual variety and contrast which are the soul of liveliness in comedy and truth in tragedy. An actor's cue is not a signal to take up the running thoughtlessly, but a provocation to retort or respond in some clearly differentiated way. He must, even on the thousandth night, make the audience believe that he has never heard his cue before.

In the final stage, when everybody is word perfect, and can give his or her whole mind to the play, you must watch, watch, watch, like a cat at a mouse hole, and make very well-considered notes. To some of them you will append a "Rehearse this"; and at the end of the act you will ask them to go through the bit to get it right. But *don't* say when it doesn't come right: "We must go on at this until we get it, if we have to stay here all night": the schoolmaster again. If it goes wrong, it will go wronger with every repetition on the same day. Leave it until next time.

At the last two rehearsals you ought to have very few notes: all the difficulties should have been cleared away. The first time I ever counted my notes was when I had to produce *Arms and the Man* in ten rehearsals. The total was 600. That is a minimum: I have run into thousands since. Do not forget that though at the first rehearsal you will know more about the parts than the actors, at the last rehearsal they ought to know more about them (through their undivided attention) than you, and therefore have something to teach you about them.

Be prepared for a spell of hard work. The incessant strain on one's attention (the actors have their exits and rests; but the producer is hard at it all the time), the social effort of keeping up everyone's spirits in view of a great event, the dryness of the previous study of the mechanical details, daunt most authors. But if you have not enough energy to face all that, you had better keep out of the theatre and trust to a professional producer. In fact, it sometimes happens that the author has to be put out. Unless he goes through the grind I have described, and which I face with greater reluctance as I grow older, he simply bothers and complains and obstructs, either saying that he does not like what the actors are doing without knowing what he wants instead, or at the first rehearsal expecting a perfect performance, or wanting things that can't be done, or making his suggestions ridiculous by unskillful demonstrations, or quarrelling, or devil knows what not.

Only geniuses can tell you exactly what is wrong with a scene, though plenty of people can tell you something is wrong with it. So make a note of their dissatisfaction; but be very careful how you adopt their cure if they prescribe one. For instance, if they say a scene is too slow (meaning that it bores them), the remedy in nine cases out of ten is for the actors to go slower and bring out the meaning better by contrasts of tone and speed.

Never have a moment of silence on the stage except as an intentional stage effect. The play must not stop while an actor is sitting down or getting up or walking off the stage. The last word of an exit speech must get the actor off the stage. He must sit on a word or rise on a word; if he has to make a movement, he must move as he speaks and not before or after; and the cues must be picked up as smartly as a ball is fielded in cricket. This is the secret of pace, and of holding an audience. It is a rule which you may set aside again and again to make a special effect; for a technical rule may always be broken on purpose. But as a rule of thumb it is invaluable. I once saw a fine play of Masefield's prolonged by half-an-hour and almost ruined because the actors made their movements in silence between the speeches. That does not happen when his plays are produced by Granville-Barker or by himself.

Remember that no strangers should be present at a rehearsal. It is sometimes expedient that strangers, and even journalists, be invited to witness a so-called rehearsal; and on such occasions a pre-arranged interruption by the producer may take place to affirm the fact that the occasion is only a rehearsal. But the interruption must be addressed to the mechanical staff about some mechanical detail. No direction should ever be given to an actor in the presence of a stranger; and the consent of every actor should be obtained before a stranger is admitted. The actor, of course, is bound to the same reticence. A stranger is a non-professional who is not in the theatre on business. Rehearsals are absolutely and sacredly confidential. The publication of gossip about rehearsals, or the disclosure of the plot of the play, is the blackest breach of stage etiquette.

I have tumbled all this out at express speed, as the best I can do for you out of my own experience, in reply to your innocent question about technique. I hope it is intelligible and may be useful.

JACQUES COPEAU

(1878-1949)

Dramatic Economy

EVERY work intended for performance on the stage involves
directing. Since there are various types of drama, there is a
directing style and method corresponding to each of these
types and—within a given type—to the specific nature of each individual work. Directing is the sum-total of artistic and technical operations which enables the play as conceived by the author to pass from
the abstract, latent state, that of the written script, to concrete and
actual life on the stage.

The freer of stage directions a script is, and the more it aims at producing nothing but immediate effects, the more leeway it allows the
directing—in the material sense of the term. This means a great many
sets, a profusion of light and color, elaborate costumes, striking ornaments, and a large number of actors and supers.

Realism brings to the stage separate segments of the world. It seeks
to make us believe in a pasteboard universe. It indulges in ingenious
make-believe, inspired by the art of the painter, the architect, and the
scene designer, in order to reproduce vast buildings, streets and squares,
and broad expanses in nature: plains, mountains, sea and sky. It makes
the sun set, the moon rise, the night fall, or the day dawn. It lets loose
storm, flood, fire, the movement of crowds, the clash of armies; it shows
boats on the high seas, trains in motion, planes in flight.

Fantasy presents, as if they were realities perceived by the senses,
objects which the human mind usually evokes only in imagination:
creatures of fantasy, monsters, gods and goddesses, the world of

Jacques Copeau: "La mise en scène," *Encyclopédie Française*, December 1935,
17'64, 1-5.

fairyland. A dreamlike atmosphere envelops them; the lands they inhabit change before our eyes.

These material refinements in staging, which the antique theatre did not have, were made possible by the inventions of Italian scene designers of the Renaissance. This was particularly true in ballet, pantomime, and opera. In our day they have been heightened by the advances in machinery and electricity, with the use of revolving stages, elevators, cycloramas, and spotlights.

But these refinements, pushed to extremes and too much at the beck and call of the engineer, risk becoming an endless game, a kind of plaything which intrigues us with its endless combinations, surprises, and tricks. When used in performances in the music hall, they achieve effects which are quite appropriate. But I fear they are contaminating some types of drama where they do not belong. Perhaps they will one day be held in check—as already seems to be somewhat the case—by improvements in the cinema, in which technicians have at their disposal more subtle, varied, and powerful means both of capturing the external world and of transforming it into a world of fantasy.

The modern trend in scenic design is in the direction of artistic simplification, in pictorial effect as well as in the choice of elements that constitute a *décor*. Our designers prefer an intelligently interpreted portrait to a photographic image; they aim at impressions rather than descriptions. They strive to evoke and suggest rather than to depict. They single out a part in order to indicate the whole: a tree instead of a forest, a pillar instead of a temple. Stylized elements replace the wealth of detail which, in the older method, went counter to nature, competing with dramatic action and wearing down the playgoer's attention.

THE ROLE OF THE DIRECTOR

The layman, ill-informed as to the secrets of stagecraft in the art of the theatre, will probably recognize the director's hand only in the tangible excesses we have described. In reality, however, the richer in literary, poetic, psychological, and emotional content a play is; the more profound it is and the more indefinable its beauty; the greater it is, the more consummate in form and original in style, the more numerous and subtle will be the problems it presents for the director.

Let us now follow the director in the successive phases of his work. He receives a script from a playwright. After his initial reading, the inanimate pages begin to come to life in his fingers. They are no longer symbols written on paper: he adds a sense of life to the meaning of the words. They are voices which speak and fall silent at his bidding, gestures which are made, faces which light up. Place, time, colors, and lights are clearly defined in terms of specific emotions and specific episodes. Later, after more methodical study, the director will deepen these various notions. But at his very first contact, a tiny universe both spiritual and concrete commences to take shape—of which the reader is more or less conscious.

What remains in the director's mind, and not only in his mind but within reach of his senses, so to speak, is a feeling of general rhythm—the breathing, as it were, of the work which is to emerge into life. But since a play is essentially action, and an actor primarily a human being who acts, before going any further our director seeks to delimit the place, form, and dimensions of this action. If it is an interior, he will give it its essential props: chairs and other pieces of furniture. If he is dealing with an open space, he will determine its contours and cubes. This is his staging plan, on which he will locate, as accurately as possible without harming the flow of the action, the actors' places or positions as well as their entrances and exits. For, in interpreting the play and setting it in its proper perspective, it is important that a given actor at a given moment and in a given situation, prompted by a given emotion, approach or draw away from a given point on the stage.

Once the stage is set in accordance with the needs of the action as envisaged in its broad lines, the action itself must be organized, act by act, scene by scene, speech by speech, down to the slightest details. As he devises the action he is going to propose to his actors—their places, their distances from one another, the movements they make, their relations with the stage set, the furniture and the props, the pace of their speeches and their silences, the varying tempo of their entrances and exits—the director bears in mind the truthfulness of the characters, the expression of their emotions, the demands of the script, the logic of events, the positions on stage, the lighting effects, the naturalness of the players, and group symmetry. He aims at achieving clear representation, well-defined movement, varied rhythm, and sustained harmony. All his steps are motivated by a unity of style and guided by an over-all idea. But he must be careful not to allow this idea to become too obvious, not to force it to the point of pedantry and abstraction, both in the stage *décor* and in the playing of the actors—for the triumph of his art is the creation of life.

This personal work on the part of the director is necessary, if he is to avoid losses of time, mistakes, and all sorts of disappointments. Yet it is not always carried through in the way in which we have just described it. But let us assume that it has been. Now the moment has come for the director to begin rehearsals.

Unless time does not permit—that precious time we so often waste because of lack of discipline and poor organization in the theatre—the director should first call together his actors around a table and not on a stage: firstly, in order to read the play to them and impress on their minds its meaning and rhythm; secondly, in order to have them read their parts. This phase will last as long as the director is capable of sustaining it, and the actors capable of enduring it. It enables the director to explain the author's intentions and his own, to nip in the bud any incipient misunderstandings, to dwell on the beauties of the script and the basic principles of its interpretation, and perhaps to correct certain mistakes in casting before the actors have entered into their parts and while they are still at ease in their mind.

The first rehearsals on the stage are devoted to the *assigning of places*. That is, the actor, guided by the director, adjusts himself to the mechanics of the action, familiarizing himself with the movements he is called upon to make, trying to understand the reasons for them, accepting them or discussing them. At the same time it gives the director an opportunity to verify his conceptions, to modify them if need be, and to make the necessary revisions in his over-all plan before the sets are built. This period of uncertainty must not be prolonged; it demoralizes the actor. So now the play is clarified, even though in summary fashion, from beginning to end. Actors and director have an over-all view of the work. They know where they are going before they plunge into the actual interpretation.

This work of interpretation becomes possible on the day that the actor, putting away his "sides," begins to speak his lines from memory and tries to harmonize what he says with what he does. At that moment, even the most gifted actors seem to hesitate. There is a critical period during which the interpreter appears as if to have lost the feel of his initial grasp. He will get it back again, and with an accent of enduring truth, if he is professional enough, if he persists in his work, and if he has sufficient power of concentration and sincerity to identify himself—first physically, then emotionally—with the character he portrays. Here too the director is the actor's guide, teacher, and mainstay. His task is not only to keep the actor in line and within the limits of his part, not only to indicate to him where he is near the truth, and not only to correct his mistakes, but also to understand the difficulties confronting the actor and to show him how to solve these difficulties. He must use tact, authority, and persuasion. But it is by means of sympathetic understanding that he will exert his most active influence, provided that his experience with his actors is long, objective, and profound enough for him to know the specific sensitivity, temperament, and ability of each one of them. It is dangerous to allow the actor too much freedom; but it is even more dangerous to stifle his spontaneity with blind coercion.

Every director has his personal method of influencing the actors. These methods should be studied individually. I believe that the Englishman Granville-Barker has found the correct approach when he says that, in his view, a director should react toward an actor as would an audience—but an ideally critical audience. He has expressed his point of view in the following terms: "The more he can leave initiative to the actors the better. And, when he cannot, let him emulate the diplomat rather than the drill-sergeant, hint and coax and flatter and cajole, do anything rather than give orders; let them if possible still be persuaded that the initiative is theirs, not his. The Socratic method has its use, if there is time to employ it; an actor may be argued by it out of one way of thinking into another. But the immediate effect of this may be depressing, even paralyzing. . . . The actor must then be heartened into starting afresh, and encouraged while he finds his way, and protected from the impatience of his fellow-actors, who have already found theirs." Granville-Barker rightly concludes that the directing of a play is most fruitful and commendable if it "could be, as it should be, fairly adapted to every one of the diverse interests involved, if the finally needed unity were evolved from these and not imposed on them." This ideal achievement presupposes, in addition to professional competence, a great intellectual and moral superiority on the part of the director; and, on the part of the actors, thorough schooling in their art and willing discipline, in order to "realize the unity in diversity and diversity in unity, the freedom compatible with order."

Without discussing the question of the ever-present pressures of the commercial theatre, the number of rehearsals depends on the length and difficulty of the work in production, the importance and complexity of its staging, the resourcefulness of the director, the zeal of his assistants, and the talent of the actors. An experienced actor, sure of his calling, rich in inner life, may rehearse for a long time and make continuous progress. A beginner or a mediocre actor quickly reaches a saturation point beyond which he loses both his freshness and his grasp. Individual temperaments and national characteristics must always be taken into account. Disciplined Germans and Russians fanatically devoted to their art can engage in an astonishing number of rehearsals. Italians, born improvisers, hardly rehearse at all. The French occupy an intermediate position. But they are lacking in method and often in seriousness.

THE ROLE OF THE STAGE MANAGER

All during his work, the director is assisted by one or more stage managers. The functions of the stage manager are closely related and complementary to those of the director, and are as sharply defined as his. For if the director stages the play and gives life to it, the stage manager watches over it and sees to it that "the show must go on." As the play draws nearer to opening night, one may say that it passes out of the hands of the director into those of the stage manager, somewhat in the same way that it has passed out of the playwright's hands into those of the director and his actors. Thus we get a picture of the various operations through which a dramatic work passes from the moment it takes shape in the writer's brain to the moment in which it is played before an audience—when it comes fully alive and flows as easily and naturally as though born upon the stage. That is what makes the theatre so difficult and often so risky an art. And that is why it really needs strict, intelligent, completely coherent, and homogeneous organization. Without such organization the playwright's thought and the life of his characters will always be cheapened and betrayed.

The stage manager notes all the various points relating to the staging, as they occur, on a copy of the play called a *promptbook*. He is in charge of the electricians, stagehands, property men, costumers, and in general the entire working crew of the play. He makes sure that the actors are on hand; sees to it that their costumes and make-up are just right; watches for entrances, places, movements, and cues; and keeps order on the stage, backstage, and in the dressing rooms. Every day he draws up a *call bulletin* and posts it on the bulletin board in the greenroom. Here the actors find the general timetable of activities in the theatre, announcements from the management, and any comments concerning behavior and breaches of discipline. The stage manager is present at every performance, guides it, sees that it runs smoothly, gives the curtain signal, decides the number of curtain calls to be taken and the length of intermissions, supervises the actual placing of sets and props, checks on the lighting, and, in an emergency, addresses the audience.

The collaboration of a good stage manager is seen to best advantage at dress rehearsals, when the director relies on him for all the practical work of running the show, so that he himself may have a little more perspective and calmly judge the over-all effect before making any last-minute changes. Dress rehearsals should be given under actual performance conditions—that is, with scenery and changes of scenery in the time taken by an actual intermission, with lights, props, costumes, make-up and wigs, music, and supers, if there are any. All the equipment needed for the play should be ordered as soon as rehearsals start and made available while rehearsals are under way, so that as

many dress rehearsals as possible can be given in the last few days
before opening night.

NECESSARY HARMONY

The director figuratively sets the stage himself (plans and dimensions, entrances and exits, essential elements). As for all the accessories
to the production (props, furniture, lights, music), if he does not
himself create them, they must in any case be created by artists working
under him, accepting his guidance and supervision. He must not allow
them to clash with one another, to step on each other's toes, or to
interfere in any way with the play. Only in this manner can harmony
be achieved within a unified framework. As a rule, this principle is
obvious. Few would question it. If it is not always practiced, if it is
more often violated than kept, we must nevertheless admit that in our
day it has been—if not discovered—at least revived and restored to a
signal place of honor.

The interdependence of music, dance, and color has produced masterpieces in the ballet. Wagnerian opera has come close to integral
unity in the theories of such a master as Adolphe Appia. Primarily a
musician in the broadest sense of the term, Appia sought to make the
flow of music, imprisoning action in time, govern action in space in the
same way. That is, he strove to make the music build up around it its
own acting space, to which the performers had to conform. Just as
music creates the spoken phrase and the gesture associated with it, so
it creates movement, which it measures in its rises or falls, on a level or
uneven surface. Thus music creates an essential *décor*. Appia conceived of the stage in relation to the needs of the action, not in response
to the demands of local color. He sacrificed pleasure to rigorous accuracy, virtuosity to inner logic. He rejected illusory *décors*, such as
picturesquely painted "flats," and replaced them with genuine three-
dimensional *décors*—in other words, purely dramatic and dynamic
décors. The main reforms in contemporary stage design took off from
there. They have been pushed to intellectual extremes, even at times
to the point of caricature; but they have achieved a salutary pruning in
dramatic style and energy.

We have found that a good script, a play that is well written for acting on the stage, contains time-spans—movements and rhythms—comparable to those in music and, as in music, capable of generating space. The question of what space or playing area to choose in a given play, or in a given scene from a play, is therefore not an unimportant matter. For there is a stage economy that corresponds to dramatic economy, a performing style engendered by a literary style; and indeed, a theatre's physical structure may serve to heighten and enhance the intellectual structure of a play or, on the contrary, to distort and destroy it.

This concept, tested by experience, is likewise verified by a study of works of the past. Let us take two very well-known examples. Aeschylus and Shakespeare did not invent their action in a vacuum. The one worked for the Greek stage, the other for the Elizabethan stage—in other words, in terms of two instruments which had their permanent architecture, their traditions, and their established laws. Aeschylus' tragedies and Shakespeare's plays were composed, so to speak, in the image of this architecture and in accordance with its rhythms. They were marked by its traditions and laws. We do not completely understand them as works of art unless we are well informed—or at least as well informed as one can be—concerning the specific techniques employed when they were performed. In our world and time, they cannot really regain their fullness of expression unless they are played on a stage under conditions analogous to those of the Greek or Elizabethan theatre in which they were born. I say analogous, because where direction is involved the mind must have some leeway and we must shun any attempt at slavish reconstruction. But it is probable that if the French public today understands Shakespeare better and enjoys his plays more, it is thanks to the efforts our directors have made to recapture the living spirit of the text and the dynamics of its action, by drawing closer to a stage tradition which ignorant or inept adapters had too long neglected.

When we evoke the stylized architecture of the theatre of Aeschylus and Shakespeare—just as we could have evoked that of the Chinese and Japanese theatres—we are at the opposite pole from the formless or multiformed stage, with its grandiose productions, such as we described at the beginning of this article. To illustrate more sharply the contrast between the two systems, let me point out that the modern stage, such as it has been handed down to us by the ingenious craftsmen of the Renaissance, a cluttered-up and mechanized theatre, is a closed-in space in which mind and matter constantly wage war on each other; whereas on the Elizabethan stage, with its minimum of material encumbrances, mind moves freely. In the first case, we are dealing with a bastardized convention, a compromise between realism and abstraction, which simulates a relativist universe. In the second case, we have a convention which is frank, complete, and self-sufficient, creating a universe in itself—a theatrical universe with its own style and technique, which are invaluable guides for the dramatist's imagination as well as that of the director.

CURRENT TRENDS

Direction has played so prominent a part in the work of the contemporary theatre; it has aroused so much curiosity; it has given rise to so much research, effort, and striving; and it has helped shed light on so many basic problems that it has often—and wrongly—been considered an art in itself. Some have asserted that the director possesses universal talents, ranging from those of the actor to those of the creative writer, and including those of the painter and composer. As a matter of fact, that is a portrait of the ideal director. But this ideal has turned the head of more than one director.

In the cinema as in the theatre, there is a conflict between technicians and writers for the realization of unity under the guidance of a master-creator. As cinema techniques develop and improve, and as the cinema establishes its own traditions, the director tends increasingly to take the place of the writer. But that place was left vacant; for one cannot really say that up to now we have had masters of the cinema. We usually say that the dramatist is master in the theatre; and at bottom, of course, everything does depend on the creative writer. Thus far there has been no split between creator and realizer: there is perfect unity in simplicity. But an increasing complexity in the means of realization will bring about a division of labor. The unity thus lost will be found again only in exceptional cases.

In principle there is no reason why a first-rate dramatist, with rich experience in the theatre, should not also be a first-rate director, capable of admirably directing his plays. Up to a certain point, his experience as a director may usefully influence his concepts of drama. But it must be acknowledged that in our day the playwright is usually a master who has let slip the instrument of his mastery. This has come about for many reasons not all of which are his fault. He writes for the stage; yet the stage may repel him or baffle him. He finds it indispensable to get help from a method of interpretation. So he turns to the specialist in this method: the director.

Hence the director is the playwright's right-hand man or substitute in the matter of producing the play. His work is based on an agreement, a kind of contract which he is able to sign because of his insight and to which he is bound because of his sincerity. But trouble arises the moment he makes use of some of his professional skills to distort the playwright's work, to introduce into the fabric of that work his own ideas, intentions, fantasies, and doctrines.

Technical competence, profound understanding, and genuine enthusiasm can and should develop in the director a second inspiration, which is released when he makes contact with another's work. To this extent he participates in creation. He is also a critic, and often better able than the playwright himself to discern errors in playwriting.

It is easy to understand why a gifted director is tempted to conceal the playwright's lack of skill by means of his own technical resources. Admittedly too he becomes impatient when certain masterpieces are said to be unplayable; so he toys with the idea of revising them or of removing the difficulties in them. It need not surprise us therefore if he proceeds boldly to the very source of creation and convinces himself that he can shape the entire process.

It is true that creating a dramatic work in words and actually mounting it on the stage with live actors are but two phases of one and the same intellectual operation. And it is also true that all great dramatists, from Aeschylus to Shakespeare, from Aristophanes to Molière, and from Racine to Ibsen, have been directors. We could cite many others of lesser genius—Voltaire, Diderot, etc.—who had original ideas about directing. The fusion of dramatist and director, however, is in a *descending* line; it is difficult to see how this order can be reversed.

Let us hope for a dramatist who replaces or eliminates the director, and personally takes over the directing; rather than for professional directors who pretend to be dramatists. (No matter how experienced a craftsman he may be, he is immediately too much the professional.) But since we lack great dramatists who stage their own plays personally and with authority, the great director shows his mettle only when he confronts a written masterpiece, particularly when that masterpiece is considered unplayable. Because he believes in it, he understands it; and because he has insight and respects it, he wrests from it its secret.

Does not perfection in directing arise from the friendly conflict between a great creator and his great interpreter? Whenever this salutary conflict is avoided; whenever the technician of the theatre, freed of restraints, visualizes things like an actor and only in terms of the acting, his production thins out and dries up. It resembles that of the musical virtuoso who composes solely for his instrument. He obtains perfection without depth, without nuances, without mystery. An added dimension is lacking. And artistic creation suffers a mortal blow.

EUGENE VAKHTANGOV

(1883-1922)

Fantastic Realism

April 10, 1922

VAKHTANGOV: Meyerhold understands theatricality as a performance at which the audience does not forget for a single moment that it
is in a theatre. Stanislavsky demanded exactly the reverse: that the
audience forget that it is in the theatre, that it come to feel itself
living in the atmosphere and milieu in which the characters of the play
live. He rejoiced in the fact that the audience used to come to the
Moscow Art Theatre to *The Three Sisters*, not as to a theatre, but as if
invited to the Prosorov house. This he considered to be the highest
achievement of the theatre. Stanislavsky wanted to destroy theatrical
banality, he wanted to put an end to it at once. Whatever reminded
him of the old theatres, even to the slightest extent, he branded with
the word "theatrical," this word having become a term of abuse in the
Moscow Art Theatre. To be sure, what he was berating was vulgar
indeed, but carried away by the need for ferreting out vulgarity, Stanislavsky also removed a certain genuine, necessary theatricality, and
genuine theatricality consists in presenting theatrical works in a
theatrical manner. . . .

Stanislavsky bore down on vulgarity, began to drive it out, began to
search for the truth. This quest after truth led him to the truth of inner
experiences, that is, he began to demand a genuine, natural inner
experience upon the stage, forgetting that the actor's inner experience
must be conveyed to the auditorium with the help of theatrical means.
And Stanislavsky himself was compelled to use theatrical means. You

Eugene Vakhtangov: *Zapiski, Pisma, Stati.* Moscow: Iskusstvo, 1939, 254–
262, *passim.* Excerpts from stenographic reports of two conversations between
Eugene Vakhtangov and his disciples Boris E. Zakhava and K. I. Kotlubai during
his final illness.

know there is not a production of Chekhov's plays without a backstage language of its own—none of them takes place without the sound of the cricket, the noise of the street, the shouting of the hucksters, the striking of a clock. And all those are theatrical means found for Chekhov's plays.

K. I. KOTLUBAI: And what is a mood? Isn't this a theatrical achievement?

VAKHTANGOV: No, there should be no moods in the theatre. There should be pure joy and no moods. Altogether there is no such thing as theatrical moods. When you look at a naturalistic picture are you possessed then by a "mood"? It impresses you with its content, but you forget the craftsmanship. I remember the impression made upon me by Repin's "John the Terrible Killing His Son." I stood there for hours. I was afraid to come close to the picture, but I evaluated it only from the point of view of its content. Blood, John's eyes, and especially the eyes of the murdered son. But now I look at the picture and it produces within me a feeling of revulsion. But to go back to our subject.

Meyerhold is the only one of all the Russian directors who has the feel of theatricality. He was a prophet at one time and was not accepted. He was ten years ahead of his time. Meyerhold did the same thing as Stanislavsky. He also destroyed theatrical banality, but he did it with the aid of theatrical means. Stanislavsky in his enthusiasm for real truth, brought naturalistic truth to the stage. He sought theatrical truth in the truth of life. Meyerhold, carried away by theatrical truth, removed the truthfulness of feelings, and truth there must be in both— the theatres of Meyerhold and Stanislavsky.

Feeling is the same in theatre and life, but the means and methods of presenting them are different. The grouse is the same, whether served in the restaurant or at home. But in the restaurant it is served and prepared in such a manner as to have a theatrical ring to it, while at home it is just a homemade piece of meat. Stanislavsky served truth with truth, water with water, grouse with grouse, while Meyerhold removed truth altogether, that is, he left the dish, the method of preparing it, but he prepared paper and not a grouse. And so he obtained paper feelings. Meyerhold was a high-grade master and he served his dish in a masterful restaurant-like manner, but it was not fit to eat. The removal of theatrical banality with the means of the conventional theatre led Meyerhold to genuine theatricality, to the formula: the audience should not forget for one single second that it is in a theatre. Stanislavsky arrived at the formula: the audience has to forget that it is in the theatre.

A perfect work of art is everlasting. A perfect work of art is one in which is present a harmony of content, form and material. Stanislavsky found only a harmony with the mood of the Russian society of his period, but not everything that is contemporary is eternal. But whatever is eternal is always contemporaneous. Meyerhold never felt the "today" but he did feel the "tomorrow." Stanislavsky never felt the "tomorrow," but always felt the "today." But one has to feel "the today in the morrow," and the morrow in the "present day."

April 11, 1922

VAKHTANGOV: Well, gentlemen, I am ready for questions.

B. ZAKHAVA: I believe we should speak about theatricality, genuine theatricality.

VAKHTANGOV: All right. I seek in the theatre modern methods of solving the problem of play production in a form which would have a theatrical ring to it. Let us take, for instance, the problems of locale. I am trying to solve them in a manner different from the Moscow Art Theatre—that is, not by reproducing the locale upon the stage, by giving it the truth of life. The method of solving the problems of locale by the Moscow Art Theatre does not give birth to artistic works, for creativeness is absent there. There is only a refined, skillful, keen result of one's observations of life. I should like to call the work I do upon the stage "fantastic realism."

K. I. KOTLUBAI: What you call "fantastic realism" is to me pure and simple realism.

VAKHTANGOV: Let us try now to point out the difference between naturalism and realism.

ZAKHAVA: In my opinion, naturalism reproduces precisely what the artist observes in actuality. Naturalism is photography. But the artist who is a realist distills from the actual only what appears to his eyes as the most important, the most essential. He rejects minutiae, selects the typical and important. But in the process of his creative work he operates all the time with the very materials of actuality. Such an art exists and it should not be confused with naturalism or what Vakhtangov is seeking now. If you name it just pure and simple "realism" what will you put in place of the form intermediary between naturalism and what Vakhtangov is seeking?

VAKHTANGOV: I might name the thing I am seeking not fantastic realism, but theatrical realism, but that is worse. In the theatre everything should be theatrical. This is taken for granted.

K. I. KOTLUBAI: I am convinced that somewhere there is a well-formulated definition of realism. Zakhava says that the artist who is a realist separates the important from the nonimportant. That is not so, as far as I see it. To me realism in art, and particularly in the theatre, is the ability on the part of the artist to create anew whatever he gets from the material by which he is inspired. The material gives the master realist a definite impression, a definite idea, with which he then creates with the aid of means germane to his specific art.

VAKHTANGOV: So you say that Zakhava gave us a wrong definition of realism. Let's discuss specific examples. What is Andreyev's *Life of Man* upon the stage of the Moscow Art Theatre?

K. I. KOTLUBAI: From my point of view it is not true realism for the following reason: it is an attempt to carry over the symbolistic content of the play with the aid of the very symbolistic means that are given by the author. It is not creating anew a symbolic play upon the stage. Whatever Andreyev wrote has been carried over to the stage in its pure form.

VAKHTANGOV: This is not so. All the acting characters were created by the director and not by Andreyev. Andreyev did not write that such and such a character is fat. He wrote a text. And the artist actor makes the figure, dresses it the way he feels, imparts to it a definite (in this case schematic) movement, tries to find out how it should walk, speak, sit, etc. *A Man's Life* and *The Drama of Life* are fantastic realism.

ZAKHAVA: And *The Lower Depths?* What do you hold that to be? Naturalism?

VAKHTANGOV: Of course that is pure realism. In my opinion, the theatre did not interpret Gorky in the right manner. Gorky is a romantic, and the theatre interprets him not romantically, but naturalistically.

Kotlubai says that what we are seeking is realism. Here is an example of our work: In the wedding scene of *The Dybbuk* we had to insert a small scene which would justify an interval. It was necessary for the audience to believe that the orchestra was successful in finding the bridegroom, otherwise it would appear as if the orchestra just left and then came back. That is why I inserted a scene of two girls watching the orchestra and performing all kinds of stunts in the Chekhov style—jumping upon benches, gloating, clapping their hands. It made a wonderful scene which was greatly liked by the actors. They themselves came to feel something of Chekhov in it. However, the scene had to be thrown out, since it clashed with the rest of the play. Now we even have a special term—"the Dybbuk method."

And what, for instance, would you say of *Turandot?*

KOTLUBAI: That is true realism.

VAKHTANGOV: That is fantastic realism. Meyerhold's staging of *The Booth* by Blok was similar to *Turandot.* There you had only the external portrayal of the theatre, that is, the side scenes were there and so was the prompter's box. But all that was pointed out by the author. The actors were the impersonators of the characters drawn by the author. This kind of histrionics could be found in the older theatres—those of Shakespeare, Molière. Now we have only a few great actors—Duse, Chaliapin, Salvini—who in acting *show* that they act.

Realism takes from life everything but what it needs for the reproduction of a given scene, that is, it brings to the stage only that which has a histrionic value. It takes life, truth and gives genuine feelings. Sometimes it even gives the minutiae of life, then we have naturalism, for minutiae is photography. The Pushkin production in the Moscow Art Theatre is realism. Did you ever notice there or in *Tsar Fyodor* any minute details? And still, in *Tsar Fyodor,* you may see certain details in the presentation of the character of a Boyar which will be naturalism. The author overlooks certain minute details but the director-naturalist introduces them: if the character enters from the street where it is snowing, the director will invariably make him shake off the snow in the hall, etc.

Attempts are made to approach the opera in a naturalistic, or rather a realistic manner. I would approach it in the way it sometimes is by talented singers. The audience should never be deceived. The singers should always stress: I am singing and that is why I am performing out on the forestage. Stanislavsky produces operas in a realistic manner. He will not permit the singer to come out to the footlights.

Now, in *Anthony* we have mixed forms: the convention of external setting, realism and fantastic realism. Naturalism is completely absent. Of outstanding importance for fantastic realism is the solving of the means and the form. The means must be theatrical. It is very difficult to find a form harmonizing with the content and presented with the aid of the right means. If we begin to work upon marble with wooden mallets, nothing will come of it. Marble demands an instrument adequate to its structure.

Why was *Turandot* successful? Because harmony was achieved in it. The Third Studio performs an Italian fairy tale by Gozzi on the 22nd of January, 1922. The methods are modern and theatrical. The form and content harmonize like a musical chord. It is fantastic realism, it is a new trend in the theatre.

Gogol's world is the world of fantastic realism. In the Moscow Art Theatre production of *The Inspector-General* we have Volkov playing the role of Osip as a naturalistic character, Lilina and others as realistic, but Khlestakov acted by Chekhov is already a character interpreted with the methods of fantastic realism. Volkov is not theatre, but Chekhov is.

In the theatre there should be neither naturalism nor realism, but fantastic realism. Rightly found theatrical methods impart genuine life to the play upon the stage. The methods can be learned, but the form must be created. It has to be conceived by one's fantasy. That is why I call it fantastic realism. Such a form exists and should exist in every art.

ARTHUR HOPKINS

(1878-1950)

Capturing the Audience

THE chief criticism of temporary producing is that it lacks either policy or design. The average production is the result of no fixed co-ordination. It has frequently been said of my productions, that they conveyed a certain sustained illusion that seemed not to be of the theatre. I believe this in a sense to be true, for it is the result of a definite experimental policy which I have followed vigorously, bringing it more and more to bear in each new production.

What was originally experimental has now become a fixed method, and I hope definitely to demonstrate that there is a way to insure invariably the projection of nearly all the values a play may possess.

From the very beginning I had an abhorrence of all that is generally termed theatric. It seemed cheap and tawdry, the trick of the street fakir. I thought for a long time that my prejudice was personal and not well founded. But, finally, all protest and all new seeking began naturally to fall into line with a theory of direction that had slowly been evolving in my mind—the theory which for the want of a better term I have defined as Unconscious Projection.

Briefly, the basis of the theory is this: Complete illusion has to do entirely with the unconscious mind. Except in the case of certain intellectual plays the theatre is wholly concerned with the unconscious mind of the audience. The conscious mind should play no part.

The theatre is always seeking unanimous reaction. It is palpably evident that unanimous reaction from conscious minds is practically impossible. Seat a dozen people in a room, present them any problem which you ask them consciously to solve, and you will get nearly as

Arthur Hopkins: *How's Your Second Act?* New York: Philip Goodman Company, 1918, 23–33, 34–36, 45–50, *passim.*, 58–61.

many different reactions as there are people; but place five thousand people in a room and strike some note or appeal that is associated with an unconscious idea common to all of them, and you will get a practically unanimous reaction. In the theatre I do not want the emotion that rises out of thought, but the thought that rises out of emotion. The emotional reaction must be secured first.

The problem now arises: "How can we in the theatre confine ourselves to the unconscious mind?" The hypnotist has supplied us with the answer: "Still the conscious mind." The hypnotist's first effort is to render inoperative the conscious mind of the subject. With that out of the way he can direct his commands to an undistracted unconscious and get definite reactions. The subject has no opportunity to think about it.

In the theatre we can secure a similar result by giving the audience no reason to think about it, by presenting every phase so unobtrusively, so free from confusing gesture, movement and emphasis, that all passing action seems inevitable, so that we are never challenged or consciously asked why. This whole treatment begins first with the manuscript, continues through the designing of the settings, and follows carefully every actor's movement and inflection. If, throughout, this attitude of easy flow can be maintained the complete illusionment of the audience is inevitable.

At first glance one might say that any method which discards conscious digestion must necessarily be limited in scope. The answer is that we begin by discarding conscious irritation, proceed to an unconscious introduction, and then abide by the conscious verdict, for, inevitably, all the unconscious reaction is wasted if the conscious ultimately rejects us. Or to put it more simply, if you give our story complete attention and then reject us, we have no complaint; but if we feel that you have not properly felt our story because of confusing distractions, we must necessarily feel guilty as to our way of projection.

This method entails sweeping readjustments. To begin with, author, director, scene designer and actor must become completely the servants of the play. Each must resist every temptation to score personally. Each must make himself a free, transparent medium through which the whole flows freely and without obstruction. No one at any moment can say, "Ah, this moment is mine! I shall show what can be done with it." There is no part of the play that is done for the benefit of anyone. It must all be inevitable, impersonal and untrammelled. It requires a complete surrender of selfishness. In fact, it demands of everyone the honest rigidity of the true artist, who will stoop to nothing because it is effective or conspicuous or because "it goes."

It is the opposite of all that has become traditional in the theatre. It is the establishing of the true community spirit in a work that is essentially community work, and it is not the glorious adoption of an ideal, but the stern necessity for self-preservation which the very method impresses. For woe be unto the one person who is out of key with the scheme once it has been set in operation! He will inevitably make himself look hopelessly out of place, and the more he struggles to stand out the farther aloof and more hopelessly adrift will he become.

It commands honesty and unselfishness, and nothing recommends it to me more than this—nothing could be more convincing proof of its rightness.

The note of unconscious projection must first be struck by the director. If he cannot get his effects in this way, he can scarcely hope that the people with him will succeed. It is always my aim to get a play completely prepared without anyone realizing just how it was done. I want the actors to be unconscious of my supervision. I want whatever direction they require to come to them without their realization. I want them to be unconscious of the movement and the "business" of the play. I want it all to grow with them so easily that when time for the first performance comes they scarcely realize that anything in particular has been done.

The first step in unselfishness must be taken by me. I must renounce at the outset all temptation to be conspicuous in direction, to issue commands, to show how well I can read a line or play a scene, or slam a door; to ridicule or get laughs at a confused actor's expense, to criticize openly. I must renounce all desire to be the boss, or the great master, or the all-knowing one. I must guide the ship by wireless instead of attempting to drag it through the water after me. There are any number of actors who have been with me who firmly believe that they received practically no direction, and that is exactly as it should be. When I discover that an actor is becoming conscious of me I know there is something wrong some place, and it is usually with me.

The two essentials in this kind of direction are for the director to know exactly what he wants and to make sure that he can get what he wants from the people he has selected. These two conditions put an end to all confusion at the outset.

Uncertainty in direction must inevitably result in uncertainty in performance. When actors discover that a director cannot make up his mind just how a scene should be played, and when they see him experimenting with them they instantly become conscious of something lacking, either in the play itself or in the director. This is a dangerous thought to set up. A company under these conditions becomes wabbly, and the first tendency of a wabbly actor is to overplay. Once an actor believes himself to be on thin ice he invariably steps down harder. A scene that is born in uncertainty is rarely well played.

The director is the guide. The play is the unknown region through which he leads the actor. He must know the paths and the turnings so well that he never hesitates. For once he falters, wondering if he is headed right, the actor inevitably begins to look around for his own way out.

My feeling about the birth of a play is that it gradually becomes an individuality, that it becomes a personality of which the different actors are organs or members. I do not see ten or twenty individuals moving about. I see only one thing made of ten or twenty parts that is moving. So long as it moves properly I am totally unconscious of its parts. The moment I become conscious of a part and lose the movement of the whole I know that something is wrong. It is the unfamiliar sound in the engine that warns one that some part is not functioning properly. That is the time to stop the play and investigate. It may be a very tiny thing—a movement at a time when all should be still—a speech when there should be silence—a pause when something should be happening—an unwarranted change of tempo, or any one of a hundred minor or major things that remove concentration from the whole.

The stripping process begins early. I eliminate all gesture that is not

absolutely needed, all unnecessary inflections and intonings, the toss-
ing of heads, the flickering of fans and kerchiefs, the tapping of feet,
drumming of fingers, swinging of legs, pressing of brows, holding of
hearts, curling of mustaches, stroking of beards and all the million
and one tricks that have crept into the actor's bag, all of them betraying
one of two things—an annoying lack of repose, or an attempt to attract
attention to himself and away from the play.

Every moment on the stage should mean something. The spectator
follows every movement, and no movement has any right to his attention unless it has some significance.

I never plan the "business" of a play in advance. I know where the
entrances are as the scene is first designed, but frequently after going
over an act once these are changed.

I am opposed to the old method of marking out the "business" in
advance, because at the outset it confines the movement and tends to a
fixity that hampers free flow. The first two or three times through an
act I let the actors roam about the scene and invariably the "business"
solves itself. The movement arrived at in this way has the advantage
of having been born in action, and there is essentially a feeling of life
about it that one cannot get by marking directions in a manuscript.
Automatically all falseness of movement is denied admission, all
crosses, dropping downstage, falling upstage, exchanging chairs, cir-
cling pianos, wrestling with furniture, and all the strange conduct that
directors of past years have relied upon to keep actors busy. The police
crusade of some time ago that kept actors moving along Broadway was
only an open-air phase of stage direction, as most actors have suffered it
for years.

Extreme simplification—that is what I strive for incessantly—not
because I like simplicity. It isn't a matter of taste or preference—it is a
working out of the method of Unconscious Projection. It is the elimi-
nation of all the nonessentials, because they arouse the conscious mind
and break the spell I am trying to weave over the unconscious mind. All
tricks are conscious in the mind of the person who uses them, and they
must necessarily have a conscious appeal. I want the unconscious of
the actors talking to the unconscious of the audience, and I strive to

eliminate every obstacle to that. I finally become a censor. I must say what shall not pass—and therein I believe lies the whole secret of direction.

The true test of performance is the ease with which it is accomplished. My chief objection to all theatric devices is that they indicate a straining for effect which defeats itself. The strain is a thing personal to the author, actor or director, and it instantly distracts the audience from the effect to the effort. Just as an audience suffers for a singer who is struggling for a note that seems dangerously out of reach, it suffers for an actor who stresses himself for an effect. An actor should be given nothing to do that he cannot do easily, and furthermore he should find the very easiest way he can accomplish whatever is assigned to him. This is an essential part of his self-elimination. He must think of the play as a clean ball. Whenever it is tossed to him he should pass it on without smearing it with his perspiration. An ideal company would end the performance with a spotless ball. An actor must say to himself, "How can I do this without being noticed?" instead of, "What can I do to make myself stand out?" With the latter query he begins to try, and with trying comes strain, and with strain artificiality and discomfort. He accomplishes what he set out to do. He stands out much as a carbuncle does.

The whole system of personal emphasis in the American theatre has led to the present unadvanced state of the actor. There is no greater proof of its fallacy than its failure. All are straining for personal success. If they only knew that the greatest success will come to those who can most completely submerge the personal. Theirs is essentially an art where they must serve unreservedly, and the great vacancies in the theatre are awaiting actors big enough in mind and character to surrender themselves completely, strip themselves of every conscious trick, disdaining to court approval by commanding it by the very honesty of their aims.

I firmly believe that an actor's mental attitude is instantly conveyed to an audience. I further believe that an audience unconsciously appraises his character. It soon discovers if he is all actor or part man,

and its appraisal of his performance is more determined by its unconscious exploration of his unconscious than by any particular thing he
does. Invariably the actors whom the public has loved have been people, who, in themselves, possessed great lovable qualities. They were
not people who in their roles assumed a lovable nature.

We cannot give actors qualities they do not possess, but I am only
seeking to point out that the audience usually gets what is inside of an
actor much more clearly than what he actually does, and an actor cannot approach his work selfishly without conveying his attitude to the
public. We let all of this pass under the vague terms of personality and
magnetism, but I do not believe there is anything vague or mysterious
about it. I believe unconscious appraisal reveals to us the character of
many people we do not know in the least. We get their intent from
what they do, and it is by their intent that we know them. . . .

As to the "new" scenery, much has been said and written, and most
of it beside the point.

One's position in the matter is entirely determined by which mind
he thinks the stage has to do with, the conscious or the unconscious.

Realistic settings are designed wholly for conscious appeal. An
attempt at exact reproduction challenges the conscious mind of the
audience to comparison. Comparison of the scene as it is offered with
the auditor's conscious knowledge of what it is supposed to reproduce.
If a Childs Restaurant in all its detail is offered it remains for the
audience to recall its memory photograph of a Childs Restaurant and
check it up with what is shown on the stage. If the butter-cake stove is
in place and the "Not Responsible for Hats" sign is there, and if the
tiling is much the same, then the producer has done well. He has been
faithful to Childs, and whatever credit there is in being faithful to
Childs should be unstintedly awarded him.

Unfortunately while the audience has been doing its conscious
checking up, the play has been going, and going for nothing, since any
form of conscious occupation must necessarily dismiss the play.
Further than that the result of the whole mental comparing process is
to impress upon the auditor that he is in a theatre witnessing a very
accurate reproduction, *only remarkable because it is not real.* So the

upshot of the realistic effort is further to emphasize the unreality of the whole attempt, setting, play and all. So I submit that realism defeats the very thing to which it aspires. It emphasizes the faithfulness of unreality.

All that is detail, all that is photographic, is conscious. Every unnecessary article in a setting is a continuing, distracting gesture beckoning constantly for the attention of the audience, asking to be noticed and examined, insisting upon its right to scrutiny because it belongs. . . .

Detail has been the boon of the American theatre for twenty years, detestable, irritating detail, designed for people with no imagination—people who will not believe they are in a parlor unless they see the family album.

And on the other side of the world the unenlightened Chinese for centuries have been presenting drama to unimaginative people wherein scenes were never changed, and palaces, forests, legions and hordes were summoned by the wave of a property man's bamboo stick.

But, thank Heaven, there was a Gordon Craig, who brought the imagination of the Orient to England, and of course England would have none of him. Germany swallowed him through the gullet of Max Reinhardt, and the "new" movement was on. It spread to Russia, to France, to Italy, to America, to every place but England, where it was born.

Here we have failed to grasp its full significance. There is still a feeling that it is some sort of affectation. It would be like us to call a revolt from affectation affectation.

What is all the discussion about? How can there be any discussion? Isn't it a palpable fact that the only mission of settings is to suggest place and mood, and once that is established let the play go on? Do we want anything more than backgrounds? Must we have intricate woodturning and goulash painting? If so, we have no right in the theatre. We have no imagination. And a theatre without imagination becomes a building in which people put paint on their faces and do tricks, and no trick they perform is worth looking at unless they take a reasonable chance of being killed in the attempt.

The whole realistic movement was founded on selfishness—the selfish desire of the producer or scene painter to score individually, to do something so effective that it stood in front of the play and shrieked from behind it.

It was my good fortune to find an unselfish artist, Robert Edmond Jones. Jones hopes only for one thing for his settings—that no one will notice them, that they will melt into the play. Naturally for this very reason they were conspicuous at first not because of what they were, but because of what people had been accustomed to. But gradually his work is being noticed less and less, and Jones knows that that means he is succeeding. That's the size man he is. And when the day comes that no one ever mentions his settings, he will breathe deeply and say, "I have done it."

He is the true artist. He wants nothing for Jones. He wants what is right for the thing we are doing. Given twenty actors with a spirit as fine as his, and I will promise you a reaction such as is now only a dream.

LOUIS JOUVET

(1891-1951)

The Profession of the Director

IN AN EMPTY theatre, alone in the middle of a velvet glacier of empty seats, a man is seated. Tense with concentration, all eyes and ears and nerves, he leans toward the stage where the actors are rehearsing. Eyes fixed on that gaping hole—without scenery and almost without light, where persons in incongruous moods and costumes are going through varied convolutions—he contracts his brow, strains his ears to hear the lines that are still imperfectly pronounced or interpreted. This man is the director, or *metteur en scène*.

In the limbo where the production takes form, in the slow growth during which its features are shaped, where it is foreseen in imagination, where the dramatic leaven is mysteriously at work, the director watches with patience, discretion and tenderness over the straggling elements he has assembled to give life to the playwright's work. His job is accomplished through intuition, understanding, foresight, through a special alchemy composed of words, sounds, gestures, colors, lines, movements, rhythms and silences, and including an imponderable which will radiate the proper feeling of laughter or emotion when the work appears before the public.

The director, or *metteur en scène*, has been called the gardener of spirits, the doctor of sensations, the midwife of the inarticulate, the cobbler of situations, cook of speeches, steward of souls, king of the theatre and servant of the stage, juggler and magician, assayer and touchstone of the public, diplomat, economist, nurse, orchestra leader, interpreter, painter and costumer—a hundred definitions, but all of

Louis Jouvet: "The Profession of the Producer, II," *Theatre Arts Monthly*, Vol. XXI, January 1937, 57–64. Copyright, 1937, by *Theatre Arts Monthly*. By permission of Rosamond Gilder, translator; and Robert M. MacGregor, Theatre Arts Books.

them useless. The director is indefinable because his functions are undefined.

The director, when he is also the producer, first selects the play, distributes the parts to the actors of his choice, designs (or has designed for him) the rough models of the settings and costumes, oversees their making, and during all this time organizes and manages rehearsals. He determines the entrances and exits, the positions of the actors, serving as choreographer to that dance which is the sum of the play's movements; he regulates the off-stage noises, the music, the lighting. In short, he arranges in ensemble and in detail all the generalities and all the particulars of that complex ceremony which the performance will be.

To direct a production is to live in terror, to delight in anguish; it is what Paul Valéry calls "the tragedy of execution." It means administering to the spiritual welfare of the playwright and at the same time taking into account the temporal needs of the theatre; establishing the point of view of one evening and of eternity; handling the text of a play, hand in hand with the author, as if it were a magic formula. Directing is the opposite of criticism: the critics, zigzagging between laws and rules on one side and their own pleasure on the other, navigate in the theatre by trying to sound their reactions with an old fathom-stick in one hand and with the other sighting the play through a pair of old marine-glasses. Directing a play is the exact opposite of this. It means constantly searching for reasons that will explain liking and admiration. It means living according to poets' rules. It means comporting with the gods of the stage, with the mystery of the theatre. It means being honest and straightforward in the art of pleasing. And sometimes, too, it means making mistakes.

The director is the kind of lover who draws his talent, invention and joy in his work from the talent, invention and joy which he borrows from or inspires in others. To direct a production means to gather together all the people and things that make up a performance and to create, through them, a certain atmosphere, arousing and serving their capabilities and their personalities. In the setting—the whole play's material surroundings—such things, for example, as wood, paint, nails and light are not, as one might suppose, lifeless, inorganic things but formidable entities whose favor toward the play and its interpreters is to be won only by a secret and long-premeditated accord.

To direct a production means to help the actors with their memorizing and to mold the text in rehearsals so that it is freed of bookishness and takes on the feeling of the players, to make the actor comfortable and to know how to do this. It means nourishing, sustaining and revitalizing the actors, encouraging and satisfying them and finding their proper theatrical diet; it means bringing forth and raising that family—formed according to a different formula for each new play—which we call a theatre company.

To direct a production means serving the playwright with a devotion that makes you love his work. It means finding the spiritual mood that was the poet's at the play's conception and during its writing, the living source and stream which must arouse the spectator, and of which even the author is sometimes unaware. It means realizing the corporal through the spiritual. It is a way of dealing with a work, with the places and properties necessary to the setting, with the performers, with the poet who has conceived it, and, finally, with the audience for which it is destined. Charged with the interests of this audience, the director must unite the stage and the auditorium, the spectacle and the spectators. He must organize that area where the active players on the stage and the passive players in the auditorium meet each other, where the spectators penetrate and identify themselves with the action on the stage, and where the actors satisfy their need to prove and free themselves by reflection in the people who listen and look on.

Jean Giraudoux modestly says that the playwright does not make his play, that the audience makes it out of the elements furnished by the playwright. "The audience," he declares, "hears and composes as it pleases, following its own imagination and feelings." He compares a dramatic work to a piece of pottery painted in false colors, whose true colors and finished design do not appear until after it is fired. A play receives the finishing process of an ordeal by fire through contact with an audience.

One could go on forever analyzing the work of the director but, in trying to define it, I only prove that it is easier to do a job well than to write well about it. To sum it up, the directing of a play is a turn of the

hand, a turn of the mind and of the heart, a function of such sensitive-
ness that everything human can enter into it. No more, and no less. I
do not believe in theories, and there is no theory to cover the directing
of plays. The method fits a theory only after the fact.

There are two kinds of director: the one who expects everything from
the play, for whom the play itself is essential; and the one who expects
nothing except from himself, for whom the play is a starting point.
That is to say—perhaps too summarily, but in order to be clear—there
are two sorts of dramatic works, and two sorts of playwrights.

There is the spectacular or theatrical theatre in which entertainment,
rhythm, music, lines and appeal to the eye—all the spectacular elements—are the important things, and here the director can indulge
himself to his heart's content. In this theatrical theatre can be included the mimes of Roman decadence, the theatre of the market-
place, a good part of opera and all operetta, ballet, fairy-plays, melodrama, and the productions of the majority of present-day foreign
directors, in which the actor, the singer, the setting, the machinery, are
the essentials of the entertainment.

Then there is the theatre of dramatists and poets which makes of
dramatic art a literary form of the highest order. Here the important
thing is the text, and the spectacular elements are admitted only as
side-issues and supplements. The literary theatre includes the Greek
and Roman dramatists (Aeschylus, Sophocles, Euripides, Seneca); the
humanistic renaissance with Shakespeare; the classic with Corneille,
Racine, Molière; then Marivaux, Beaumarchais, Musset. These peaks
of dramatic art have been defined by one of our directors, somewhat
cavalierly, as "men of letters who wrote for the theatre."

There are works of lasting character, and others whose value is only
momentary. It is an accepted fact that fashion affects the writing of
plays and their conception; but whenever one attains universality,
where the characters are dealt with purely as human beings, we have
what the text-books call a classic. This type of play contains within
itself its own method of staging; that is, the work of the director is to
observe how the play responds to his suggestions, to make his devices

disappear into the text, so incorporating them that the play absorbs his directions without being deformed by them.

In the spectacular theatre, on the other hand, external direction is required; the work is swathed in personal contributions and inventions. The text is no more than a pretext or a support for the setting, the actors and the stage devices; and the director, relying heavily on the storehouse of the theatre or of his imagination, often rivals the leader of a cotillion. So true is this that we can say that the text of a classic or literary play is written for the audience, the text of the other kind for the actors and the director.

The natural tendency of a director is to see his plays with a definite personal bias that is the index of his temperament. Almost all directors, after a few years of modest service, dream of showing their own stature and the scale of their imagination. And, like the apprentice who thought himself a past-master of his trade, like the shoemaker whom the painter Apelles put in his place by advising him not to criticize anything above shoes, they are seized with a violent desire to make over masterpieces and to express at last their own personal conceptions.

As an illustration of this mentality, this professional deformity, I should like to quote a sentence that has been in print, on the film production of *A Midsummer Night's Dream:* one of the greatest directors wrote it: "The dream of my life was to produce a work without having anything hamper my imagination." That in itself is not bad for a man whose profession is to serve others. But he adds, "I have set the condition that this work should represent Shakespeare, and nothing but Shakespeare." I hope you can feel in this avowal both the homage he intended to pay to Shakespeare and the opinion he held—comparatively—of himself. And, as a final touch, he adds, "My dream has just been realized." That is, this dream is at your disposal in the motion-picture houses. You may see Shakespeare adapted to the use of commercial New Year's calendars.

The greatest director will never be able to equal in his achievements the dreams and imagination of the most humble of his audience.

In reality, a play stages itself; the only necessity is to be attentive and not too personal in order to see it take on its own movement and begin to manipulate the actors. Acting on them, mysteriously, it tests them, magnifies or diminishes them, embraces or rejects them, nourishes them, transforms and deforms them. From its first rehearsal a true play comes alive, just as wood warps, wine ferments and dough rises. It gathers impetus and gradually the director, like the sorcerer's apprentice, terrified and enraptured at the same time, sees it sweep over the actors and bring them to life, rejecting or carrying away all his directions like straws in the wind, in a kind of blossoming or birth.

The profession of the director suffers from the disease of immodesty, and even the most sincere do not escape it. Their license to work freely with the plays of other people, to dabble with them and make them over, is an established and accepted convention, and after a few hours of conversation with himself or with a colleague a man must have a steady head and firm foothold to resist the dizziness in which, convinced of what he would like to believe, he approaches the conclusion that Shakespeare or Goethe understood nothing of the theatre. Great dramatic art is a mystery. No work can be judged outside of its age, and its transposition into another atmosphere requires long adaptation and very great respect. But here is a formula:

One can recognize a great dramatic work with certainty when the director, deciding in all good faith that it should be otherwise constructed or written, has, nevertheless, nothing more to say; when, in spite of all his desire to make over the play, he accepts it practically as it is written. A conversation I had with a director who confided to me that he was in despair because he had just been working for two months, without any result, on *Le Malade Imaginaire* illustrates this definition. When I expressed astonishment, he said, "Yes, I've just spent my whole summer at it. I've tried lighting it from above, and below, and from the side; I've experimented with settings and movement on the stage. There's nothing, nothing, to be done. It's the perfect play. It is a work of genius."

This was the same man, moreover, who one day defined for me his ideas on staging a play: "My work begins and the play interests me at the moment when the text ends."

I have also heard one of the greatest directors declare, in an impulse of revolt and disgust, "I've had enough! All plays are the same. I get tired and disheartened by my work. I am greater than what I do."

If I had space I would speak here in praise of restraint and success in the theatre, and say too that the inner joy necessary to good work should not be confused with the taste for indulging one's own pleasure.

In general, the director follows his instinct and directs the plays he feels and loves, and distorts most of the others to his personal taste. That is the fundamental fault with this authorized intermediary who is so valuable when he directs a theatre. It is not because I have a taste for disparagement that I say these things, but because I want to point out everything in the director's function that can be an obstacle to the free development of the theatre.

If there is any conclusion to be drawn to this subject of the producer, it should be a commendation of the profession. To be professional is to be authentic. It is the only way of being real, to possess and practice the virtue of truth. For nothing counts unless it be true, unless it has roots. Nothing counts but honesty.

In our time, among so many other errors, there is a social lie which allows the relative and the contingent to pose as authentic. I do not know what kind of commercialism or industrialism it is whereby the middleman, the retailer and the *passe-partout* producer have taken precedence over the craftsman; but the theatre has been thrown into disorder by these ill-qualified executives and incapable producers. (It has reached a point where, in the movie industry, the generic name for the man who works and labors is strictly reserved, in unconscious mockery, for the man who does nothing and does not know how to do anything: the producer. The only man in the business who knows exactly nothing about casting, cutting, camera-angles, montage—nothing about anything—is pompously entitled the producer.)

It is perhaps evident by this time that my wish is not to humiliate anyone, but to restore justice and equity by having the true workers become aware once more not only of their dignity but of their rights. In continuing to allow the so-called organizers—the merchants in the temple—to be kings in the kingdom of workers, we are in danger of compromising all we have.

In the short life given to us, there is still time for those whose sincerity and talent are expressed not in gain or glory but in the legitimate satisfaction of their taste for perfection, to recover a serenity as necessary to their inner peace and equilibrium as it is vital for social equilibrium. There is still time for the professional to be set apart, encouraged and protected by the society for which he works, and for the government—God on earth—to give some recognition to its own.

BORIS E. ZAKHAVA

(b. 1893)

Work with the Actor

IN ORDER to clarify fully the relationship between actor and director it is necessary to understand two particular qualities of theatre art. The first is the collective nature of theatrical production, and second, that the basis of production is the actor, a human being who, though he may be the material with which a director practices his art, is in his own right a creator.

The production of a play calls for the use not of a single artistic medium as in other arts, but for the combination of many art forms. The playwright, director, scene designer, musician, costumer and the actor each invests his share of artistic energy in the whole production. Hence theatre art emerges not as the expression of an individual but of a collective; the collective is the author of the finished dramatic result, the production itself. . . .

In the theatre, the director, dramatist, scene designer, musician, etc., each speak to the public, not directly, but through the actor. The actor then is not only the basic element in the theatre; he is the *central figure* in theatre art. He alone steps out on the stage to establish that vital communion between audience and the artists. They can talk only through him. Each craft must bring him ideas so that he may realize them; otherwise these ideas will be forever inert. The actor accepts what is offered him, evaluates it, separates the wheat from the chaff, and having allowed it to permeate his artistic being can then project these spiritual treasures across the footlights. Those words of the playwright which the actor does not endow with life, which he does not make his own, will remain dead; a beautiful prop or a beautiful piece

B. E. Zakhava: "Principles of Directing," *Theatre Workshop*, Vol. I, No. 3, April-July 1937, 43-58, Vol. I, No. 4, September-October 1937, 14-33.

of scenery placed on the stage, but never touched by the actor either physically or sensually, will also remain dead and should be removed from the stage. The dramatic significance of every theatric idea on the stage is communicated by the actor. *The contributions that go to make up the art of the theatre are essential only so long as they furnish material for the creative activity of the actor. . . .*

CREATIVE RECIPROCITY

The director starts work on a script. He determines its theme. In terms of the theme offered him by the script he begins to study. To do this he rallies all his senses, his memory, his personal and social experience. He tries to absorb as great a store of observations as possible and is always on the lookout for new concrete impressions from actual life. He subjects this wealth of material to a careful analysis to establish the difference between appearance and the unchanging facts of living reality. As a result of this research he arrives at what is *his* conception of the theme. This conception, or idea, lives in his consciousness surrounded by the wealth of factual data he has acquired. Armed this time with his own idea of the given reality, he returns to the author's ideas and enters into creative co-operation with him—as he begins to formulate his production plans.

When the production plan is ready the director presents it to the actors. He asks that each actor understand his role in terms of the whole play and also in terms of his central idea.

The actor, if he is an honest creator, having received the script given him by the director, will, before starting work on it, mobilize his own personal experiences, observations, and conceptions; he will begin to enrich these experiences and consider them in the light of the script. Correlating his ideas with the director's, and finding himself in general agreement with the director, he is eventually ready to start work on his role, building his own creative interpretation in collaboration with the director. . . .

Let us assume that there are no outstanding differences or that they have been eliminated by mutual persuasion, that the actor and director are working in the same direction as far as the social and ideological interpretation of the play and the characterizations are concerned. Rehearsals begin. The director gives the actor a concrete instruction pertaining to a particular movement or a given moment, or a certain phrase or intonation. This order may take the form of an explanation or a demonstration—this is for the present unimportant. The instruction arouses in the actor a whole series of associations from his observations of actual life, with the result that the direction given him and this experience fuse, synthesize, and a complete interpenetration takes place. The actor has done more than mechanically carry out a directorial request; he has utilized his creative personality. Having given the actor his formulation the director has it returned with interest, so to speak, in the form of the actor's stage technique. For while its meaning was being digested in the creative personality of the actor it became enriched with all the added resources of the actor, and not only those of the director who conceived it. The director, in this fashion, gets in return from the actor somewhat more than he gives. It follows that in fulfilling the director's instructions the actor influences the director. This will be an incentive to the director not to repeat himself in giving further instructions. Consequently, there will always be a quality of freshness about these instructions which would be lacking should the actor merely execute mechanically the task set by the director. New directions will go through the same process within the actor's consciousness and again serve to stimulate the director. In other words, each new phase of the progress is dependent upon the preceding one. In this way a director's creativeness is rooted in the actor's creativeness, and is not merely a rigid control over the actor's physical being. At one of his rehearsals Vakhtangov reproached his students: "You'd like to get by with only the material I give you. It's not enough. If you continue in this way those who see you will say, 'There is no individuality in these actors.'"

What did Vakhtangov recommend to his students to help them toward a creative approach? First of all he asked them to work on their roles at home and to bring the results of this work to the rehearsal. "Make it a habit to reflect on your role," said Vakhtangov. By "reflect" he meant to allow the imagination full play.

But whether the human imagination is sufficient source material for work as a substitute for living experience is questionable. An understanding of life is the true prerequisite for the productivity of the imagination. Let us take, for example, even such a highly fantastic thing as a mermaid. What is a mermaid anyhow? A creature with a female human face and the tail of a fish. Such creatures do not exist in real life. But the elements of which a mermaid consists are real enough. A female face and the tail of a fish are sufficiently familiar to all of us. If, however, you try, with the help of your imagination, to create a single thing which is outside of human experience, you will soon find that to do so is quite impossible.

The work of the imagination, then, is based wholly on experience, on a knowledge of life. Poverty and sterility of the imagination are, for the most part, due to the absence of a well-rounded human background and powers of observation.

If the artist is familiar with many phases of life he then has food for the imagination. All that remains for him is to learn to correlate this knowledge for a self-set purpose and toward the harmonious solution of an artistic problem. Which brings us back to the argument that in order to be able to "reflect" on his role the actor must be familiar with the realities which are its prime ingredients. And only by this same method can a director guarantee a creative, and not a mechanical production. . . .

THE CREATIVE WORK OF THE ACTOR

The first problem of the director in relation to the actor involves his full exploitation of the actor's creative resources. The correct channeling of the actor's energy will determine the entire course of the production. It is the director's job to see that his instructions are always within the grasp of the actor. The actor should be asked to take nothing for granted. He must maintain complete creative flexibility throughout the course of his work. The director must not merely avoid mechanical domination of the actor, he must constantly strive to preserve the actor's creative freedom and to see that nothing disturbs it during the course of the production.

What is the creative state of the actor? *The creative state of the actor exists when his response to an expected stimulus is as spontaneous and true as his response to an unexpected stimulus.*

Let us analyze this. The creative work of the actor involves complete freedom of reaction. This means simply the expression of the free associations of the actor without hampering or conditioning by any outside force. It lies in his spontaneous, characteristic manner of speaking. He does not do a thing just because the director has told him to. A response slips out unpremeditated; totally uninhibited. If the actor in rehearsal feels constant pressure on him from the director, his free initiative is bound to be cramped. However, in our definition of the creative state we demanded not only freedom but also truth. The actor will readily comprehend given stage directions if he feels them to be logical in the given situation and in the whole production. This specific gesture, that specific tone, this specific piece of business will then appear inevitable, and he will not grope about for any other.

But to put this principle into practice is very difficult. The director may say to the actor: "This is how you should react." The actor agrees, since he sees the logic of this proposed reaction in the light of his own analysis of the role. However, when he tries to realize this reaction it appears artificial, studied, forced. The director will then say: "Go ahead on your own in this instance." The actor does what he wants, but still it does not fit the situation or the general scheme of the play. It is only when the correct thing is done with perfect freedom that the logic of it and the freedom of its execution combine to make it right.

The actor must respond to every stimulus he receives in the stage environment in such a manner that it is fresh and totally effortless, which means that he reacts in this specific manner because *he cannot react otherwise.* At the same time this reaction must coincide with a consciously set plan (either the director's or the actor's). This demand is very severe but absolutely necessary.

The arbitrary demand for immediate results from the actor at the very beginning of work on a production is the most harmful of all directorial practices. Unfortunately, this occurs very often.

By "results" we mean particularly when the actor "emotes" in terms of stage patterns, voice, and movement. If the director, in the course of early rehearsals, demands a finished product from the actor (a specific emotion to be registered in a specific form), he demands something which cannot be done. "Here you should laugh a little," the director says, and the actor, embarrassed, makes an effort to laugh. Inevitably the product is artificial, strained, insincere. "Here you should cry," and the actor musters all his resources to simulate a measure of grief. But it is obviously false and melodramatic. Feeling, and the genuine form in which it is expressed, is the result of a long chain of processes. To express an inner state the actor must follow a systematic path. There are no short cuts, but if led along this route, the actor will reach his true destination.

How shall this process be developed? Every emotion, together with the true form it assumes, is a result of the individual's conflict with his environment. Any human want leads to an attempt to satisfy that want. Should the want be satisfied, a pleasant sensation results. If, on the other hand, difficulties lie in the way of the satisfaction of this want, suffering may ensue. Also, hand in hand with the attempt to satisfy these wants, go all the sensations of pleasant anticipation or fear of failure.

Thus we can see that each sensation grows out of the satisfaction or lack of satisfaction of an individual desire. First, we have the will or desire, then our activity is directed toward the satisfaction of the desire. In the course of this process emotions arise as a result of circumstance and often in spite of the individual (I don't want to cry but I can't help it).

The actor must first of all consider what he (as the character in the play) wants, and then what he is going to do about it. His feelings, and the methods of their expression, are conceived involuntarily in the course of his attempt to satisfy one or another of his specific desires. . . .

The director should not exact the imitation of emotions from the actor but the execution of specific actions. He must tell the actor what to do, and not how to feel.

Doing differs from feeling chiefly in the element of will which is present in it: to persuade, to quiet, to beg, to mock, to bid farewell, to wait, to drive away, to hold back the tears, to hide one's joy or suffering; these are all verbs inferring a will-power (I wish to persuade and I do persuade, I wish to quiet and I do quiet, etc.). The actor can undertake to execute such action at any given time provided he understands the motives behind them. These verbs may and should be used by the director to guide the actor in his work. Other verbs: to get excited, to pity, to laugh, to get angry, to be impatient, to despise, to love, and so on; all express feeling and therefore should not be used as stage directions. The director must know how to present a production problem to the actor, hinting, at the same time, the answers to two basic questions concerning the situation and the character:

1. What is the character doing, and
2. For whom, or why, is he doing it? (In other words, what does he want at the given moment?)

We see then, the three elements of the actor's stage task as:

1. Action—What I am doing
2. Volition—Why I am doing it
3. Solution—How I am doing it

The first two become quite clear at the outset after a discussion and analysis of a role. The third arises involuntarily and is the product of reciprocity and inter-activity between the members of the acting company. Let us take an example. Suppose the actor has to portray a man who has just been imprisoned in a small dark cell, in solitary confinement. The director decides that the state of mind of the character is one of utter despair. However, the director would be making a colossal error if he asked the actor to register despair. Despair is an emotion and we have agreed that we are not going to try to enact emotions. We have to act a stage problem, the emotion will follow. If the director immediately poses the problem of despair, the actor will inevitably seek the path of least resistance and become a stereotype. He will grab his head, pull his hair, groan, etc. All this will be unconvincing. Instead of a vital and fresh artistic solution the spectator will be given vulgarized and trite samples of the actor's stock-in-trade.

If the director will say to the actor: "You are looking for an escape from this prison, you will examine the strength of the bars, look for loose stones in the floor, etc.," the actor will have a chance to get busy immediately. In the course of all this business, the director will warn the actor that the walls of the prison are very solid, the bars very strong, the stone floor impossible to undermine. Thus the actor, having fulfilled all these suggested instructions with sincerity, involuntarily begins to feel his confinement, the hopelessness of his position. If the director will now tell the actor to find something to occupy his attention, to help him forget his sad plight, the actor will realize, in carrying out these directions, the impossibility of any kind of escape and will feel despair in his heart. By posing a series of closely connected improvisations the director can, unknown to the actor, raise him to almost any emotional state. The attention of the actor will be constantly occupied by the things he is doing. He won't be thinking of how he should be feeling or what forms his feelings should assume. Thus the artistic result, the emotion and its expression, will be a by-product of the process of activity. . . .

The director may demand outright the display of emotion only when he is certain that the actor will be able to translate the directions into terms of stage technique, and then only if the director sees that the actor is already in the creative mood and can absorb the directions with great flexibility no matter in what terms they are couched.

THE DIRECTOR'S DEMONSTRATION

The director's order may be given in two forms: as an explanation or as a demonstration. The first of these is superior since no matter how the director phrases his explanation it demands the active participation of the actor.

However, if we accept the demonstration as a form of directorial technique we must examine its values, and the ways in which it can be used to best advantage. There are certain dangers in this method. It may make the actor a mere carbon copy of the director's personality, completely subjecting him to the director's will. But we cannot utterly ignore this method. Such an evasion would rob the director of one of the best ways to stimulate the creative resources of the actor. It is often only by demonstration that the director can communicate his ideas dynamically, since only through demonstration can he show the organic unity between word and movement. This method often has the effect of inspiring and exciting the actor when long explanations have proved barren. Last but not least, it is a great time-saver. Where an explanation may take effect only after an hour or two, a demonstration will do the trick in a couple of minutes. Clearly this method possesses usefulness for the director. Since we do not discard it, we must lay down some principles to guide us in the use of this valuable but dangerous instrument. What are these principles?

Before we set these down it should be absolutely clear that this method cannot be considered basic in the director's work. The basic method is not demonstration, but explanation, elucidation. The demonstrative method should be a last resort used only under certain conditions.

One condition essential to its success is the developed creative state of the actor. This will insure the actor against copying mechanically the details of the director's demonstration. It is only when he finds the actor already independently creative that the director can enrich and broaden the scope of his work through demonstration. If the actor is in a passive state, demonstration will not only fail to help him, but will do untold damage. The more brilliant and penetrating the director's demonstration, the more shocking it will be to such an actor, who will either creep back into his shell at the comparison between the scintillating talent displayed by the director and his own puny efforts, or he will try to imitate the director's exhibition mechanically. Both are equally bad.

But even when the director uses this method he must suit his demonstration to the peculiar situation. It is important, for instance, that the demonstration cover a *general* situation to describe a *specific* one, and a *specific* incident to throw light on a *general* state. This means that the director is not to show the exact tone and gesture to be used on a specific line, but should merely give an idea of varied approaches. It is wiser for the director not to use the script but rather to improvise lines similar in meaning; not to apply special movements to the bit of characterization under discussion, but to use other patterns which might generally characterize and vitalize the person. The most appalling of all faults in a director is the pedantic insistence upon a particular inflection and particular movement in a particular bit in the role.

Unusually apt in the use of demonstration was the late Vakhtangov.

His demonstration had a generosity. He never attempted to lay down an arbitrary speech or movement. Rather he improvised so richly upon the text that he gave the actor a choice of interpretations. By the actor's reaction he could tell which was the most suitable and he then gave the actor the greatest encouragement to expand upon it.

The director must show the *general*, never the *specific*. The director should never, in demonstrating, give a finished product, a little masterpiece of acting. He should only suggest to the actor, giving him a friendly shove in the right direction, hinting to him the potentialities of a part. Having made these suggestions, he should permit the actor to find the needed artistic materials to give them polish. The actor will develop and complete for himself what he has received from the director in a sketchy form. The creative initiative to do this will come from his experience and observation of life.

We know that very often the director is a former actor. Having been talented in his work he now demonstrates to the actor he is directing how he would act the part were he cast in it. This is a serious mistake. The director, showing how he might have acted the part, inevitably uses his own individual peculiarities, his temperament, his physical make-up, the mobility of his face, voice, etc. This is exactly what an actor must do in approaching a role. But this is not the case with a director demonstrating it. The director should not only forget about *his own personal acting materials, but also those of the actor whom he is directing.*

Before entering into a working relationship with an actor the director should place himself in the actor's position and be able to adjust himself to the actor's degree of expressive power. He should keep that degree of expressive power as a measuring rod in any demonstration he gives to the actor. Only then can the director safely judge, not only how *he* would act a certain role but how the actor in point could perform it. An honest director never gives exactly the same instructions to two different actors even though they are rehearsing the same role. Only through an appraisal of his capacities can the director establish a genuine reciprocity between himself and the actor.

A director worthy of the name always seeks to develop the creative individuality of the actor. He discovers these individual assets, guards and expands them. On the other hand, a director who ignores this creative material present within the actor and chokes this individuality vitiates his most productive source of creativeness. He uses actors arbitrarily and opportunistically. No matter how great and fine such a director may be, and no matter into what raptures he sends the exclusive audiences who watch his demonstrations, the majority of his actors remain mediocrities, uninspired, stereotyped. Their work appears as a pale shadow of the brilliant directorial rendition, and leads to fond reminiscences of that original perfection. With such a director, actors don't grow creatively; they stagnate, and at parting they will remain what they have been made, helpless parasites feeding on the pap of the director's vitality.

The director should be able to help in the labor pains of those unborn ideas in the actor which are blindly searching for an outlet and expression. These ideas come to the very threshold of his mind pleading to be allowed in, but he cannot crystallize them and lift them from obscurity. Here is where the director must help the actor perceive what already exists in himself, but which has been unable to find a true artistic outlet. The director must have his tentacles sunk deep into the psychologic mold of the actor. Only then will he be able to regulate and organize the actor's creativeness without coercion or imposition.

Again I can't help remembering Vakhtangov. I know of no director who penetrated more closely into the inner life of the actor. I often watched some performance or rehearsal, where Vakhtangov, having observed the actor, would amaze and shock him by relating in detail every experience which the actor, as a human being, had passed through in the course of his appearance on the stage. He would say: "In such and such a spot you were frightened, then gathered your forces and improved. Then, pleased at how well things were going, you wanted to be even better, and so over-acted, became disgusted with yourself and then acted passively, just any old way from then on."

Vakhtangov made observations such as these about more than one of his students and often about all in a scene at once. It is difficult to realize how anyone could remain so observant at so many points of concentration. It is a faculty every director should strive to achieve. . . .

In conclusion, we may say that the demonstration, like any other method of work, is only one of many means toward an end which is the correct channeling of the creative energies of the actor. Only with this approach to the demonstration method on the part of the director and actor, will it lead to a rewarding artistic co-operation between them. . . .

THE IMPASSE

. . . Before placing the blame for a creative impasse upon the actor, the director should check and re-check his directions for possible errors. This is how experienced directors work. They are careful. They try over and over again, feeling their way. Young and inexperienced directors, especially those inflated by self-importance, often evade the responsibility they have toward the actor. It is painful to see the perseverance, worthy of a better cause, with which such a director hangs on to the actor to demand a precise bit of business or a phrase. Every bright idea that pops into his head he regards as an inspiration and he sticks to it to the bitter end.

A director who understands the nature of acting and of the actor (the clay of his art) behaves very differently toward the actor whom he loves and values. Such a director, before blaming an actor, always seeks the reason for failure in his own mistakes. He is his own severest critic. He tries to make all his instructions to the actor not only true, but also clear, simple, and easily understood. He knows that a direction given in vague, diffused ideas is not effective. He does not fatigue the actor with excessive theorizing. He talks little, but encourages the actors to discuss their roles at great length. He is attentive. He is severe when necessary and also, when necessary, he is gentle and kind. He adapts himself to each actor as the demand is made of him. He never forgets that the material of his art (the actor) is the most delicate, most perishable, most temperamental, most sensitive, most complicated mechanism in the world: *a human being.*

Now let us assume that the director has carefully examined all the demands he made on the actor. After serious and extensive research, he has found no errors which can be traced to his direction, so it becomes necessary to seek the reason for the impasse in the actor. How shall he remove the impediment? Let us first consider what common impediments exist for the actor.

1. *Lack of attention.* One of the primary rules for stage behavior is that during every moment he spends on the stage, the actor must have his attention fixed upon an object. He must see the person with whom he is playing, not pretend to see but actually *see*; he must also hear all that is said by his partner, not pretend to hear, but actually *hear*; and not only listen, but understand what is said to him.

"If the actor on leaving the stage," says Stanislavsky, "remembers only how well he played, it means he played badly. On the other hand, if he does not recall how he himself acted, but remembers only how beautifully his colleague did, then he acted well."

This is easy to understand. If the actor remembers how his partner performed it means the latter was the constant object of his attention. He watched and listened, observed his face, his gesticulation, his mimicry, his intonation. Having observed, the actor was able to adapt himself to his partner, to influence and be influenced by him. He lived and functioned not for himself, nor for the spectator, but for his colleague. He was *creating*.

2. *Muscular tension.* One of the basic requisites for the creative work of the actor is the free flexibility of his muscular system. This means that for each movement and position of the body, he must use a precise amount of energy, no more and no less. The proper distribution of energy throughout the body, which is achieved unconsciously in daily life, often disappears when the actor goes on stage. He finds himself full of muscular tensions. Since the nervous and muscular systems are in such close co-ordination, this tension causes much of the nervous agitation which often plagues the actor at openings or troubles him in the course of performance. The result is woodenness and the loss of all rhythm or plasticity of movement through nervous constriction of the muscles. If the actor can concentrate his attention on various objects and persons he loses a great deal of his initial nervousness and fear. This gradually loosens up the muscular constriction.

However, the reverse process is also possible. If the actor frees himself from muscular tension it will be easier for him to overcome his nervousness, which in turn helps his concentration on the stage problem. The director should be alert to the danger of wasted motions and whenever muscular tensions become obvious the director should instruct the actor, "Relax your face, your forehead, or your neck," so that the actor, freeing himself from pressure, will at the same time feel free of oppressive barriers to creative work.

3. *The absence of justification.* Creative activity on the part of the actor is only possible when his stage environment, including the play and its development, have reality for him. Everything on the stage must have an established significance; every passage, every prop, every part of the set, every word, every movement, every sound, every fact, every incident, every trifling detail, must have its *raison d'être.*

How is this stage reality achieved? It is primarily based on the understanding of motivations. Every action on the stage must spring from a logical motive. This motive must be in complete accord with the character and situation. A given motive must "feed" the actor: must give him the opportunity of arriving at newer and more distinctive creative images. Actors playing the same role will arrive at individual interpretations in this way. One actor playing Hamlet will explain his love for Ophelia by one reason; another by another. All of the justifications may be inherent in the script, but the tendency of the actor is to select the one closest to his own personality and temperament. In terms of his own ideas he can convert the stage activity into personal conviction. This conviction is the essential quality demanded by his audience.

If, therefore, there is anything in the play which remains obscure to the actor, as, for instance, why he must say so-and-so to his partner, or why he must assume such-and-such a position, these must be clarified and motivated or else the actor cannot create. That is why it is so necessary for the director to be certain that nothing remains obscure to the actor, even though it may seem like a completely trivial matter.

4. *Lack of creative "food" may also be the cause of an impasse.* It often appears that the accumulated mass of observations and facts pertinent to the stage problem have been exhausted in past rehearsals. The work has not yet been completed but the raw materials appear to have been consumed. Repetition of yesterday's ideas won't do. The words and ideas no longer have any freshness. The rehearsal is at a

standstill. The actor has reached an impasse. It is obvious that if the actor ceases to move forward he will fall behind, even losing the ground he has won.

What shall the director do? The best thing to do is to stop rehearsals and look around in search of new "nutritive" material for the actors. To do this, the director must again encourage the actor to do research in the sphere of life pertinent to his character. It is inconceivable that the actor will fail to find something new and genuine in the honest pursuit of information concerning his character's background. Then, together with the actors, the director should discuss and reflect upon this new information. The new ideas will supply the material for continued rehearsals.

5. *Attempts of the actor to enact emotions.* The first suspicion a director has of the actor's attempt to give an imitation of self-styled superimposed emotion, should be a warning to him to stop the actor immediately. Give the actor a specific task to perform.

6. *When falsehood creeps in.* Very often the creative impasse is the result of seemingly unimportant falsehoods which creep in unnoticed by the director. Let a falsehood reveal itself in some trivial detail, such as a physical bit of business, and disastrous results will follow. The presence of even a suggestion of falsehood is a symptom of the fact that a true feeling of conviction does not exist in the actor. If this conviction is lacking, the actor cannot create.

That is why we stress the need for the director to remove every possible shred of doubt from the mind of the actor. This is why Stanislavsky attached such significance to the execution of the slightest physical task. It is actually through the fulfillment of these simple tasks that the feeling of conviction is fortified. Having established a command over the simple tasks, the actor is in a better position to grasp complicated psychological problems. A contempt on the part of a director for these simple tasks is, to say the least, very harmful.

This is a basic principle for directors. *It is never worth while to continue until unquestionable honesty of execution has been attained in a given bit.* It should not irk the director to spend one or two rehearsals on some elusive phrase. The loss of time will be more than compensated. Having spent two rehearsals on seemingly trivial details, the director will be surprised at the facility with which the actor goes through the subsequent scenes. The point is that a falsehood will entrench itself just as firmly as a truth. It is particularly hard to root out a falsehood which has gained strength by repetition. Repeat only what is true, at all times. It may not yet be entirely clear and sharp, but that is no cause for concern. Expressiveness, brilliance, and polish can be cultivated at rehearsals only if the basic actions are true.

Now we have arrived at certain basic principles concerning the creative state of the actor, the violation of which results in an intellectual and artistic impasse. The director must determine, in each specific instance, what is needed to preserve the actor's creativity. The director must, in each case, give the correct diagnosis, the basic cause of the creative impasse. He must be able to put his finger on the weak link if he expects to mend the chain.

From all this it is clear how carefully the director must treasure the actor as the material of his art; what understanding, what keenness and discernment he must possess. All these qualities will arise naturally if the director values the actor; if he remains unsatisfied up to the perfection point where the expression of the actor attains inner artistic truth.

TYRONE GUTHRIE

(b. 1900)

An Audience of One

ᴘRODUCING a play clearly requires the co-ordinated efforts of many people, and the producer is no more than the co-ordinator. His work may, and I think should, have creative functions, but not always. The important thing is gathering together the different pieces and welding many disparate elements into one complete unity, which is never, of course, fully achieved in artistic matters.

The work of the producer can be analyzed—indeed has been ana-lyzed—in many different ways. I propose to deal with it under two headings: firstly, the producer in relation to the script of the play, that is to say the raw material of his work; and secondly, the producer in relation to actors and staff, that is animate collaborators.

It seems to me that the producer's business, when faced either with a new script or with being asked to revive a classic or an old play, is first of all to decide what it is about. Clearly, that is not entirely simple. To take an obvious instance, who is really going to give the final word as to what *Hamlet* is about? As we all know, more books have been written about *Hamlet* than almost any other topic under the sun. I am told that, as far as biographies are concerned, the three champions about whom the most has been written are Jesus Christ, Hamlet and Napo-leon Bonaparte, in that order. *Hamlet* is an obviously difficult case in which to decide what the play is about, but take a nice simple little play called *Charley's Aunt*. What is that about? Is it just a question of telling the story, or is it a question of finding a meaning to the story? Are Charley's "Aunt" and all those jolly undergraduates symbols of this or that, or are they to be taken at face value? Is the thing to be—as

Transcript of a talk delivered before the Royal Society of Arts, London, March 10, 1952.

I have seen it done in Scandinavia—a serious study of English university life, or is it just to be made as funny as possible? Personally, I think the latter; but before you can make it funny you have got to decide why it is funny, what is funny about it, and what the joke is, which is quite a tricky little problem.

I think very often the lighter the play is the more it is composed of thistledown and little else, the more difficult it is to pin down. One has often seen little tiny plays absolutely slain by the great mechanism brought to bear on their own interpretation. An obvious case in point is *Così Fan Tutte*. I do not know whether anyone has seen a satisfactory performance of that. I have seen it a great many times, but it always seems to me that a great many steam hammers in human form are assembled to crack a little jewelled acorn.

With regard to what the script is about, the last person who, in my opinion, should be consulted, even if he is alive or around, is the author. If the author is a wise man, he will admit straight away that he does not know what it is about, unless it is a very perfunctory work indeed. If it is just a little piece of journalism on the minor problems of psychoanalysis, then he probably will know all too well what it is about. But if it has the potentialities of being an important work of art, I am perfectly convinced he will not have the faintest idea of what he has really written. He will probably know what he thinks he has written, but that will be the least important part of it. Were it possible to find out, I would lay any money that Shakespeare had only the vaguest idea of what he was writing when he wrote *Hamlet*; that the major part of the meaning of it eluded him because it proceeded from the subconscious. A great work of art is like an iceberg in that ninety per cent of it is below the surface of consciousness. Therefore, in my opinion, the more important the work of art, the less the author will know what he has written.

I had the great privilege and pleasure to know the late James Bridie extremely well. I worked with him often, but he would never even discuss what his plays were about. He would say, "How should I know? I am the last person you should ask. I am only the author. I have written an armature, inside which, possibly, are the deepest ideas which have never quite formulated themselves in my consciousness. If, as I hope and believe, I am a poet, there will be something in these, but I am the last person to know what it is."

The producer has to decide what he thinks the play is about, and of course I am largely joking when I say that he does not really take the author seriously. Naturally he does, but not as to the deeper, the inner and the over-and-above, the between and through, meaning of the lines. If somebody does not decide at an early stage what the play is about, obviously the casting will be made for the wrong reasons. Ideally, a play should be cast because the actors chosen are people that somebody—be it the producer or be it the manager—thinks will express the play best. In fact, in the exigencies of commercial production and the exigencies of practical affairs, all too often plays are cast because somebody thinks that Mr. X will help to sell the beastly thing, and Mr. X happens to be living with Miss Y so she is a cinch for the leading lady, and all sorts of vulgar and extraneous considerations of that kind which really have nothing whatever to do with art but everything in the world to do with the practical business of putting on a play. I cannot sufficiently differentiate between the two, but seeing that we are speaking in these almost hallowed precincts I am going to try to behave as though we were in an ideal atmosphere and plays were cast solely with artistic considerations in view, or at all events very much in the foreground with practical things far away in the background.

In theory, the artistic way to cast a play is to decide who, of the available actors, seems to be the most like the principal part in the script that we are given, and who would best understand the thing. Let me qualify that. It is not entirely a question of who is the most like the principal character, because very often the last thing that an actor does well is to portray a character that is like himself as one conceives him to be in private life. Very many actors do their best work when they are hiding from themselves behind a mass of hair and make-up and fantasy, when they present something entirely unlike their real selves.

One must think which of the available actors would seem to give the best interpretation of a given part. That is why, at a very early stage, the whole business of producing a play has to move into conference. It is, in my opinion, very unwise for the leading actor not to work step by step from the very earliest stages with the three or four people with whom he is going to collaborate most closely: the manager, or whoever is responsible for the budgetary financial side of the production, the leading actors, and certainly the designer, the man who is ultimately going to be responsible for the pictorial look of the thing. All their work should grow together and should, I think, be the result of a productive exchange of ideas.

Therefore, it is clearly necessary that, if the thing is going to work well, they should be people who can to some extent speak one another's language, who can exchange ideas, who can admit themselves to be wrong without red faces in the company of the others, and so on. So that, long before the thing gets to the stage of rehearsal and parts being read or movements made, there should have been a quite extensive exchange of ideas about the look of the thing, about the sound of the thing, about the shape of the thing in predominantly musical and choreographic terms.

To elaborate that a little, the performance of a play is clearly analogous to the performance of a symphonic piece of music. By the time the play is ready, if it is properly rehearsed, the diverse voices, the group of people who are playing the thing, will have found a music for their parts. Why acting, in my opinion, is so much more interesting than opera singing is that the actors invent the music of their parts to a very great extent. In an operatic score, the composer's intention is made extraordinarily clear. The rhythm, the inflection, the loudness and softness, the pitch and the pace at which the idea is to be conveyed, are all clearly defined in the score. Almost the only creative piece of work left to the conductor and the singers is the color, because so far no form of notation has been found for musical color. The actor has to find nearly all those things for himself. Supposing you are an actor who is playing Hamlet. "To be, or not to be: that is the question: whether 'tis nobler in the mind to suffer . . ."—those infinitely familiar lines. You have to find the inflection, that is to say the tune, to which they are sung or spoken, the pitch, the pace, the rhythm and the color. That is, in fact, very highly creative.

Parallel with the creation of the actor must, I think, come the co-ordination of the producer. Supposing two of us are playing a scene, and one has decided that the scene must be played lightly and forcibly, and the other person takes a different view of the scene and feels that it must be managed in a very dark and very black way with long pauses. It is the business of the producer to co-ordinate the two without necessarily making either man feel that he has been a fool or stupid. It is a point of view which way the scene should be taken, and somebody has to be the chairman, somebody has to decide. That is really in most cases what the producer is.

I know there is an idea abroad, largely cultivated in popular fiction, about the theatre and films, that the producer is a very dominant person who goes around doing a lot of ordering about, saying, "Stand here, stand there, copy me, do it this way, do it that way." Of course, with experienced and accomplished actors that would be complete nonsense. Imagine my saying to Dame Edith Evans, "Do it this way, dear, copy me."

The performance of a play should be able to be observed by anybody who knows it well just like a graph, like a patient's temperature chart, like a graph of the sales statistics of a firm or anything else. One should be able to see the peaks and the hollows, and it should be possible to delineate the shape of each scene in a graph, which helps to make the scene more intelligible, which helps to make it illuminate the scene preceding it and the scene following it, which helps it to contrast, and at the same time to blend with the neighboring scenes; and, while each little scene should have a graph, similarly a graph of the whole act should arise from that.

Now on to the second main heading about production.

First of all, and very briefly, there is the question of organization, discipline and that kind of thing. If the company is any good and if the producer is any good, that is simply a matter of general convenience. I do not think the producer has any difficulty over discipline provided the rehearsals are not boring, and provided they are kept moving not at the pace of the very slowest person present but at a fairly decent tempo.

Then comes the question of coaching. How far is a producer to coach the interpretation? How much is he to say to the actors, "Do it this way"? I do not think one can give a complete answer to that. If you are taking the first production that has ever been done by the dramatic society attached to the Little Pifflington Women's Institute, you will probably have to do a great deal of coaching and coaxing to break down the self-conscious giggling of people who are quite unaccustomed to impersonation and pretending to be someone they are not. But if you have a good professional cast the amount of coaching you have to do is very small.

I do not think one should be at all afraid of saying to actors in a quite dogmatic way, "Play this scene sitting on the sofa, and if you are not comfortable let me know later on, but don't decide until we have done it once or twice. Later on, maybe you would feel like getting up half-way through and going to the window." Otherwise, if the actor is allowed to grope it out too much for himself, there is a waste of time, and the dominant personalities start bullying the milder, more unselfish and co-operative ones, which is what we have to be on the lookout for.

Then comes what I have tried to indicate is very much the main business of the producer, the work of co-ordination from the departments inwards.

Clearly, the co-ordinating of an idea, so far as it is concerned with visual matters, lies to a considerable degree in the hands of the person responsible for the lighting. Here, as elsewhere, I feel there should be the minimum of dogmatism. A good designer will have been working from quite an early stage in collaboration with the leading actors. Actors on the whole are sensible people about their clothes. Most actors have not at all a vain idea of their own appearance, but a very realistic appreciation of their good points and bad points, and they can be very helpful to a designer in suggesting things like the length of their coats or the width of their sleeves. If an actor says, "I want a long sleeve because I think I can do something with it," that should be taken very seriously; and, in my opinion, an actor should never be forced to wear a dress he does not like, unless it is for economic or disciplinary reasons. You could not expect people to feel free, unself-conscious and at ease on the stage in dresses they feel to be unsuitable.

Where I think the producer's work of co-ordination requires the greatest amount of time and care spent upon it is in the vocal interpretation of the play. As I have already tried to indicate, the performance of a play is, on a smaller scale, a performance of a musical work. The script is, as it were, sung, because speaking and singing are, after all, the same process. Although I am speaking now and not singing, I am uttering a definable tune all the time. Every syllable I utter is on a certain pitch and a musician could say precisely where it was. Every sentence that I phrase is consciously phrased in a certain rhythm. The pauses, although I am not conscious of it, are expressing an instinctive need to pause, not merely to breathe, but for clarity and various other interpretative purposes. This is even more pronounced in the perform-ance of a play, where all that has been most carefully thought out in terms of pace, rhythm, pitch, volume and all the rest of it, to make a certain expressive effect. That is particularly where the co-ordinating hand of the producer is required, joining up the various songs that are being sung and making them into a unit; and similarly, joining up the various patterns that are being danced, because even in the simplest realistic comedy, in the most ordinary kind of realistic set—the actors have to move, and their movements have to tot up to some kind of choreographic design which expresses the play, which has some mean-ing over and above the common-sense position in which one would pour tea or put sugar into it. For long stretches of the play the positions have to be guided not at all by anything that is afoot. Of course, it is mere journalism to think that plays are concerned with action. They are not. Plays in the cinema may be, but in the theatre the action is a tiny point.

In almost every play for the stage, there is scarcely any action. The movements of the play are almost all concerned with the expression of ideas and not of action. If there is action, it is very short-lived and very brief. The choreography is much more concerned with the subtle delineation of emotions by the way people are placed, with the subtle changes of emphasis by putting people into the brighter light or taking them out of it, by having them face the audience or turn their backs, by putting them in the center or near the side. It is all very much more delicate and allusive than simply getting them into common-sense positions to perform certain actions.

Finally, I should like to discuss what to me is the most interesting part of the job, the blending of intuition with technique. If I may elaborate those terms, by intuition I mean the expression of a creative idea that comes straight from the subconscious, that is not arrived at by a process of ratiocination at all. It is my experience that all the best ideas in art just arrive, and it is absolutely no good concentrating on them and hoping for the best. The great thing is to relax and just trust that the Holy Ghost will arrive and the idea will appear. The sought idea is nearly always, in my opinion, the beta plus idea. The alpha plus idea arrives from literally God knows where. Prayer and fasting can no doubt help, but concentration and ratiocination are, I think, only a hindrance. And yet I think no artist worth his salt will feel he can rely on inspiration. Inspiration must be backed up by a very cast-iron technique.

It is the case that as one gets older one's technique, if one is an industrious and intelligent person, tends to become better; but there is also the danger that it becomes a little slick. I think not only artists, but anybody engaged in any activity must feel the same thing. The record begins to get worn, and we slip too easily into old grooves, the same association of ideas comes back too readily and easily. I notice with my own work in the theatre—and I have been at it now for nearly thirty years—that I have to check myself all the time from slipping into certain very obvious and, to me now, rather dull choreographic mannerisms. I instinctively think, "Oh, obviously the right place is so-and-so, and the right way to group this is such-and-such." Then I think, why do I think that? And usually the only reason is that one has done it that way a good many times before. That is obviously frightfully dangerous in any creative work. It is the negation of creation; it is just falling back onto habit.

Yet there are certain very valuable things about experience and about technique. It is now comparatively easy for me, in late middle age, to establish a good relation with actors. They think because I have been at it for a long time that I know something about it, and they are readier to take suggestions from me now than they were twenty-five years ago when I was a beginner, though I am inclined to think that most of the suggestions are duller ones. Twenty-five years ago, intuition functioned oftener and more readily. That is, I think, one of the very difficult paradoxes about production.

Clearly, for practical reasons, it is very difficult to put the highly intuitive, gifted youngster in charge of a responsible production. He will make too many mistakes. He will be too dependent on the things that experience and authority bring easily from the older people. Also, it is difficult for the senior actors. It requires enormous tact, both on the part of the young producer and the old actor, to be helpful to one another. Yet the young producer is precisely what the experienced actor with a cast-iron technique—and consequently a great many mannerisms, too many clichés and short cuts—needs. He needs a very bright, sharp, critical young person of twenty-five to say, "No, Sir X, don't do it that way. You have been doing it that way for twenty-five years and it has been fine for twenty-five years, but that is just the reason for not doing it that way now." Well, you can see that unless that is done with supreme tact it is all too easy for Sir X or Dame Y to cast down their script and summon their Rolls-Royce.

I should like to conclude by telling a little anecdote which was told to me by a distinguished producer now resident in this country, who began life in Czechoslovakia and early in his career went to Germany. He soon got quite a good position while still in his early twenties in one of the German provincial theatres. He was a fine-looking young fellow and very "castable" in hero parts, and the management of the theatre sent him to see Reinhardt, then at the very apex of his celebrity and power in Berlin. My friend was still young enough to be madly thrilled, not only with the great opportunity of meeting this god and the possible advancement that it might produce, but with such childish and naïve, but extremely natural, things as the overnight journey in a first-class sleeper and all that kind of thing. All that was a terrific thrill, and he described very touchingly how he enjoyed it. He arrived in Berlin on a delicious crisp autumn morning, and went to the theatre at which Reinhardt was working, the Grosses Schauspielhaus. He described the grand chandeliers, the polished floors, the gentlemen in livery who collected him at the door, how he swept up the marble staircase, along a passage with portraits of eminent people all down the side, through a less important door in the side of the passage, down some stairs with no polish and carpets at all, through a very squalid little passage, round various corners, and across a courtyard, until he

came to a room really more like a kitchen. He said at first the only
things he could see were the long windows all down one side with the
sun streaming in. Then, as he began to get accustomed to that, he saw
a group of rather drab-looking actors rehearsing at one end. Then he
suddenly saw that one of these actors was somebody whose face had
been familiar to him all his life, a great star of Germany, and I think
he had that experience which anybody has who suddenly comes face-
to-face with a very familiar face that he has seen illustrated, whether
politician, film star, or anybody else. You suddenly think, "How small
they are! I thought they were much bigger." He was busy taking all
this in and thinking what a small person this gentleman was whom he
had always thought so great when suddenly, at the end of the room, he
saw a very unimportant-looking gentleman sitting on the kitchen table
swinging his legs and looking at his hands. It was Reinhardt. He
thought, "Now the great moment has come and I shall hear Socrates
pour out words of wisdom and technical advice to these people. Eminent they may be, but they will not be above getting a little tip or two
from Reinhardt." But nothing happened. Then he thought, "Well,
they must be so bad that he is going to give them a hell of a slating at
any minute. There will be a few glorious minutes when high-powered
abuse will pour from the golden lips and the boys down there will get
very hot under the collar." Nothing happened, and nothing continued
to happen for quite a long time until the actors came to the end of a
scene. Then there was a short pause, not a rudely long pause at all, but
quite a pause, and my friend was agog with excitement to know what
would be said. Reinhardt just looked up and said, "Thanks very much.
Now can we go back to the maid's entrance?" That, or something like
it, went on through the whole morning, and he said that, far from it
being a dull rehearsal, it was clearly—he was artist enough to perceive
it—an immensely constructive rehearsal, and he began to think why it
was, because nothing was being said, no instructions were given, no
abuse poured forth and no praise. He analyzed it this way, and the
more I think of it the more profoundly convinced I am that he is right,
that Reinhardt was performing the one really creative function of the
producer, which is to be at rehearsal a highly receptive, highly concentrated, highly critical sounding-board for the performance, an audience
of one. He is not the drill sergeant, not the schoolmaster, and he does

not sweep in with a lot of verbiage and "Stand here and do it this way, darling, and move the right hand not the left." He is simply receiving the thing, transmuting it, and giving it back. When you come down to analyzing what the creative part of acting is, it is the giving of impressions to the audience and then, on the part of the actor, the taking back of their impressions and doing something about them. The best simile that I can make is that the actor throws a thread, as it were, out into the house which, if the house is receptive, it will catch. Then it is the actor's business to hold that thread taut and to keep a varying and consequently interesting pressure on it, so that it is really pulled in moments of tension and allowed to go as slack as possible in moments of relaxation, but never so slack that it falls and cannot be pulled up again. The producer at rehearsals can be that audience. He can perform that function, and if he is a good producer he will perform it better than the average audience; he will be more intelligently critical and alive, and the rehearsals will not be dreary learning of routine; they will be a creative act that is ultimately going to be a performance.

That is why, in my opinion, the analogy between the producer and the conductor holds good. A *good* conductor is a man with a fine technique of the stick. He has a clear beat and an expressive beat, and is an interesting chap for the audience to watch. He can bring one section in with a fine gesture and blot another out. He knows his score, and so on, but it is all interesting showmanship. But the *great* conductor does not require any of those things. He can have a terrible beat and look like nothing on earth, but if he is a great conductor every man in the orchestra will give, under his baton, not only a better performance than he would under another conductor, but a better performance than he knew he could give. That is not got out of them by instruction; it is a process of psychic evocation. Precisely the same thing holds good for the producer of a play. His function at its best is one of psychic evocation, and it is performed almost entirely unconsciously. Certain conscious tricks can come in the way or aid the process, but this evocative thing comes from God knows where. It is completely unconscious. Nobody knows when it is working, and nobody knows why it is working. Some people, and only the very best, have it; others do not. I could not answer why or wherefore, but I am just convinced that that is so.

JOSHUA LOGAN

(b. 1908)

The Art in Yourself

"L OVE THE art in yourself rather than yourself in the art." Thus wrote Konstantin Stanislavsky across the bottom of his photograph which he had inscribed to me as a parting gift.

I had been studying with him throughout the cold Moscow winter, sitting by his side while he directed productions for the Stanislavsky Opera, an offshoot of the Moscow Art Theatre. Now summer had come and I had to go back to America.

My only diploma was this photograph with these few written words, but these words have grown deep in my belief. When I think I have found anything that resembles creative art in myself, I try to care for it, to cherish it, to hold it in my mind as I would an enlightening dream, so that it will not vanish.

Therefore, to write about creative work in the theatre, particularly my own—how I direct, how I feel about acting; in fact, for me to say anything which smacks of theories or opinions on the theatre—is a very uncomfortable experience. It makes me wonder if I am "loving myself in the art."

So please understand that these words are not put down for you but for me, as guides for my future work. I will be flattered if you read them, but then be sure to forget them and make up your own rules. Those are the only ones that will be useful to you.

The first obligation a director has is to the audience. No matter how great theatrical art may be, it becomes nothing if it is not shared. Theatre is not giver; theatre is giver and receiver.

An audience must be made to care early about the people in a play.

"The Art in Yourself" was written expressly for this book.

The problems must be made to matter, to make a difference to the audience, and the problems should be made desperate. Mildness is not a virtue in the theatre.

And the audience cannot be fooled. The old statement, "I don't think the audience noticed it," is a falsehood. The audience notices everything—every hit and every error. It senses insecurity in acting or directing immediately, as a horse knows fear in its rider.

And the director must give a chance for the audience to express its approval. Sometimes, at the exit of an actor or at the end of a scene, directors or actors do everything in their power to keep the audience from applauding, thinking it will break the magic spell. I think they are then robbing the audience of one of its chief pleasures. There is a great emotional contact between the cast and the audience. If the play is going well, love flows back and forth across the footlights. The audience likes the cast and the cast likes to be liked. It needs the reassurance of the audience's approval. Therefore, I think a director should allow an audience to applaud at any time it shows the tendency to do so. This is accomplished by punctuation—making a period instead of a comma. Then immediately the actor and director must say by a change of mood or position, "That's enough. We're going on with the story now."

If this hiatus is effected with taste and delicacy, the audience will not even know that it has applauded, except subconsciously. The web is intact.

I do not by any means mean that applause should be forced, encouraged, or even recognized. There must never be a tiny bow of appreciation or beaming look center which breaks the illusion and reveals the happy actor peeking through the face of the character he is playing.

When I was very young I thought it was a very splendid and original and artistic idea to direct my actors so that quite often their backs were to the audience or their faces were upstage. "A lot can be told with a back," was the phrase I used. Someone had told me that there was a "fourth wall" and that wall was along the footlights and the actors must be conscious of it always. One director even put an invisible fireplace in the footlights so that actors would warm their hands at it. They had to pretend to be looking out of imaginary windows cut through the unseen wall along the footlights. All evening I watched the hands warming themselves at the unseen fire and pulling back the window curtains which were not there. Of course I forgot the play.

The climax of another play was the suspenseful question: what would be the expression on a woman's face, a suspected murderess, when the murder was described to her? Would the face betray her guilt? The director had felt it was most original and clever to play this scene with the woman's back to the audience and her reaction to the gory details was seen only by the other actors. The entire audience wished for giraffe necks so they could look around the back of her head into her eyes.

At that moment I made up my mind where the "fourth wall" was in a theatre. If there are three walls showing on a stage, the fourth wall is in back of the audience. The audience should think of itself as being in the room, eavesdropping. The moment it is made conscious of the "fourth wall" along the footlights, it will become conscious of the footlights, then of the proscenium arch, then of the people sitting alongside, then of what time it is, then will it make the 11:37 or the 11:53. And the play has gone where the woodbine twineth.

Therefore, I try to arrange movement on the stage so that the audience can see the eyes of the actor who is making the point of the moment, and if I can't manage both eyes I'll settle for one. This is very difficult to achieve. Actors want the moral support of looking into each other's eyes. The director has to find a real dramatic reason for the actor to look away and thus allow his face to be visible. But all ingenuity must be summoned, because watching two profiles can soon become tedious.

During rehearsals I believe that the actors must have as good a time in the creation of the play as the director has. They should never feel as though they are being moved about by a great puppeteer, and too many days of sitting around tables reading lines and perfecting readings can make the rehearsals a bore for the actor. Actors like to move, even though they may not be terribly sure of how the line is to be read. Perhaps the movement will help them decide. The sooner the actors are on their feet, the sooner the fun begins.

Although I think a director must know his script thoroughly and see the general mood and the general picture of the stage at all times, he must never specifically settle on a rise or a cross or a gesture of the hand until he has given his actor a chance to use his own creative instinct.

I first go through the play quickly, indicating only by vague sketches the movement of each scene. In this way I hope to keep the play in a state of flux until it takes its natural and spontaneous form.

The next time through, a little more detail is added. And always I impress on the actors the fact that they are telling a story and it is not important to settle on the actual detail of their performance until they are sure of what the whole play means and what everybody else in the play is doing.

A director must never steal an actor's creation. If the actor makes an effective turn or gesture or suddenly gives an illuminating reading to a line, the director must never take credit for it himself. This is the actor's expression of himself. He can be asked to repeat it so that it will not be forgotten. Or it can be emphasized or clarified. But the director must be carefully honest in such a case and say clearly, "This is what you did. It was your idea. I just don't want you to lose it." If the director should go back over the scene and then make the suggestion to the actor as though he had thought of it himself, he will never be trusted or respected by the actor as long as he lives. He has stolen the most precious thing an artist has: his self.

In the American theatre today, technique is an ugly word. Reality, mood, emotional images are in fashion. Groups of actors, led by well-meaning teachers, get together in rooms and work on acting exercises. By recalling some real emotion of their life: grief felt at the death of a father or mother, pity experienced while watching an accident, fear suffered on waking at night as a child in a strange room in the dark— with concentration these personal experiences can be reimagined until a mood or state of mind is attained which can be used to color the interpretation of a written scene at hand. Acting groups sitting close to the actors involved have seen tremulous, pulsating, often brilliant performances achieved by the actors experimenting in this manner.

However, these same scenes transferred to the theatre in front of a large audience without the technique of diction or redirection to aid projection, often become jumbles of obscurity. Not hearing the words or seeing the faces of these actors, the audience cannot share the thoughts or participate in the story. Boredom suddenly flowers all over the theatre. The actor is so engrossed in his own personal image that he has achieved only self-gratification while his poor audience has achieved only frustration. All such intercourse has been found wanting.

For many years, during rehearsals I had intimate talks with actors where we discussed special, secret ways of playing scenes. But I have found that rehearsals are no fun when two people are whispering and nobody else knows what is going on. So now I bring all problems out into the open where even the smallest-part actor can know what the star's, leading man's and director's problem is at every moment. In this way everybody can feel a part of the entire project and can become deeply involved, even in the scenes in which they do not appear.

We continually analyze what the audience might be thinking at the moment or at least what the author is trying to make the audience think.

The director must play the part of the audience while the show is in rehearsal, encouraging the actors, minimizing their fears, giving them words of encouragement when a scene is well played.

And he must always be in charge of his cast. There should always be a feeling that he is their leader and that they can rely on him and that he will protect them when confusion sets in.

And above all, he must fight those greatest enemies of the theatre, fear and doubt—the fear of facing an audience, the fear of not being good enough, the fear of forgetting lines, the doubt of self that is in all of us.

In the high state of tension that is reached toward the first facing of an audience, the director must be on guard against panic, for should the actors begin to doubt their director or their play or themselves, all is lost.

> "He who doubts from what he sees
> Will ne'er believe, do what you please.
> If the sun or moon should doubt
> They'd immediately go out."

In directing the musical play, the main problem is of course the songs. How can the audience be made to accept the fact that a change of chemicals has occurred and that the actor is now singing his lines instead of speaking them?

This has been a cause of many sleepless nights for me, and I have come to the conclusion that a song must be treated as a scene, a high emotional scene, something that comes out of a nervous mood that is *started in the dialogue scene preceding the song.* If the spoken scene has become high enough, ecstatic enough, then the audience is not shocked by the intrusion of song. Therefore, it is a case of working in all departments to bring the audience into the state where it is ready to accept a song.

A song is about to start. Perhaps the author will have to write a little more of a scene before the song begins to establish the approximate feeling of the song. The actor and director heighten the emotion of a scene by performance. At the moment the apt emotional state is reached, the orchestra starts playing quietly under the dialogue to underline the emotional state. Just before the actual beginning of the song, perhaps the actor's voice can rise in emotion until, still speaking, this tone is colored to resemble singing. When he actually sings there should be a feeling that there is nothing left to do but sing. The song is simply a high moment in the story, never a departure from it.

The actor's voice must be as close to the audience as possible to obtain its full effect—the moment an actor sings toward the wings or upstage, the impact of the melody and tone is lost. Therefore, props, chairs, boxes, etc., must be brought 'way downstage earlier so that if the song is to be sung while sitting on them or resting against them, it seems a natural, spontaneous movement rather than a signal that a song will start.

The effect of a song can be heightened by using all of the sounds of the orchestra as a background for the actor's performance. A musical figure in the orchestration can be accompanied by a change of expression, a move of the head, a gesture of the hand, or simply a change of emotion which has no definable physical attribute.

All the artists and technicians of the theatre combine to produce the final effect—the author, actors, scenic designer, choreographer, costume designer, stage manager, carpenters, electricians, prop men, orchestra. Each of these people must put as much of his own self into his work as he possibly can. It is his duty to bring out that thing that makes him different from another person—and bring it out passionately.

Quite naturally, a point comes where one particular self clashes with another particular self. This is the point at which each self must make a creative compromise—make a slight, painful, but healthy adjustment so that the clash is not so violent that it destroys the play.

The director should be the Solomon of this very necessary compromise who decides which self must be most apparent at which moment. If the costume designer has designed a dress that will not go through the scenic designer's door, the director must decide which shall be slashed, the costume or the door. The director must edit an actor's performance, bring out his strong points, hide his weak ones. For instance, if the actor is more forceful when he is sitting down, the director must arrange that he is seated as much as possible.

The author may also have to make a lifesaving sacrifice. Certain lines are dear to him; the actor has tried them in various ways; something is still wrong. Perhaps it's the actor's voice or face or personality which doesn't fit with the lines. At this point the author must be persuaded to cut or rewrite the lines in order to make it easier for the actor to project the author's scene. Any agreement is worth while if it is made for the sake of clarifying the play for the audience. All really great authors are ruthless with their work. No word is sacred. Every second of every line must be heard, seen, understood, felt, shared by the audience. Confusion may seem artistic but it is fatal.

I think of an audience as a tremendous, terrifying animal—a behemoth that wants to be conquered. It is many people suddenly fused into one being, with one heart and one eye. It can be loving and docile and happily approving. Or suddenly it can turn and be vicious and make loud booing sounds. Or most terrifying of all, it can even turn over and go to sleep.

When the curtain goes up there is a sense of challenge from the audience to the performers. "Do you think you're good enough to make me enjoy myself?" asks the audience.

The director and his actors must meet this challenge with the calm, attractive arrogance of a champion. "You fortunate people," they must say. "You're going to see us in this splendid play! Look how relaxed we are, how confident! You don't frighten us! Look how calmly we walk across the stage and sit on this chair! If we make a pause, you're going to pause with us and you're not going to cough. And you're not going to make us nervous so that we'll grow louder or talk faster in a vain effort to please you. We'll talk like this because this is our emotion. This is the way we feel; therefore, it is the way you feel. Be calm. You're in the hands of masters."

Only then the great temperamental animal feels reassured that its precious evening is not going to be wasted. It settles back with a contented smile and avid, eager, childlike eyes. "Yes, yes, go on!" it says.

André Antoine reading to the company at the Théâtre Libre.

Stanislavsky and members of the Moscow Art Theatre hear Chekhov read *The Seagull* (1898).

George Bernard Shaw takes a hand in the direction of *Androcles and the Lion*.

David Belasco explaining a scene to the company of *Tiger Rose* (1917).

Vsevolod Meyerhold rehearsing a scene from his production of
The Final Conflict (1931).

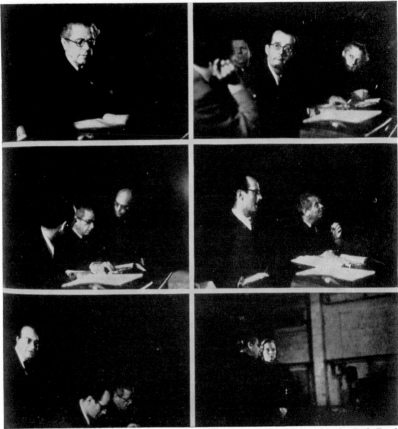

Max Reinhardt and his *Regiebuch* in action during the production of
The Eternal Road (1937).

The Group Theatre rehearsing *The Case of Clyde Griffiths* under the direction of Lee Strasberg (1937).

Joshua Logan directs the chorus of *Wish You Were Here* (1952).

Part III

THE DIRECTOR
AT WORK

&

KONSTANTIN S. STANISLAVSKY

(1863-1938)

Director's Plan for *Othello*, Act III, Scene IV

In May, 1929, Stanislavsky went to Nice to recover from a grave illness that was to keep him from ever appearing on the stage again. During his convalescence he sent to his colleagues a projected mise en scène for the Art Theatre's production of Othello. *It is from his notes, which were not completed beyond Act IV, Scene 1, that the "Director's Plan for* Othello" *was collated. The passages from Stanislavsky's "score" which follow reveal his methods of work on the play, his analysis of the leading characters, and afford us a glimpse into the "creative laboratory" of this great master of the stage.*

IN OTHELLO's part not a single scene is irrelevant in revealing the whole mountain of the hero's growing passion. Therefore this mountain must be before us through the whole part, the image of it must be kept before the actor's eyes all the time.

I keep thinking of auxiliary technical devices to intensify and vary the shades of passion experienced by Othello to prevent the actor from acting on pure temperament and voltage (pressure).

Here is a device. One can intensify not only by pressure or force alone, but by color. Imagine, as it were in painting, that next to pale pink appears a pale mauve shade, and next to the pale mauve a dark green strip, followed by a pale blue and then red. The very suddenness

---

Konstantin S. Stanislavsky: *Stanislavsky Produces Othello*, translated by Dr. Helen Nowak. London: Geoffrey Bles, 1948, 157–161, 163–166, 205–218, *passim*. By permission of Geoffrey Bles, Ltd., England.

of the change carries in itself the power of the effect. In our case colors
are replaced by devices. Acting the curse scene which is spread over
several pages, it would be very difficult to proceed at high voltage all
along, but if for every piece a scale of colors or devices is chosen, and
the choice is skillfully made with the view of intensifying the scale in
power, considerably greater results will be obtained with much less
expenditure of energy.

Let the actor therefore bear in mind this method with the intensification of the force in the role of Othello. As to the voltage, save it in the
accelerating crescendo period for the two final notes only. This is how
it is also done in music: only the last note or two require a *forte-fortis-
simo*, while everything that precedes it, sometimes spreading over several pages, increases only relatively, from *piano* to *forte*.

In order to keep the part on *piano* notes as long as possible, since the
élan of the part and the actor's sentiments will constantly develop, I
would conduct this scene on the desire to acquit Desdemona. Othello
frightens her with the story about the magic handkerchief, he takes
her hand, looks into her eyes, and talks in the hope that in her reply she
will give him proof of her innocence. In short, he asserts because he
wants to be told that he is wrong. When it becomes clear, however,
that the handkerchief is gone, he is ready to demand it, to obtain it by
threats, only not to suffer a disappointment in his hope to convince
himself of her uprightness.

It must not be forgotten that they arrived only yesterday. Today he
discovered things about her. By the time the sun was setting he fled to
the Tower. There he was when evening descended and the stars came
out.

Now the question arises: when could Othello have gone to see Desdemona? (The handkerchief scene). Had he called on her the following day, *i.e.* had he been missing all night, there may have been another
meeting between the two; would it therefore not be correct to play this
scene as happening in the evening of the same day? Here, however,
another doubt arises: another scene with Desdemona—that before the
murder in the last act—is also played at night; would the repetition
prove tiresome or not?

I cannot decide on it; at times it seems to me good, and then again it seems all wrong.

I can imagine that after the vow, with the coming of evening, Othello has suddenly grown very sad. The first flash of indignation gone, the vow made, a little reaction sets in. The same voice coming from his adored Desdemona speaks again, and he longs to convince himself once more that she is innocent. As to the time, it could have happened in the evening or at night, because the reaction would require some time. True, Shakespeare introduced the scene with the clown which makes it difficult to fix it for the evening, but as we have eliminated the clown, there is no reason why we should not act it in the evening.

There is another difficulty: the fact is that Desdemona's chamber was ordered for this scene and for the one preceding the murder, but somehow, I do not know how, it was forgotten. Therefore nothing remains but to play both scenes in the bedchamber. I know it is not good; but we have no other choice. Speak to I. Y. Gremislavsky about how to escape this predicament.

I imagine the following solution: Desdemona's chamber is round— what if we show in these scenes different parts of the same room? It will be the same room, the same walls, with the difference that the stairs leading up will not be on the right side of the audience but on the left, and when ascending the actors will face, instead of turning their backs to, the audience as proposed in Act V. The scene can be differently furnished; there may be a dressing table, maybe a divan and a window. It is moonlit, and the window could be open while Desdemona prepares for bed.

I continue along the play. And so, Othello's wounds smart more than ever. Of course, Desdemona is no longer what she was. Her heavenly purity is gone. She is a cheat like all women. It is these words—like *everybody else*—that are so disappointing, that have cooled his ardor. It means he made a mistake. Everything was a dream, the product of his imagination, and now all is frustration. There can be no question of going upstairs to share her bed. On last night's purest and exalted love he now looks in quite a different light. It was not exalted love on her part, but the common passion of any woman. This sentence "She is like everybody else" burns his soul. He walks further and further away from the bedchamber, from people, wanting to try and understand his feelings and what to do now; he opens a door and finds himself in a blind alley, sits down on the steps and crouches there all night hardly knowing it, his thoughts stretching in a long unbroken chain like gray rain clouds in the autumn. But Iago, the detective, watches him all the time. In the morning, when the first rays of the sun light up the little window of the back room or passage end, where household articles, or perhaps arms, are dumped in a heap, Iago who has been watching for some time through the peephole in the door, decides to enter and talk to him. He has taken a new line—he defends Desdemona and tries to excuse her, applying the yardstick of an average woman to her. Othello, however, was used to measuring her qualities on quite a different scale, that of a superior being. Therefore Iago's words only make Othello indignant. He finds it hard to live with the idea that Desdemona is no goddess but an ordinary woman "like everybody else."

But as it turns out, she is much worse than any other woman, she is depraved. The mere assumption of it, the mere fact that this can be said of Desdemona is enough to stun him. He feels the ground sway under his feet, loses his balance and falls into a paroxysm.

It must be noted that now that Iago has Othello in his clutches, he revels in his power over him. Iago, by the way, presents himself to me as follows: he is first and foremost a virtuoso of provocation, there is much of an actor in him, much temperament and the capacity of all human vices. At the same time he is courageous, deft, and the soul of a company; he knows how to make people laugh, he can sing a song, tell a story and organize a drinking bout. He has it in him. "*Figaro sì, Figaro là.*"

Finally, he possesses a certain breadth in whatever he does. This is why when he drinks, he drinks his fill, and when he jokes he jokes his fill too. When at war he fights with all his might; his revenge is as powerful, and so is his jealousy and power over people's souls when he gets hold of them, be it Roderigo (of whom he makes a slave and a clown) or Othello (with whom he plays like a cat with a mouse).

This is why my Iago is not satisfied with an ordinary brawl among the officers in Cyprus to precipitate his rival Cassio into trouble. He needs to rouse the island. He will subordinate Othello to his will as if he were his slave. And all this is done not because Iago is something of a satanic superman, but because he is an actor, an artist and virtuoso in the art of provocation. He loves a big plan, the large scale, because he is an artist at his job, and has excellent powers of imagination.

Now, when he has complete hold of Othello, he calmly and coldly enjoys the possession of the other man's soul like the great technician of art he is, like Svengali who possessed the soul of Trilby, like the lion tamer who makes the strong beast yield to his power.

Othello writhes in the convulsions of epilepsy, and Iago coldly stands by watching his work and enjoying it.

Now that he has reached the stage of indolence, he, like an actor on a professional tour who has full confidence in himself, acts on technique alone, calmly and with a cold heart.

Othello revives, and Desdemona appears to him in a new light. She is not like everybody else, *she is worse*. This is the approximate heading of this scene.

After the scene with Cassio he is not merely disappointed in her. He begins to hate, to abhor her; this is the beginning of the revenge. The notion is born that so much meanness must not be allowed to walk on this earth; from this moment punishment is under way. There can be no more hope for salvation or for the revival of an illusion.

From this moment and until the end of the play he conducts the investigation (the Desdemona-Emilia scene), passes judgment and fulfills the verdict.

After all that has been said the only thing that remains is the planning and appointing of places. This I am setting out to do now.

I am staging the Desdemona-Emilia scene in order to touch at least somewhat on Desdemona's part, up to now neglected.

I dislike Desdemona's constant pestering of Othello to forgive Cassio, as the play shows it. I think Desdemona is always doing it at the wrong moment. It becomes particularly bad when the actor portraying Othello displays passion and jealousy all through his part. The result is that the spectator, seeing the husband in a bad mood, asks himself: Why does she bother him just now, couldn't she find a more opportune moment? Placing myself in the actress' position I find it necessary to excuse this awkwardness. How do I go about it?

First, it is essential that the actor who plays Othello should help in the scenes with Desdemona and behave so that her pestering becomes possible and natural.

Secondly, one will have to use one's imagination and this is what I am about to do now.

Let us enter into Desdemona's position. The young girl with romantic ideas lived shut up with a widower-father, surrounded by nurses, servants and two or three friends. Imagine how boring it must have been in that big house, with the father always busy, with book-reading as her only distraction. And then, suddenly, she escapes this seclusion, enters into a secret marriage, bids farewell to her husband, there and then, perhaps forever. A day later she herself leaves her native country, is caught in a terrible storm, is saved, lands on a strange eastern island, is anxious for news of her husband; finally, there is reunion, and the next day she finds herself mistress of the island, the wife of the Governor. She gives receptions, there is a dinner, a *soirée* with herself as hostess. Then follows the first night of love, and already on the next day she is asked for protection and help because people recognize the power she holds over her husband. Is it possible that all these romantic events of the last few days could have passed without so much as leaving a mark on her? She is delighted at everything that has happened. Life in these days seems like a fairy tale. She feels as if she were reborn. Naturally, she will nurture the desire to display her new authority, to carry off her new part with dignity. There is even a certain new self-confidence about her. The question of Cassio becomes more than a mere question of protection or sympathy, but one of personal ambition for her as the mistress of the island, and more than that, as a woman.

Is it possible for him to refuse me? Is it possible for him not to do this trifle for me? Have I no power over him? After all, it would be most embarrassing because of Emilia, of Cassio, because of the whole retinue if she fails in this, her first debut.

But I should like to add to this something that is even deeper. This is what my imagination pictures for me. Desdemona has spent her secret meetings with Othello not only in love-making, she was also educating him at every conceivable opportunity. Women love to exercise their power over men, they like instructing them, teaching them, turning them into nobler and kinder beings. I can imagine that she gave him books to read. I can see this big man sitting up all night and sweating over his homework like a schoolboy cramming for an exam, so as to be able to talk to her about it the next day. There is a great deal she can teach him he did not know and had no time to think about in his war-filled life. There are questions of love, marriage, co-habitation, attitudes toward people, decency and other problems born of culture, and a culture as advanced as that of Venice at that time. And the question of religion! Othello is a Christian of course, but he never gave much thought to religious dogma. Desdemona, a devout Catholic, can teach him a great deal in this respect.

But I can also see other scenes. Othello is ignorant of the way one is supposed to kiss a woman's hand and to bow in a worldly fashion. There are many naïve and ludicrous habits of the savage in him, and Desdemona would try to eradicate them. She would teach him how to approach a woman and kiss her hand, and this big man, embarrassed and panting, wiping the perspiration from his forehead, would make every effort to master the things he is taught.

He likes all this because he has a beautiful and noble nature and is easily inclined to accept cultured behavior. Thus Desdemona would become his tutor, and this attitude, I fancy, colors her request to pardon Cassio. It is the right thing to be human and forgive people if they are loyal to one; one must be grateful. Questions of military ethics and discipline are of little interest to Desdemona. I imagine that her pestering of Othello is to a certain extent influenced by this attitude on her part to be his tutor. . . .

ACT III . . . SCENE IV

THE BEDCHAMBER

1—Staircase. In the last act it is on the right and those ascending have their backs to the audience. In this scene it is on the left and those ascending face the audience. 2, 3—Trunks with Desdemona's dresses and linen. 4—Praying desk with a Bible on it and a crucifix behind. 5—Carved Turkish cupboard. 6—Narrow Turkish divan. A canopy over it. On the side of the canopy hangs an embroidery done in gold on red velvet. Probably such embroidery is being sold in Eastern shops to this day. They can easily be copied, *i.e.* painted on velvet. 7—Toilet table with an Eastern mirror. 8—Revolving Turkish chair.

DESDEMONA: Where should I lose that handkerchief, Emilia?

Desdemona is preparing for the night. She wears a semi-day, semi-night outfit. Her hair is not down (she will need her hair up in the next scene, Lodovico's reception, which takes place without an interval; if, however, there should be enough time to arrange her hair during the "Cellar" scene, it would be better to have it down, ready for bed).

Emilia is putting Desdemona's jewels in a box: a brooch, bracelets and other things. She may prepare the combs for her hair (or anything else you may think of to occupy her). One might object to that as she is no maid, but would a close friend not undertake at times the duties of a maid? Desdemona has obviously just done her hair and conducted a conversation with Emilia. What about? About Othello, of course, with whom her mind and heart are full. In the midst of the conversation she remembers the handkerchief, and we find her looking for it. Remember how this is done, or more correctly, *what* one has to do if one wants to find an article one has mislaid.

For the time being Desdemona thinks that she must have dropped it here; therefore she looks under furniture, into corners, under cushions or the carpet covering the divan, under the dressing table, near the stairs, behind the trunk.

Emilia, who has a finger in this pie, takes no part in the search. She pretends to be occupied with more important things. She would have to sham if she looked for it, and that would be disgusting; she would be ashamed to do it.

The asterisks stand for pauses during which Desdemona bends down, looks, searches, etc.

EMILIA: I know not, madam.

DESDEMONA: Believe me, I had rather have lost my purse
  Full of crusadoes;* and, but my noble Moor
  Is true of mind, and made of no such baseness
  As jealous creatures are, it were enough
  To put him to ill thinking.*

EMILIA: Is he not jealous?

Emilia's reply is so important to Desdemona that for a moment she leaves off searching to convince her that her lover does not possess this mean vice, jealousy.

The line about the sun having drawn "such humours from him" is said in a gay tone, like a joke. Desdemona is altogether in a cheerful mood. And why not, it is only the second day of her honeymoon!

DESDEMONA: Who, he? I think the sun where he was born
  Drew all such humours from him.*

After "Drew all such humours from him"—laughter, and a pause during which she continues to search.

Everything that has taken place up to now will thus represent the *first action of the scheme,* and the piece could be headed *"the search for the handkerchief."*

EMILIA: Look, where he comes.

In the last pause Emilia hears steps below. She rushes to the stairs, sees

Othello coming and then hurries to Desdemona so as not to be compelled to call out. Her movement shows alarm and excitement.

Emilia thinks differently from Desdemona. She did not like
Othello's behavior during the day. It does not seem the way to spend
one's time during the first days of one's marriage.

Hearing that he is coming and thinking of last night's wonders, Desdemona wants to meet him suitably. She runs to the mirror to touch
up her hair.

Emilia waits respectfully at the stairs to disappear at the first opportune moment and not to disturb the husband and wife.

DESDEMONA: I will not leave him now till Cassio
   Be call'd to him.

She speaks these words while smartening herself up. Her hair done, she
runs to the banisters to meet Othello.

(*Enter Othello*)

Pause. Othello's entry should be delayed to underline its significance.

He enters trying to seem cheerful and cordial at all costs and not
make Desdemona see how he feels inside.

How is 't with you, my lord?

She speaks, leaning over the banisters. Thus their meeting takes place
as follows: flirting lightly, Desdemona at the banisters, looking at him
questioningly and trying to find out how he is, while Othello stops on
the stairs, having had no time to come up yet. Their heads are on a
level.

OTHELLO: Well, my good lady. O, hardness to dissemble! (*Aside*)

He tries to sound cheerful. Desdemona suddenly puts her arm round
him over the banisters, leaving his head uncovered.

His face is turned to the audience, she is showing the back of her
head.

How do you, Desdemona?

Desdemona stops dead still in the embrace. He starts at it. The embrace is intolerable, but he restrains himself. One can see by his arms
how he would like to, but cannot make himself, put them around her.
His face shows suffering. The embrace over, however, he will try again
to seem, if not gay, at least calm.

By the way—it would be better were the actor to make it his task to be cheerful; should he not succeed in being sincere about it, even better: this failure will accentuate the artificiality which Othello requires at the moment.

Pause. This scene of meeting and embrace must be played right through to the end; do not be afraid of prolonging the pause.

Othello has said: "O, hardness to dissemble!"

N.B.—Emilia may be out of place here. If so, she ought to go before Othello makes his entry.

The embrace is over. Desdemona is happy. Playfully, as in the "Fountain" scene, she pulls him along again and makes him sit on the divan. He obeys, but when Desdemona is not looking his face expresses all that he suffers within.

Sitting down Othello asks: "How do you, Desdemona?"

On her knees next to Othello, Desdemona replies with delight and passion: "Well, my lord!" and throws herself to kiss his hand which Othello inconspicuously tries to draw away. With the last of his strength he forces himself to restraint. He has taken his hand away. Pause.

DESDEMONA: Well, my good lord.

OTHELLO: Give me your hand;* this hand is moist, my lady.

Embarrassed pause.

She is squatting on the cushions and he, having taken his hand away, looks at her, trying to seem calm and even gay. There is a misunderstanding.

N.B.—I forgot to give a warning of a general nature at the beginning of this scene. What it is about is the following: Othello as well as Desdemona has much material here in order to set into action every sentiment—sarcasm, suffering, tragedy, Othello's jealousy and Desde-

mona's fright and perplexity. I am refraining from it on the grounds
of the *piano-forte* law (I shall send you the explanation later). For the
time being I want to mention only that the longer one delays every
kind of excess on both parts, the better for the following, the easier for
the actors, the more force and color they save for those places in which
a full *forte* is required. This is why I try to present the author's text in
a slightly different shade, using a slightly softened sub-text.

After the embarrassing pause Othello wants to examine his feelings.
Just now when she kissed his hand, he felt the warmth, moisture and
magnetism of her hand. Now he verifies it.

Pause. His eyes are not grim, but searching.

After a short pause of reflection during which he touches her hand
and admires the hand as well as Desdemona, Othello notices that her
hand is moist.

More verifying and questioning.

DESDEMONA: It yet has felt no age nor known no sorrow.

OTHELLO: This argues fruitfulness and liberal heart:

Othello speaks this monologue with great emotion, looking at Desdemona as though he sees through her and probes her heart with his
glance, studying her hand and watching her intently. The actor must
not give himself away to Desdemona, but on the other hand the audience must be made to realize his state of mind. This might be done
by looking away from her under various pretexts so as to cover up expressions which Othello cannot conceal otherwise. Or, under the
pretext of wiping his face, smoothing down his hair, rubbing his temple
he may, in a moment of need, conceal his face from her. He may also
resort to his voice, when by intonation or the lowering of his voice he
will disguise the real meaning of some sentences from his wife.

> Hot, hot, and moist: this hand of yours requires
> A sequester from liberty, fasting and prayer,
> Much castigation, exercise devout;
> For here's a young and sweating devil here,
> That commonly rebels. 'Tis a good hand,
> A frank one.

DESDEMONA: You may, indeed, say so;

Desdemona continues in the same carefree tone.

> For 'twas that hand that gave away my heart.

OTHELLO: A liberal hand: the hearts of old gave hands,

Othello—concealing the sarcasm from Desdemona, but not the audience.

But our new heraldry is hands, not hearts.

DESDEMONA: I cannot speak of this. Come now, your promise.

Difficult place for both. It will not shock the audience if Othello has succeeded in his former sentences to hide from Desdemona his true state of mind. Otherwise Desdemona's position is rather difficult; she must pretend not to see what is so obvious to everybody. She will need some help from the actor playing Othello. He must give her the opportunity to go through this scene without tension.
Desdemona has made herself even more comfortable at his feet; not without coquetry she puts her head or chin on his knee. (Othello can hardly stand this close intimacy but he still holds out.)

OTHELLO: What promise, chuck?

Pause, and a penetrating glance from Othello. Already he knows what she is going to say, and he watches her like an examining counsel, trying not to startle his victim.

DESDEMONA: I have sent to bid Cassio come speak with you.*

Playfulness and coquetry, rather tactless at this moment; or serious womanly persistence on Desdemona's part. May the spectator say to himself at this moment, his heart contracting slightly: Oh, why is she doing it now!

OTHELLO: I have a salt and sorry rheum offends me;
    Lend me thy handkerchief.

Pause. Piercing glance of Othello, the examining counsel. After this he tries to bring forth his lines about the cold and handkerchief as unconcernedly as possible.

DESDEMONA: Here, my lord.

Desdemona jumps to her feet and runs to the dressing table.
Othello, who has imagined for a moment that the handkerchief is there and everything will turn out well, runs after her, cheerful and young all of a sudden, expecting that when he sees the handkerchief he will recover on the spot and yesterday's bliss will come back to him.

But alas!—After the momentary exaltation follows a terrible collapse and acute disappointment.

The handkerchief is not there; that means everything is true.

Pause. At once Othello is withered. He is hardly capable of concealing his condition. Pause. He cannot make himself speak the following lines straightaway.

OTHELLO: That which I gave you.

He speaks these words in a lifeless voice. His glance is questioning her.

DESDEMONA: I have it not about me.

Slight embarrassment, almost unnoticeable, because Desdemona does not as yet understand the meaning of what is happening.

OTHELLO: Not?

In a low, almost inaudible voice, halting at words important to Othello by their inner meaning.

DESDEMONA: No, indeed, my lord.
OTHELLO: That's a fault.*
        That handkerchief

Before the words "to my mother give" etc. Othello is almost at a loss, as much as to say: what is one to do, how is one to act now?

        Did an Egyptian to my mother give;

Othello has thought of a new means to obtain the handkerchief. He reveals to her its magic secret. He even wants to frighten her, because, if the handkerchief exists, it may help to produce it. If, however, this last measure fails, everything is lost.

Speaking this monologue Othello acts more with his eyes and by suggestion than with words. In his story about the handkerchief I depict three phases, one more forceful than the other.

How can one underline the monologue to deprive it of its elocutionary effect and turn it into a *productive and cogent action of words?* I would suggest an inner task, a warning, *i.e.* she should know that, first, the handkerchief has been given to his mother by an Egyptian; second, that the Egyptian could almost read the thoughts of people (this is very important); thirdly, to warn her that while she is in possession of the handkerchief (as if it were something like an engagement ring) everything will be well; should it disappear, however, everything is finished.

She was a charmer, and could almost read
The thoughts of people; she told her, while she kept it,
'Twould make her amiable, and subdue my father
Entirely to her love; but if she lost it
Or made a gift of it, my father's eye
Should hold her loathed, and his spirits should hunt
After new fancies:* she dying gave it me,

After the words "or made a gift of it" a pause. Searchingly Othello watches the impression he made while Desdemona grows slightly pensive and walks up to trunk 2 concentratedly, opens it and goes through it thoughtfully and worried. The handkerchief is not there.

Meanwhile Othello pierces Desdemona with his gaze. Pause. She slightly averts her face from him.

And bid me, when my fate would have me wive,

Othello pronounces the second part of his warning. Another chain of consequences: first, second, third . . . etc.

To give it her. I did so: and take heed on 't;
Make it a darling like your precious eye;
To lose or give 't away, were such perdition
As nothing else could match.*

After "as nothing else could match" another pause; Desdemona searches with even greater concentration and grows more serious. She goes to trunk 3, thoughtfully lifts the lid and unconvincingly searches among her underclothes. (It must be done so that the trunk is not higher than up to her chest when she is standing.)

Othello follows at her heels with even more searching eyes and urgent warning.

DESDEMONA: Is 't possible?

While Desdemona searches Othello delivers another warning with even greater persistency, with its first, second . . . etc.

OTHELLO: 'Tis true; there's magic in the web of it:
A sibyl, that had number'd in the world
The sun to course two hundred compasses,
In her prophetic fury sew'd the work;
The worms were hallow'd that did breed the silk,

And it was dy'd in mummy which the skilful
Conserv'd of maidens' hearts.

DESDEMONA: Indeed, is 't true?

Desdemona grows increasingly thoughtful and worried. Cautiously
she glances at Othello.

OTHELLO: Most veritable,* therefore look to 't well.

Hurriedly, alarmed and with a worried face she quickly goes to the
divan where her bag lies. This is the last place where she could find it,
and therefore she does it with growing anxiety. It is not in the bag
either.
Othello watches her, close on her heels as before.

DESDEMONA: Then would to God that I had never seen 't!

In despair Desdemona sits down on the divan. She tries to hide her
face. Othello watches her the more intently.

OTHELLO: Ha! wherefore?

Do not forget that it is for the first time since they knew each other
and became engaged that Othello has frowned on her.
    Desdemona never imagined that he could be severe with her. If the
actor overdoes Othello's sternness at this moment he will so stun Desdemona that in confusion and surprise she will hardly be able to say
another word. A very agitated and serious tone of voice should suffice.
No more so far, because by the end of the page a stronger note will
have to be introduced, and yet it must not be the strongest in the
whole score of the part. There will be more scenes, such as the Lodovico scene, the scene where he interrogates her and Emilia, not to mention the last act.
    But this unexpected serious tone already startles Desdemona into
dumfoundedness, and for a little while she looks at him in great
astonishment. Therefore the words (indicated by an asterisk, see the
text) "Why do you speak so startingly and rash?" are preceded by a
pause. In this pause Desdemona looks perplexed and as if she does not
recognize Othello, while he, feeling that he has given himself away,
tries to smooth out his outburst.

DESDEMONA: *Why do you speak so startingly and rash?
OTHELLO: *Is 't lost?* is 't gone?* speak,* is it out o' the way?

Not taking his eyes off Desdemona and having forcibly calmed himself (outwardly, but not inwardly), Othello sits down in order to see every line in Desdemona's face closer and better.

Wherever there are asterisks there should be pauses of questioning while Othello drags out her replies from her as if with pincers.

Do you feel how during these pauses the inner tempo-rhythm of the scene grows increasingly intense?

DESDEMONA: *Heaven bless us!

Poor Desdemona is completely at a loss. She is not used to being spoken to like this, and apart from that, it is so incredible that Othello should talk like that to her. She looks at him and turns away in embarrassment. It seems she is facing another person, in no way resembling Othello.

The words "Heaven bless us!" are preceded by a helpless pause as if to say: What is happening here? What shall I do now? What is one supposed to do in a case like this?

OTHELLO: *Say you?*

But Othello does not give way, he presses on with his demand.

DESDEMONA: *It is not lost;* but what an if it were?

Desdemona first tries to pacify him, and then, during the pause, searches for a way to tell the truth.

OTHELLO: How!

Othello catches his cue, not giving her time to finish.

DESDEMONA: I say, it is not lost.*

Desdemona is in an even greater hurry trying to pacify him, but having said that the handkerchief is not lost, she again does not know what to do and searches for a solution, but her thoughts will keep dissolving in space at this moment as if on purpose and it seems impossible to gather them together.

OTHELLO: Fetch 't, let me see 't.

The scene continues to be conducted with the eyes and as though by means of inner conversational rays. After a short inquisitive pause Othello says: "Fetch 't, let me see 't."

DESDEMONA: *Why, so I can, sir, but I will not now.*

But Desdemona has not made up her mind yet what to do: therefore, while searching for a solution, she needs again to delay the answer concealing as best she can her great embarrassment.

Her further replies, broken by pauses, the searching for a solution and concealment of her embarrassment are also caused by the fact that she cannot concentrate her attention and find a way out.

> This is a trick to put me from my suit:*
> Pray you let Cassio be receiv'd again.

At last she has found it, and now hides behind the sweet and slightly coquettish plea on Cassio's behalf, which she has made on more than one occasion *today*.

I underline this *today* to help you keep in mind that it was only this morning and yesterday that the lovers had been making love to each other. All the greater is Desdemona's astonishment that the change should have occurred in these few hours.

> OTHELLO: Fetch me the handkerchief;* my mind misgives.

In his impatience to get an answer Othello changes his position, perhaps gets up. (Asterisks indicate inquisitive pauses.)

> DESDEMONA: Come, come;
> You'll never meet a more sufficient man.

Having somewhat regained her composure Desdemona steps to another line of acting—without pauses. She gives him no time to think and tries to draw him into conversation. With growing agitation she too may have risen.

> OTHELLO: The handkerchief!

Othello interrupts her, not allowing her to finish.

The actor will have to repeat the words "The handkerchief!" three times. There must be an intensification, and it must be done clearly and impressively, but remember, there is much intensification of this kind still ahead. In cases like this when one does not wish to strangle the temperament which is bound to carry you away, and yet keep it from exhausting itself, one will have to resort to coverings. One of them would be intense inner suffering and not just wrath acted on pure temperament and high voltage.

> DESDEMONA: *I pray, talk me of Cassio.

Now Desdemona cannot stop any more, driven on by the nervous state of mind, the whole scene and confusion. Now her embarrassment makes her go on talking, just as it reduced her to silence before. Her eyes are on Othello like those of a frightened child who cannot stop for fear of bursting into tears.

OTHELLO: The handkerchief!

What can be placed beneath these exclamations "The handkerchief!" to make them more effective? Another warning—Othello is implying as it were: I warn you, no tricks will help you! or: Bear in mind, truth is the only thing that can save you! If even more covering is needed, one could entreat Desdemona to tell the truth instead of warning her, using the same grade of temperament.

If, on the other hand, intensification is needed (not of the kind, however, that will be required in the following act) one should make a definite request, saying: "The handkerchief!"—and no more excuses.

Or all this screening of the temperament could be done in the order of intensification, *i.e.* the first exclamation "The handkerchief!" as an entreaty, the second—warning, the third—a definite request.

DESDEMONA: A man that all his time

The longer Desdemona pleads her case for Cassio, the more she becomes embarrassed, helpless and at a loss.

Hath founded his good fortunes on your love,
Shar'd dangers with you—

OTHELLO: The handkerchief!

After the third and most powerful exclamation "The handkerchief!" is a pause. Both are surprised and embarrassed at the fact that they have reached such a tone so soon.

Confused pause. They look at each other in astonishment and cannot adapt themselves to this new relationship.

Othello tries to calm down and repair what has been done.

DESDEMONA: *In sooth, you are to blame.

Desdemona makes a slight attempt at reconciliation. In addition to the words she speaks and the intonation she uses she tries to go up to him and makes not even a step, only a movement, in his direction, but . . .

OTHELLO: *Away! (*Exit*)

As if defending himself from an attack Othello stops her. He struggles with himself. Pause. Then . . . whatever happens, an inspiration. May

the actor give way to his feeling completely. It will be worse than anything if he begins to run away, as is frequently done. Best if a moan
or a desperate movement escapes him, and he drags himself away, crest-
fallen and not knowing where he is going. At this moment he looks
like a man who has lost his reason. He even fails to find the way out,
the stairs. Perhaps he stumbles over things, goes in the wrong direction. This cannot be foreseen from afar, it must be tried out.

After Othello's last exclamation: "The handkerchief!" Emilia (her
head) is seen on the stairs. She has heard that something has gone
wrong, and she is ready to stand up for her mistress. Now she cautiously enters the bedchamber (before Othello's exit).

After Othello is gone there is a pause. Desdemona, hardly capable
of realizing what has happened, sits down at a loss what to do. Both
women look at each other in perplexity.

EMILIA: Is not this man jealous?

They try to understand and explain what has happened.
Asterisks indicate pauses of reflection.

DESDEMONA: I ne'er saw this before.*
Sure there's some wonder in this handkerchief;

At the mention of the handkerchief Emilia, who has a finger in this
pie, is slightly embarrassed.

I am most unhappy in the loss of it.
EMILIA. 'Tis not a year or two shows us a man:

She steps aside under the pretext of doing something, to hide her face.
At the divan she folds up some clothes left there by Desdemona.

They are all but stomachs, and we all but food:
They eat us hungerly, and when they are full
They belch us. Look you, Cassio and my husband.

How this scene is to be finished without a curtain and the transfer to
the next scene will have to be decided on the spot. I am afraid the
noise made by the revolving stage may be injurious. How could we
disguise it? The striking of a tower bell is old and hackneyed, but as
it is night-time one can hardly find anything else.

One could produce the following effect. While the stage revolves
the tower clock strikes twelve. Pause; then it strikes one. Meanwhile
dawn begins to creep in on the "Cellar" scenery. The clock strikes

two. Pause. Another change of light. The clock strikes three—it grows lighter again. Then it is four. Othello still sits motionless, his head leaning against the wall.

Should one cut out the scene with Emilia and end with Othello's exit and a pause displaying Desdemona's perplexity? It would be more effective.

MAX REINHARDT

(1873-1943)

Regiebuch for *The Miracle*, Scenes I and II

The Reinhardt Regiebuch *has long been a legend in the theatre. A staggering number of annotations makes it extremely difficult to transfer a typical Reinhardt* Regiebuch *to the normal printed page. We are fortunate, however, in having a relatively uncomplicated* Regiebuch *which was prepared by Reinhardt in close collaboration with the designer Norman Bel Geddes for* The Miracle, *a wordless play by Karl Vollmoeller, with score by Engelbert Humperdinck. The first time such a* Regiebuch *was made public was in* Max Reinhardt and His Theatre, *edited by Oliver M. Sayler, an elaborate commemorative volume published in 1924, during the run of* The Miracle *at the Century Theatre in New York. It is from this source that the two specimen scenes which follow are drawn. The brief credo that introduces them—one of Reinhardt's rare statements about his work—originally appeared in the program for the New York production.*

IT WOULD be a theory as barbaric as it is incompatible with the principles of theatrical art, to measure with the same yardstick, to press into the same mold, the wonderful wealth of the world's literature. The mere suggestion of such an attempt is a typical example of pedantic scholasticism. There is no one form of theatre which is the only true artistic form. Let good actors today play in a barn or in a theatre, tomorrow at an inn or inside a church, or, in the Devil's name,

---

Max Reinhardt: "*Regie* Book of *The Miracle*," *Max Reinhardt and His Theatre*, edited by Oliver M. Sayler. New York: Brentano's, 1924, 64–66, 251–267.

even on an expressionistic stage: if the place corresponds with the play, something wonderful will be the outcome. All depends on realizing the specific atmosphere of a play, and on making the play live. And yet, do not banish from the temple merely the traders and money-mongers, but also the over-zealous high priests who desire to rob the theatre of all its brilliancy and sensuousness, who would like nothing better than to turn it into a preacher's pulpit, who swear by the written word, and who after having murdered the spirit of that word, would like to press it back again into its place in the book.

Just the contrary is the true mission of the theatre. Its task is to lift the word out of the sepulchre of the book, to breathe life into it, to fill it with blood, with the blood of today, and thus to bring it into living contact with ourselves, so that we may receive it and let it bear fruit in us. Such is the only way; there is no other. All roads which do not lead into life, lead us astray, whatever their name may be. Life is the incomparable, and most valuable possession of the theatre. Dress it up in any manner you wish, the cloak will have to fall when the eternal human comes to the fore, when, in the height of ecstasy, we find and embrace each other. The noble dead of a hundred, of four hundred, of a thousand years ago, arise again on the boards. It is this eternal wonder of resurrection which sanctifies the stage.

Therefore, do not write out prescriptions, but give to the actor and his work the atmosphere in which they can breathe more freely and more deeply. Do not spare stage properties and machinery where they are needed, but do not impose them on a play that does not need them. Our standard must not be to act a play as it was acted in the days of its author. To establish such facts is the task of the learned historian, and is of value only for the museum. How to make a play live in our time, that is decisive for us. The Catholic Church which aims at the most spiritual, the most supernatural, does so by means which appeal directly to the senses. It overwhelms us with the pathos of its temples towering in the sky; it surrounds us with the mystical dimness of its cathedrals; it charms our eye with wonderful master-pieces of art, with the brilliancy of its colored windows, with the lustre of thousands of candles, which reflect their light in golden objects and vessels. It fills our ear with music and song and the sound of the thundering organ. It stupefies us by the odor of the incense. Its priests stride in rich and precious robes. And in such a sphere of sensuousness, the highest and the most holy reveals itself to us. We reveal ourselves, and we find the way to our innermost being, the way to concentration, to exaltation, to spiritualization. . . .

SCENE I . . . CATHEDRAL

Characters

THE NUN	THE LAME PIPER
THE ABBESS	THE KNIGHT
THE OLD SACRISTAN	THE MADONNA

Nuns and Novices. Peasants, Townsfolk and Children. Bishops, Priests, Monks and Pilgrims. Cripples, Blind, Lame and Lepers. Patricians of the Town, Knights and Troops of Soldiers.

1. The interior of an early Gothic Church.
2. High, massive columns rise into mystic darkness.
3. Gothic arches, stone ornaments representing tendrils and lace work, a richly decorated iron grating, entangled scrolls and figures.
4. Narrow, high church windows in deep, rich coloring.
5. Aisles, corridors, doors, an unsymmetrical arrangement of mysterious openings, windows, stairways.
6. Votive statues on columns, small statues with candles and flowers before them, crucifixes, offerings brought by grateful people, wax flowers, embroideries, jewels, a child's doll, decoratively painted candles.
7. In the background a richly carved altar, with a golden shrine and candles seen through a grilled screen.
8. The eternal lamp burns before it.
9. A Cardinal's hat hangs above.
10. Altar, with table, to divide and open, with steps through it.
11. The floor is of large gray stones, some of which are tombstones.

In the center of the floor the stones are to be glass with lamps below, so wired as to spread the light from the middle outwards.

12. Flickering light from behind columns as from invisible candles throws fantastic shadows.

13. Shafts of sunlight, coming through the high windows at the right, project patterns on the floor.

14. At left and right of auditorium [stage directions read "right" and "left" from the point of view of the audience], cloisters with vaulted ceilings and stone floors.

15. Chandeliers of various sizes in the auditorium to cast light downwards only, adding depth and mystery to the ceiling.

16. Several poles for flags and lanterns fastened to the seat ends in aisles of auditorium.

17. Panelling of balcony rail to show here and there between flags.

18. A clock above pulpit. This clock is to strike at various times during the dream parts, to suggest the existence of the church. Remember the sound before the clock strikes.

19. On top of the clock two figures to mark the hours, by striking a large bell between them. One of these figures symbolizes life; the other death.

20. Clerestory windows around upper part of auditorium. Choir stands and triforium openings below windows.

21. All doors have heavy bolts, locks and knockers to create business and noise.

22. Large keys on rings for various doors.

23. The doors immediately behind proscenium lead to sacristy.

24. The doors below the loges lead to exterior.

25. Small midnight Mass bell, near top of tower, to be rung from rope on stage floor.

26. Wind machines, thunder drums and voices also to be there.

27. When audience take their seats, everything is dark.

28. The sound of a storm far away.

29. Soft candle-light in the auditorium, only where it is absolutely necessary, and flickering behind the columns around the altar screen.

30. Clusters of candle-lights in distant places in the auditorium and stage, high up in the tower to produce an effect of tremendous size and of incredible distance.

31. There are to be candles around the altar screen and on the altar itself. The candles should be of various lengths and the bulbs of very low voltage and of various pale colors.

32. In chapels tiny candles suggest side-altars against darkness. Prominent clusters of them unsymmetrically chosen. Flickering candles on the columns in the apse and cloisters throwing shadows.

33. Candles on altar, altar screen and in chapels to be wired individually and lighted or extinguished by nuns. Candle bulbs to be no larger than one-half inch in diameter. The bulb must not show.

34. Candle extinguishers and wax tapers.

35. The large altar is dark.

36. One recognizes gradually among the towering columns several dark figures huddled together absorbed in prayer.

37. From a distant tower a bell sounds.

38. Large bells are located in ventilating shaft over auditorium and controlled from orchestra gallery.

39. A praying voice from behind the triforium windows is indistinctly heard; now and then a Latin word is audible.

40. Chairs are pushed about, some one blows his nose, others cough. The echo resounds through the church.

41. After that, silence.

42. An old sexton appears carrying a lantern.

43. His stick taps the pavement, and his steps drag over the stone floor.

44. He pulls back the green curtain over the Madonna statue.

45. He goes to the tower. Up the winding staircase the lantern shows through little windows and finally at the top.

46. He crosses a bridge and disappears through a doorway in the wall.

47. The organ starts and bells ring high above the church.

48. Nuns in pairs march through the cloisters toward the altar in two long columns, to take part in the coming ceremony.

49. The windows of the church become more brilliant from sunlight without.

50. Outside a young bright spring morning has awakened.

51. Sixty nuns dressed in ivory-colored garments trimmed with black. They all wear ropes. The black nuns' costumes appear like shadows passing in the dark and must be cut in such a way that the white undergarments show conspicuously when the nuns flutter like white doves in their excitement at the loss of the Madonna.

52. The chin cloths must be drawn very tightly, so that they never look slovenly. In fact they are to be made so that they can not be worn otherwise.

53. One column is headed by the Abbess.

54. The Abbess may be dressed either in white or in black, wears a crown and carries a silver staff, like the Bishop's, but smaller.

55. In this column the aged feeble Sacristan of the convent is carried in on a chair by four nuns.

56. In the other column a young nun, still but a child, is led in. She takes a tearful farewell of her mother, father, and grandmother who are seated at the right.

57. In an impressive ceremony the young Nun is dressed in an overgarment similar to that of the old Sacristan and receives the keys and office.

58. The Abbess sits in a special chair during the ceremony. She sings while one nun holds a music book for her and another holds a lighted candle.

59. This is accompanied by responses without music from the choir gallery.

60. In front are the holy pictures and the statue of the Madonna which stands on a column. It is a stone statue, painted in blue tempera and gold-leaf and wearing a crown set with precious stones.

61. The statue is to look as stone-like as possible and heavy, even if clumsy.

62. She must wear the white muslin nun's garb, as an undergarment.

63. The white head-cloth always has to remain on and be drawn as tightly as possible.

64. The Madonna holds the child in her arms.

65. The pedestal is decorated with many flowers, and large and small candles.

66. Crutches stacked around the base.

67. This pedestal altar conceals steps, covered with soft rubber. There must be supports for the Madonna under her arm-pits, at her waist, a seat, and recesses cut in floor for her feet. Her shoes are rubber-soled.

68. There are five statues of saints at other positions.

69. Large bells in the distance begin to sound as the Convent Church is revealed in its full glow of light.

70. The Nun, for the first time as the new Sacristan, opens all the doors with her keys.

71. A great commotion and the hum of voices come from without.

72. The sound of music grows nearer, the organ starts with massive tones.

73. A great procession pours into the church through all the doors. Men and women who are making the pilgrimage to the celebrated miracle-working statue of the Madonna.

74. First come the visiting orders of nuns in white.

75. Then peasants with banners.

76. Women in vivid-colored clothes, some bare-footed.

77. Towns-people following, carrying banners with coats-of-arms of towns.

78. Tradesmen carrying the various emblems of their trade on poles.

79. A group of peasants bring in an enormous cross.

80. A great crowd of children with a May-pole.

81. Priests carrying church banners.

82. Acolytes swinging incense.

83. Choirboys with their large books.

84. The Archbishop carries his staff and walks beneath a canopy carried by four men.

85. Under another canopy is carried the monstrance. Church dignitaries follow.

86. Then monks carrying wooden statues of saints on poles.
87. A great mass of cripples on primitive crutches and stretchers, wearing dirty ragged clothes.
88. Blind people, who are led.
89. Widows in mourning.
90. Mothers carrying sick children on their backs, in their arms, and with others clinging to their skirts.
91. Lepers with clappers.
92. Pilgrims with broad-brimmed hats, staves, bundles and flasks.
93. Finally the knights in vivid color.
94. Followed by heralds, squires, men-at-arms, in full dress.
95. No one comes empty-handed. All who have nothing else to carry bring full-leafed birch-branches.
96. The procession fills the whole stage and all the aisles in the auditorium.
97. There is much singing and waving of the yellow green branches. It looks almost like a green forest, waving to and fro.
98. The voice of a priest, whom no one sees, is heard.
99. The music stops.
100. A bell rings at the altar.
101. A white vapor begins to rise from the vessels containing the incense.
102. The crowd falls on its knees.
103. The sick crowd up to the statue of the Madonna and pray without halt. The Archbishop leads the prayers from the pulpit.
104. The tension grows. A breathless silence.
105. Finally there arises in the audience a completely lamed man, who had been carried in on a stretcher. He gets heavily to his feet, with convulsive twitching, and raising his arms high in ecstasy strides to the figure of the Mother of God, where he dances with joy.
106. A cry, the organ, rejoicing of the crowd. A miracle has come to pass.
107. The pilgrims leave the church singing.
108. The candles are extinguished and the nuns slowly pass out.
109. The young Sacristan goes about her duties of locking the doors.

110. In the last doorway there stands the healed fellow blowing harm-lessly upon a flute. This demoniac figure, who runs through the play and has an evil influence upon the fate of the young Nun, is the lure of sensual life. At this moment his appearance resembles that of the Pied Piper. He wears a broad-brimmed hat over his faun-like ears.

111. Children surround him in their curiosity and listen to his music.

112. The Nun stands still as if under a spell and hears his tunes with the same astonishment and naïve joy as the children.

113. The children, unable to resist longer, fall into the rhythm, crowd into the church and force the Nun, who resists, into their ranks.

114. An unconscious yearning for the spring without causes her mo-mentarily to forget her new office.

115. In her childishness, the Nun lets herself be forced into the dance.

116. She lets her keys fall and dances joyfully.

117. In the meantime, the Piper's tune has attracted a young Knight, who quietly enters and is fascinated by the graceful dancing of the Nun.

118. Suddenly, on seeing him, she becomes frightened and rooted to the spot as they exchange glances.

119. The Nun hears nothing as the bell rings for vespers.

120. Nuns approach in a column, the Abbess at their head.

121. They become enraged on seeing this pair in the church.

122. The children and the Piper slyly escape through the open door.

123. The Abbess rebukes the young Sacristan who stares about her, dazed.

124. At a nod from the angry Abbess the keys are taken away from her and the heavy bolts locked behind the Knight who has slowly gone out.

125. She is sentenced to spend the night in prayer before the statue of the Madonna.

126. The nuns again depart and the church sinks gradually into night and silence.

127. The Nun prays fervently before the statue of the Holy Virgin.

128. In her confusion she scarcely knows what is happening to her.

129. Her thoughts, which she seeks vainly to discipline, escape through the stone walls and wander tirelessly into the night in the direction of the young Knight.

130. The poor child returns again and again to her prayers, seeking peace and comfort there.

131. Her youth, awakened for the first time, struggles against the cold discipline offered her.

132. She runs to the font and sprinkles herself madly with holy water.

133. Her heart beats wildly, she throws herself about on the steps leading to the miracle statue.

134. She wrings her hands and plunges desperately into passionate prayer.

135. At this moment something happens that can just as well be a raving dream of fever as a fantastic reality. With the rapid pace of dreams, one experience chases after another and drives the Nun back into the church after a moment of actual happiness through a martyrdom of indescribable suffering. Dream, or reality, it is intense, terrible, vital, as endlessly long as an intense dream, as horribly short as a full life.

136. Suddenly there is a light but insistent knocking at the gate. The Nun grows tense.

137. The knock is repeated. Is it her own heart-beat? She tries not to hear and prays aloud.

138. The knocking continues, always louder, and finally sounds from all sides and from all doors. Each door should have a heavy knocker.

139. She springs up involuntarily, takes several steps toward the door.

140. She stands still in fright, throws herself on her knees, wrings her hands, is torn back and forth.

141. Finally like an excited but caged bird, she flutters anxiously to and fro, beating her head against the cold walls.

142. The knocking grows wilder, her yearning more uncontrollable.

143. She shakes the locked doors with all her strength.

144. Throwing herself on her knees, she begs the Mother of God to set her free.

145. The moon shines through the windows.

146. As if mad, she dashes toward the Holy Virgin and points fiercely at the child in her arms. She is yearning for the child, for everything out there.
147. Completely out of her mind she finally takes the holy child from the arms of the Madonna and holds it high.
148. A warm glow radiates from it and then suddenly the child disappears in a flash of light.
149. Everything grows dark. A sound like thunder resounds through the high church.
150. When it is again light Mary has heard the passionate pleadings and has performed a miracle.
151. The high altar glittering with candles, slowly opens, forming a Gothic arch, with a knight in silver armor and a blue mantle, visible through the high candles on the altar tables.
152. The Knight and the Nun stand regarding each other.
153. The Nun shrinks back frightened and flees to the foot of the Madonna.
154. The Mother of God smiles as graciously as ever. Her will is plain.
155. The altar table, with the candles on it, opens slowly, exposing a flight of steps.
156. The Knight slowly approaches the Nun. She rises shyly.
157. He offers her his hand to lead her forth. She looks at her clothing and hesitates to go out in her holy costume.
158. She removes the black nun's veil, the white cape, the rosary with its large cross, the belt and finally her dark dress and lays them all tenderly on the steps of the miracle statue.
159. Rising, she shudders at the sight of her underdress, feeling that she is without clothes.
160. The Piper who was behind the Knight brings in the blue cloak of the Knight and covers the young Nun with the dress of life.
161. Again she kneels, and the Knight with her, at the foot of the Virgin.
162. Then he catches her in his arms and runs off with her into the world.
163. The church is deserted.
164. A sigh comes from somewhere within the walls.

165. The Madonna statue begins to glow with an unearthly light.
166. It seems as if she were opening her lips and smiling. The figure moves.
167. The light on her face changes from unearthly to the pink of life.
168. She opens her eyes.
169. She smiles.
170. She turns her head.
171. She drops her robe.
172. She descends.
173. She lifts her arm.
174. She removes her crown.
175. She holds it up high.
176. She lays it on the pedestal.
177. Then she gives a sign for the altar to close, and it becomes as before.
178. The Virgin bends low, and in sweet humility puts on the simple costume of the Nun.
179. She goes to the tower and rings the bell.
180. Voices of singing nuns. The Virgin kneels and prays in front of her pedestal.
181. The nuns come into the church for mass.
182. The Abbess glances at the supposed Nun, sunk in prayer, and chuckles fondly at the repentance of her favorite.
183. By accident her glance falls on the spot where the miracle statue has stood, but now where only her cloak and crown lie. She does not trust her eyes, stares, consults the sister.
184. A terrible fear seizes all the nuns.
185. They scream, run around enraged, cry out, weep, threaten their supposed sister, fetch the priest and ring the alarm bell.
186. With clenched fist and swinging cords, all rush at the poor Nun, who has obviously permitted the theft of the precious treasure in her impious sin.
187. The Nun's head remains humbly bowed.
188. Whenever the threatening sisters surround her in a wild rush, she gently floats a short distance into the air without changing her position. This is done on a trap on the right.

189. In silent awe they draw back from her; staring at this miracle speechlessly, they recognize that a higher power is obviously at work here, and that the young Nun is the chosen agent.
190. Returning to the earth, she goes about her duties like an ordinary nun, taking a jar of oil to fill the eternal lamp.
191. The nuns form open rows and follow their holy sister spreading their arms wide and singing in ecstasy.
192. The scene grows dark.

SCENE II . . . SUMMER FOREST

Characters

THE NUN	THE ROBBER COUNT
THE KNIGHT	THE SHADOW OF DEATH
THE PIPER	HUNTSMEN AND FOLLOWERS
	OF THE COUNT

1. The bells on high ring and the narrow lacy church windows light up in their dark, varied colors.
2. Thirty men in costumes, suggestive of green bushes, stand at the foot of the altar replacing branches that had been placed there.
3. The organ peals softly and one hears an old Gregorian chorus in the pure high voices of girls in the choir gallery.
4. Soon the interior of the church becomes visible. In the flickering candle-light one sees the dark figures of people praying.
5. With a wax taper a church servant lights the candles on the altar and between the piers there moves a shadowy column of nuns.
6. Then while the choir is still singing, everything sinks again into darkness.
7. In the vague darkness comes a procession to the altar. A priest, acolytes swinging incense, and nuns following.
8. The priest reads a quiet prayer and rings the little bell at intervals.
9. Incense floats upwards. The stage has to be piped for smoke behind the columns and around the edge of the glass floor. It finally fills the stage and becomes a fog, while it is still dark.

10. At the elevation of the Host, through the mist glows a light as though in it, which rises slowly, appearing like the moon.

11. The lights in the windows die out, the nuns come downstage and the fog thickens.

12. In the ensuing forest scene and in all following changes the Cathedral remains standing with its columns and walks, galleries and lacy figures, and only through separate decorations, drops and lighting does it receive the necessary changes, whereas the all-enclosing church remains in the darkness and is more felt than seen.

13. Through the mist one can still dimly see the candles on the altar which now seem like glowworms in a mist.

14. Some rise very slowly while others fall. The windows have disappeared.

15. The nuns begin to dance. Their clothes become but a film and they appear like nude elves. Their hair-dresses have vanished and in their stead is green hair.

16. These fine-limbed elves form rings about the trees and twist and turn in the wind. They float about noiselessly and dance the joy of a young spring night.

17. During the dance, the fireflies have all gradually risen in the mist and now appear like stars in the sky.

18. Moonlight comes as if through dancing foliage from the center left of the balcony.

19. The altar looks like a group of young trees in spring.

20. Out of the mist has risen a great tall forest.

21. The Knight and the Nun come into view through the trees.

22. The Piper as a faun precedes them, jumping about merrily playing on his Pan-pipes as he drives away the dancing elves.

23. The Nun and the Knight come slowly into the foreground closely embraced.

24. The Nun throws aside her cloak and turns around in overwhelming happiness.

25. The Knight puts his arm around her, draws her close, and tries to kiss her.

26. She escapes and runs away laughing. He follows her.

27. She dances and plays around the trees as the elves did before.

28. Finally he catches her, carries her to the center and they embrace passionately, as she lies in his arms.

29. The Piper summons the green bushes, worn by invisible men, to circle around the lovers.

30. The circle gradually grows smaller as they are surrounded and finally completely hidden by the thick foliage.

31. The Piper then tiptoes to the front and calls as if up into the hills with a moose-like cry.

32. The answer is heard coming from the upper gallery, then the middle one, and soon from the lower one.

33. The blowing of horns, the barking of hounds and the crack of whips.

34. Then he hides behind two of the bushes which he had called aside.

35. A merry hunting party appears, as if from over a hill, coming down both center aisles through the audience, suggesting something of the religious procession.

36. Instead of sacred relics, they carry trophies of the chase. Porters carry deer down one aisle and game down the other.

37. The hunters have spears with glowing points like candles.

38. Trumpeters and retainers carry spears, axes, knives, bows and arrows.

39. Ladies carrying falcons on their gloved hands.

40. Men with lanterns light the way.

41. In their midst is the master of the chase, a Count, an unusually large powerful man with Mongol features. He has a hunting knife in his belt and a whip curled around his hand.

42. The party turns to the left and discovers the Piper who has purposely put himself in the way.

43. They regard him with merry curiosity.

44. He plays on his pipes and runs away. They follow him in a wild chase, as if he were an animal.

45. He runs down to the front again at the right, the hunting party at his heels.

46. Arrived in front, he looks about quickly and finally hides himself in the foliage where the lovers are sheltered. The hunters dash into the bushes and discover the lovers there.
47. The Nun rushes out and covers her face with her hands in shame. The Knight follows.
48. The company surrounds the two and the Count approaches the Nun to look at her.
49. The Knight steps in front of the Nun to protect her, and confronts the Count.
50. The Count pushes the Knight aside. The Knight draws his sword, but is seized by the other men.
51. He resists, is conquered after a brief struggle and is tied to a tree, just where the Madonna stood.
52. Lanterns are placed on the ground around the prisoner.
53. He is now obliged to observe how the Count forces his attentions upon the Nun.
54. She at first stands as if in a trance and then watches with horror how her lover is bound. She wrings her hands in despair, pleading with the Count for mercy for the Knight. The Count laughs cynically.
55. The Piper approaches the Count, whispers in his ear, points to the Nun and indicates the movements of dancing. The Count understands and commands the Nun to dance for him. The company applauds.
56. The Nun draws back in fright and hides her face.
57. The Count stamps his foot impatiently and repeats his command. The Nun merely shakes her head. The Count orders the Knight to be killed, if she refuses to conform to his wishes. The hunters draw their knives and point them at the Knight's breast.
58. The Nun cries out in horror, falls at the Count's feet and begs for the life of her lover.
59. The Count insists that she dance. She has no choice.
60. The company forms a circle about her and she dances with anguish but believing that she is saving the Knight.
61. As the Piper starts to play, the hunters constantly draw closer to the dancing girl.

62. The Knight struggles painfully in his bonds.
63. Then the Piper creeps over to the Knight and secretly unties his bonds.
64. The Knight rushes at the Count, who is making love to the Nun and is again thrown back by the hunters, severely wounded.
65. The Shadow of Death suddenly appears behind the dying man and remains by him until he collapses, dead.
66. The Count leads away the Nun, who resists violently. The company follows him boisterously.
67. The Knight's crumpled body with the knives sticking in it suggests the figure of a martyr.
68. Clouds pass over the moon.
69. Only the Piper is lighted. He stands beside the body of the Knight and blows on his pipes held aloft in a satanic manner, playing for his first victim the always recurring tones of a song of death.
70. Suddenly he jumps into the blackness.
71. The Shadow of Death shines in the dark beside the body of the Knight.

VSEVOLOD MEYERHOLD

(b. 1873)

Rehearsals of *The Inspector-General*

In the annals of the theatre it is unusual to find a ver-batim transcript of an actual rehearsal. Meyerhold, accustomed to doing the unusual, made this a possibility with his corps of assistant régisseurs who recorded the minute details of every aspect of a production. Even in the transcripts available to us of two rehearsals of The Inspector-General, *Meyerhold's improvisatory methods of directing are clearly revealed. In order to preserve the continuity of a rehearsal, the editors have taken the liberty of integrating transcripts dated February 13 and March 4, 1926, into a single reconstruction of Meyerhold at work on the opening scenes. A difficulty posed by the reconstruction grows out of the fact that Meyerhold made numerous changes in Gogol's text. Not having the text of the play as it was being evolved, we have taken the liberty of interpolating Meyerhold's directions where they most logically seem to fall in Gogol's original text.*

ACT I . . . A ROOM IN THE MAYOR'S HOUSE

(*The Mayor, Charity Commissioner, School Superintendent, Judge, Police Superintendent, Doctor and two Police Officers*)

MAYOR: I have called you together, gentlemen, to give you a very unpleasant piece of news: there's an Inspector-General coming.

The Mayor's entrance should be acted out to the hilt. Once we have agreed that the role should move along in a certain tempo, it is my duty,

---

"Na Repetitzia *Revizora,*" *Teatr i Dramaturgia,* February 1934, 40–42.

technically, to create an atmosphere in which the actor will feel at ease. The actor should be relieved of anything that makes for ponderousness.

JUDGE AND CHARITY COMMISSIONER: What, an Inspector!

When everybody says: "What, an Inspector!" there should be no uniformity. There should be a variety of accents, and also a difference in enunciations. Some break up the word: "In-spec-tor." Some speak rapidly, others with a drawl. Their reaction is an immediate one and they do not speak in character. Anyhow, the audience cannot make out who says what. They are all crowded into the sofa, nearly ten of them. [Meyerhold has added to the group.] Character quality should be toned down a little. Everybody speaks at once. Their remarks are in chorus.

MAYOR: Yes, an Inspector-General from Petersburg, incognito. With secret instructions, too.

JUDGE: Well, I declare!

CHARITY COMMISSIONER: Now we're in for it!

SCHOOL SUPERINTENDENT: Good Lord! With secret instructions!

MAYOR: I had a sort of presentiment of it: all last night I dreamed about a pair of monstrous rats. I never saw the like of 'em—so black and enormous. They came and sniffed about—and vanished. . . . Here's a letter which I will read you from Khmikov. (*To the Charity Commissioner*) You know him, Artemy Filipovich. This is what he says: "My dear friend, my comrade and benefactor . . . (*He quickly mutters over the first few sentences*) . . . and to let you know"—Ah! that's it— "I hasten to let you know, among other things, that an official has been sent with instructions to inspect the whole province, and your district especially. (*Lifts his finger significantly*) That he *is* coming I know from very reliable sources, but he pretends to be a private person. So, as you have your little faults, you know, like everybody else (you're a sensible man, and don't let what swims into your hand slip through your fingers) . . ." (*Stopping*) H'm, that's only a manner of speaking . . . "I advise you to take precautions, for he may come any moment—if he has not already done so, and is staying somewhere incognito. Yesterday . . ." Oh, then come family matters, "My cousin, Anna Kirillovna, paid us a visit, with her husband. Ivan Kirillovich has gotten very fat, and is always playing the fiddle . . ." Et cetera, et cetera. Now, here's a pretty business!

A groan. A groan helps to raise the tone of the voice and out of the groan you come directly to the words: "Now, here's a pretty business!"

The Mayor is in the chair. The two servants and Hubner, the Doctor, stand near him. This, by the way, imparts something of the generalissimo to him. He is like a Czar in this town.

It appears to me that in such an environment, in such a collection of idiots—and the Commissioner, the Superintendent, the Judge—are all idiots—that among all of these complete idiots, the Mayor does somehow stand out. He is shrewder, he does have some kind of polish. He has climbed to some position of prominence. He has lived in quite a few places. All his instructions show that he is head and shoulders above the others. His education is hard to pin down. Judging from what he says later of the teacher, he does have some vague knowledge of history. He betrays some sort of a pseudo-culture. Of course, what sort of culture can there be in that God-forsaken hole? The Mayor shows a certain fluency in his speech. He builds his phrases, for instance, better than Bobchinsky and Dobchinsky. With them, we can almost hear their brains creaking. The Mayor quickly orients himself. He can say something to the point. He is an orator, he can deliver a whole monologue.

Don't play him as an old man. He needs to be rejuvenated. How did it happen that the Mayor was always enacted as an old man? Because in the past the Mayor was always played by old actors with many years of acting behind them. Maksheyev, for instance, Vladimir Davydov—they played it when they were quite old. And when young actors undertook this role, they copied the performances of old men with big names. That is how these devices and intonations entrenched themselves.

You are young, you are about fifteen or twenty years younger than I—forget this old man's diction. Shoot it out with a free, distinct diction. No doddering right now, that will come later—we will go into it then. Perhaps we will give you a chair during the rehearsals—you sit, think it out, everything is arranged and then you begin. Give him the chair we used in *The Forest*. He doesn't feel too good and is seated in the chair. And give him a glass of water.

JUDGE: Yes, extraordinary, simply extraordinary. There must be some reason for it.

School Superintendent: But why, Anton Antonovich? Why should *we* have an Inspector?

Mayor (*Sighing*): Oh, it's fate, I suppose! (*Sighs again*) Till now, thank goodness, they've pried into other towns; but now our turn has come.

Judge: It's my opinion, Anton Antonovich, that it's a deep political move, and it means—let me see—that Russia . . . yes, that's it . . . Russia wants to make war, and the Government has surreptitiously sent an official to see if there's any disaffection anywhere.

"It's my opinion, Anton Antonovich . . . " should have more of an "into the ear" intonation. More of the confiding tone, of tale-bearing. He hasn't given a thought to it, but already he begins to elaborate. Then you can put it into the tempo.

Mayor: Ah, *you've* got it! *You* know a thing or two! The idea of treason in an inland town! As if it lay on the frontier! Why, from here you may gallop for three years before you reach a foreign country.

Judge: No, I'll tell you how it is—you don't understand—the Government looks very closely into matters; it *may* be far away, yet it observes everything——

Mayor (*Cutting him short*): It may or it may not—anyhow, gentlemen, I have warned you. I have made some arrangements on my own behalf, and I advise you to do the same. You especially, Artemy Filipovich! Without doubt, the Inspector will want first of all to look at your hospital; and so you had better see that everything is in order; that the nightcaps are clean, and that the patients don't go about as they usually do—looking like blacksmiths.

"You especially, Artemy Filipovich . . . and so on." This is blurted out in one breath.

Charity Commissioner: Oh, that's all right. They shall have clean nightcaps, if you like.

Now, the first thing the Charity Commissioner says is remarkably sugar-coated—pure honey—real strawberry. [Gogol frequently gave his characters revealing surnames. The Charity Commissioner's name is Strawberry.] I don't know how we will develop this. It does not come out right because both the Commissioner and the Judge are too reasonable in their dialogue. Some other version should be found—it should not be played according to the script. We will work on it later.

MAYOR: And you might write up over each bed, in Latin or some other lingo—(*To the Doctor*) that's *your* business, Hubner—the name of each complaint, when the patient got ill, the day of the week and month . . . and I don't like your invalids smoking such strong tobacco; it makes you choke when you come in. It would be better too if there weren't so many of them; otherwise it will be ascribed to bad supervision or unskillful doctoring.

CHARITY COMMISSIONER: Oh, Hubner and I have settled all about the doctoring; the nearer we get to Nature the better; we don't go in for costly medicines. A man is a simple affair—if he dies, he dies; if he gets well, why, then he gets well. And it isn't easy for the patients to understand our Doctor—he doesn't know a word of Russian. (*The Doctor grunts unintelligibly*)

And this is the assignment for the Doctor. [A German-speaking Doctor who has no lines in Gogol's text. Meyerhold has asked for some props to be brought in including a glass of water to be used as medicine.] Is this water all right to drink? You stir it and from time to time you hand the Mayor a spoonful. You keep on stirring. And the Mayor must take it. At times he pushes it away, at times he drinks, takes the glass with his own hands, gulps down a little. The medicine is of a kind that can be taken by the glassful. And you must have something to say in German and say it so as to overlap the Mayor's speeches. This will help him to handle the scene. You will step up his tempo. Inasmuch as there is an obstacle, there is always the need of overcoming it. You keep on talking—*perpetuum mobile*. Do you speak German? You are of German descent, aren't you?

Has anyone got a handkerchief? A muffler? (The Mayor's head is wrapped up.) There you are. Let the Mayor say a few lines and then begin to administer the drink. You will walk around him, rap at his chest, apply a mustard plaster to his feet to draw off the blood from his head. Do you know some German words? Repeat some phrases.

Every time there is a flurry of feeling, it has its effect upon the Doctor. He soothes the Mayor, and then pounces upon the others when they talk. Agitation is harmful for his patient. I don't quite know what, but you keep on saying something like *Sein Sie ruhig*. That irritates the Mayor, and this irritation enables the Doctor to put his acting into the required tempo. The Doctor exhorts everyone in his

own unintelligible manner and continues to treat the patient. It is
a very intricate thing—special instruction is needed here. *Warum
sprechen Sie so?*—something of this kind. The Doctor has a tre-
mendously bigger role here than that of the Mayor.

MAYOR: Also I would recommend you, Ammos Fyodorovich (*the
Judge*)—to turn your attention to the court-house buildings. There's
the antechamber, where the petitioners usually wait; you've let the
attendants breed geese there, and the goslings go poking their beaks
among people's legs. Of course, raising geese is a most laudable pursuit, and there's no reason why the clerk should not do so; only, you
see, the County Court is not exactly the place for it. . . . I intended to
mention it before, but it somehow escaped my memory.

JUDGE: Well, I'll tell them to take 'em all into the kitchen today.
Will you come to dinner?

(To the Mayor) The remark addressed to the Judge has an under-
tone of irritation. Then the tempo will be right. "Of course, raising
geese is a most laudable pursuit" and so on. . . . You seem to take it
in parenthesis and that is why there is that drop. The transition
should be effected rapidly. Keep in mind the phrase "not exactly the
place for it." The preceding words should not be spoken in a lowered
tone, not in parenthesis. They are the springboard in the direction of
"not exactly the place for it." The latter phrase should be kept in
mind from the very beginning of the monologue and then the preceding words will be given the right expression. The basic function of the
Mayor's role is that he carries the movement of the script forward.

MAYOR: Besides that, it doesn't do for the court chamber to get so
full of rubbish of all sorts. Why, there was a whip lying among the
papers on your own desk. I know you're fond of sports, but there is a
proper time and place for everything. When the Inspector is gone
you can put it back again. Then your assessor—he's certainly a
learned man, but he reeks of vodka, as if he had just come out of a
distillery; that also is undesirable. I meant to tell you of this some
while ago, but something or other put it out of my head. There are
ways of remedying it, if it is really, as he says, a natural failing. You

can recommend him to eat onions or garlic, or something of the sort. Hubner can help him there with some of his nostrums. (*The Doctor grunts as before.*)

When the Doctor hears his name he begins to speak: "*Das habe ich schon gesagt.*" He continues to stir the medicine.

JUDGE: No, it's quite impossible to get rid of it. He says his nurse knocked him down when he was a child, and ever since he has smelled of vodka.

MAYOR: Well, I just reminded you of it. As regards the local administration, and what Khmikov is pleased to call one's "little faults" in his letter, I don't understand what he means. Why, of course, there isn't a man living who has not *some* peccadilloes to account for. Heaven made him so—let *freethinkers* say what they like.

JUDGE: What do you mean by peccadilloes, Anton Antonovich? There are peccadilloes and peccadilloes. I tell everyone plainly that I take bribes, but what kind of bribes? Greyhound puppies! That's a totally different matter.

MAYOR: H'm, whether they're puppies or anything else, they're all bribes alike.

JUDGE: No, indeed, Anton Antonovich. But suppose, for example, one receives a *cloak* worth five hundred rubles, or your good lady receives a *shawl.* . . .

MAYOR: Yes, but what has that got to do with your being bribed with puppies? Besides, you're an atheist, you never go to church, while I, at least, am a firm believer, and go to church every Sunday. Whereas *you*—oh, I know *you*, when I hear you talking about the Creation my hair simply stands on end.

JUDGE: What of that? I have reasoned it all out with my own unaided intellect.

MAYOR: Anyhow, too much knowledge is worse than none at all. However, I only made a remark about the County Court, and I dare say nobody will ever look at it, there's an odor of sanctity about the place. But you, Luka Lukich, as School Superintendent, ought to keep an eye on the teachers. They're very clever people, no doubt, and are blessed with a college education, but they have very funny habits—inseparable from their profession, I suppose.

We'll do it this way. You—the Mayor—will be seated in a half-turned position so that when you cut loose from the Doctor you always turn toward someone. "But you, Luka Lukich . . . ought to keep an eye on the teachers." You rise, stand up in the chair on your knees. You rise and keep firing away. Nuances will come all by themselves. You rise, and Hubner removes the trousers, and, taking advantage of the change of position, applies a mustard plaster. I am suggesting all that in order to furnish the necessary crescendoes of the tempo.

MAYOR (*Continued*): One of them, for instance, the fat-faced man—I forget his name—can't get along without screwing up his phiz like this—(*Imitates him*)—when he's got into his chair, and then he sets to work clawing his necktie and scratching his chin. It doesn't matter, of course, if he makes a face at a pupil—perhaps it's even necessary—I'm no judge of that, but you yourselves will admit that if he grimaces at a visitor, it may make a very bad impression. The honorable Inspector, or anyone else, might take it as meant for himself—and then the deuce knows what might come of it.

LUKA: What can I do with him, I ask? I have told him of it time after time. Only the other day, when our headmaster came into class, your friend made such a face at him as I had never seen before. I dare say it was with the best intentions, but people come complaining to me about radical notions being instilled into the juvenile mind.

Here, Luka Lukich, with this new treatment of the Mayor, you don't get it right. He advances upon the Mayor: "What can I do with him" . . . he must keep on pushing himself forward, advancing, like one who in repudiating what you say, reviles you and thrusts himself upon you.

MAYOR: And then you should look to the master of the history class. He has a learned head, that is evident, and has picked up any amount of knowledge, but he lectures with such ardor that he quite forgets himself. I once listened to him. As long as he was holding forth about the Assyrians and Babylonians, it was all right, but when he got on Alexander of Macedon, I can't describe his behavior. Good Heavens, I thought, there's a fire! He jumped out of his chair, and

smashed a stool on the ground with all his might! Alexander of
Macedon was a hero, we all know, but that's no reason for breaking
the furniture—besides, the State has to pay for the damages.

LUKA: Yes, he is fiery! I have spoken to him about it several times.
He only says: "Do as you please, but in the cause of learning I will
even sacrifice my life!"

MAYOR: Yes, it's a mysterious law of fate, your clever man is either
a drunkard, or makes faces that would scare the saints.

LUKA: Ah, Heaven save us from being schoolmasters! You're afraid
of everything, everybody meddles with you, and wants to show you that
he's as learned as you are.

"Ah, Heaven save us from being schoolmasters!" Here again is your leit
motif. The Mayor has already dropped the subject while you still continue to advance upon him. Luka Lukich is beyond himself.

(Enter the Postmaster)

POSTMASTER: Tell me, gentlemen, who's coming? What sort of
official?

MAYOR: What, haven't you heard?

POSTMASTER: I heard something from Bobchinsky. He was with me
just now at the post office.

The Mayor not only beckons the Postmaster, but rises up, leaning
upon both the Doctor and the Postmaster. He speaks in a confidential tone, but rather rapidly and loudly, so that everyone should hear.
You understand, confidentially, but at a terribly accelerated speed.
You grab the Postmaster and smother him, so he will find it hard to
shake himself loose, while the Doctor keeps on grumbling *"Dieser
Postmeister, Gott!"*

MAYOR: Well, what do you think about it?

POSTMASTER: What do *I* think about it? Why, there'll be a war
with the Turks.

JUDGE: Exactly. That's just what I thought!

MAYOR: Well, you're both wide of the mark.

POSTMASTER: It'll be with the Turks, I'm sure. It's all the French-
men's doing.

MAYOR: Pooh! War with the Turks, indeed! It's *we* who are going to get it in the neck, not the Turks. That's quite certain. I've a letter that says so.

"It's we who are going to get it in the neck, not the Turks. I've a letter . . . " The Mayor has to turn over the letter to the Postmaster and the latter glances at it with an experienced eye. He can read the letter rapidly, this is his specialty. Take a beat and a half. You are through with the reading. Then—"Oh, then we shan't go to war . . . " That is, if it is true what is written there. The phrase should be motivated, otherwise it will not be determined by anything. And this pause becomes significant by the Mayor's action—he approaches the Postmaster and lowers his tone to a confidential whisper.

POSTMASTER: Oh, then we shan't go to war with the Turks.

MAYOR: Well, how do *you* feel, Ivan Kuzmich?

POSTMASTER: How do *I* feel? How do *you* feel, Anton Antonovich?

MAYOR: I? Well, I'm no coward, but I *am* just a little uncomfortable. The shopkeepers and townspeople bother me. It seems I'm unpopular with them, but, the Lord knows, if I've blackmailed anybody, I've done it without a trace of ill-feeling. I even think (*Buttonholes the Postmaster, and takes him aside*)—I even think there will be some sort of complaint drawn up against me. . . . Why should we have an Inspector-General at all? Look here, Ivan Kuzmich, don't you think you could just slightly open every letter which comes in and goes out of your office, and read it (for the public benefit, you know) to see if it contains any kind of information against me, or only ordinary correspondence? If it is all right, you can seal it up again, or simply deliver the letter opened.

That should be done in a different tone—more intimate and wheedling in character. To come right out and say a thing like "slightly open every letter" is rather hard for him to do. The Mayor speaks very quietly, rapidly and in a monotone. When you whisper into someone's ear, you do not embellish your speech with all kinds of melodic ornaments. Let it be done in a hardly audible tone so that the audience will be forced to strain itself to catch the meaning.

POSTMASTER: Oh, I know *that* game. Don't teach me *that!* I do it out of sheer curiosity, not as a precaution. I'm keen on knowing what's going on in the world. And they're highly interesting reading.

I can tell you! Now and then you come across a love letter, with bits of beautiful language, and so edifying . . . much better than the *Moscow News!* Just wait, wait.

As to the Postmaster, his "highly interesting reading" makes him fall into the same tone. The Mayor eyes him foolishly. He is thinking of the Inspector-General, while the Postmaster fumbles in his pockets. "Just wait, wait." The Postmaster has letters in all his pockets. He is a walking container. Why do you slow down on the tempo? Dash along, dash along. Give the Postmaster a lot of letters so that he can keep on taking them out, seeking, until he finds the right one.

MAYOR: Tell me, then, have you read anything about an official from Petersburg?

POSTMASTER: No, nothing about anyone from Petersburg, but plenty about the Kostroma and Saratov people. It's a pity you don't read the letters. There's some fine passages in them. For instance, not long ago a lieutenant writes to a friend, describing a ball in first-rate style—splendid! "Dear Friend," he says, "I live in Elysium, heaps of girls, music playing, flags flying" . . . quite a glowing description, quite! I've kept it by me, on purpose. Would you like to read it?

His hand should tremble in the handling of the letters, and many letters at that. Ordinary description should be avoided. The text of the play is no guide in this case. The description of the ball was always read realistically, while one should do it very lightly, almost in a whisper. And then "Would you like to read it?" "Let me have it"— and the Mayor snatches the letter away from the Postmaster. [Note the deviation from Gogol's text. Meyerhold evidently prefers to have the Mayor read the letter aloud.] The acting should be done with the object—the letter itself. (Question: And perhaps he puts on glasses while reading the letter? Answer: No, you shouldn't put it on too thick. He reads without glasses. A candle should be held before him.)

MAYOR: Thanks, there's no time now. But oblige me, Ivan Kuzmich—if ever you chance upon a complaint or a denouncement, keep it back, without the slightest compunction.

POSTMASTER: I will, with the greatest pleasure.

JUDGE (*Who has overheard a little*): You had better look out. You'll get into trouble over that sometime or other.

POSTMASTER: Eh! The saints forbid!

MAYOR: It was nothing—nothing. It would be different if it concerned you or the public—but it was a private affair, I assure you!

JUDGE: H'm, *some* mischief was brewing, *I* know! . . . but I was going to say, Anton Antonovich, that I had got a puppy to make you a present of—a sister to the hound you know. I daresay you've heard that Cheptovich and Varkhovinski have gone to court with one another; so now I live in clover—I hunt hares first on one's estate, and then on the other's.

The Judge has an air of self-consciousness about him. He forces himself into the group and shoves into the heap of letters, a young, slobbering, very small puppy. The Judge mumbles something, turns the puppy over and shows that it is a female: "A sister to the hound you know." A purely physiological scene, a pleasant scene, such as one sees in a surgical laboratory when a transplantation of glands is being performed. And so all the others look on, while the Judge turns the puppy over on her back, puts its feet wide apart—and everybody looks, everyone wants to see it for himself. A laboratory puppy—we'll work out this scene.

MAYOR: I don't care about your hares now, my good friend. I've got that cursed incognito on the brain! I expect the door to open any minute . . .

"I don't care about your hares now"—this should not be said, but should be rather conveyed in mimic movements. "I expect the door to open any minute . . . "—you say it by way of realization that nothing can be done with these people. The only thing to do is to leave, otherwise the Judge will insist on presenting you with a hound. I will make up those passages, the scene should be fully worked out. I will come back to the Mayor later.

(*Enter Bobchinsky and Dobchinsky, out of breath*)

BOBCHINSKY: What an extraordinary occurrence!

DOBCHINSKY: An unexpected piece of news!

ALL: What is it—what is it?

DOBCHINSKY: Something quite unforeseen. We go into the inn——

BOBCHINSKY (*Interrupting*): Yes, Pytor Ivanovich and I go into the inn——

DOBCHINSKY (*Takes him up*): All right, Peter Ivanovich, let *me* tell it!

BOBCHINSKY: No, no, allow me—allow me. You haven't got the knack——

DOBCHINSKY: Oh, but you'll get mixed up and forget it all.

BOBCHINSKY: Oh, no, I shan't—good Heavens, no! There, don't interrupt me—*do* let me tell the news—don't interrupt! Pray oblige me, gentlemen, and tell Dobchinsky not to interrupt.

MAYOR: Well, go on, for God's sake, what is it? My heart is in my mouth! Sit down, sirs, take seats! Pytor Ivanovich, here's a chair for you! (*They all sit round Bobchinsky and Dobchinsky*) Well, now, what is it, what is it?

"My heart is in my mouth"—there should be a light groan from the Mayor. A physiological determined groan. "My heart is in my mouth." He has a heart murmur and he must show it at once. Now the groan sounds somewhat stylized. Of course, by varying it somewhat, you will neutralize it. And then what will happen will be that groans will be followed by some kind of fatigue. The groans determine the music of the words, or rather the timbre of the text. Your acting will consist in the succession of such moments. He clutches at his heart, his pulse is irregular. The audience should be given to understand that the groans are not stylized, that there is, indeed, something the matter with his heart. He groans, he clutches at his heart in a way that arouses in the audience the fear that he might have an apoplectic stroke.

The first part of the scene is very well done. Sharp gesture, marionette-like quality. It will not militate against the atmosphere of illness. It will be all right if you obtain the effect of ease. Now you have just one note in your groaning, but when variety appears then we'll have real illness. Then there will be new moments, new occasions for groaning, and they will break up some of the artificiality.

There are certain achievements to be recorded. Excellent. The Mayor's part is becoming sharp. The lines are charged with a kind of trenchancy. We begin to hear the coining of italics, peculiar turns of phrase are cropping up. This, in my opinion, is a big gain. It means that you have already reached the plane where it will be easier to carry on the work of further improvement. In the later work you will have to aim at greater lightness. Now it is still somewhat ponderous; but the first half is especially well worked out in the sense of poignancy, clear-cut chiselling. We even see the old man disappearing, there is no more of the senile cud-chewing.

You have gained a great deal by finding all the colors, but when the entire system of the role unfolds, we see that since the monologue of the fifth act dominates over the rest, the role should be built up to a certain crescendo, otherwise there may be a sudden drop, so that nothing will remain but the tone of the first act.

LEOPOLD JESSNER

(1878-1945)

Staging of *The Weavers,*
Act IV, The Looting Scene

From 1919 on, Leopold Jessner, director at the State Theatre in Berlin, aroused audiences with his startling expressionist productions. On February 4, 1928, the premiere of his interpretation of the great naturalist drama The Weavers took place, and once again a Jessner production provoked controversy. The famous Looting Scene which follows, a typical example of Jessner's ingenious embellishment of a text, was the high point of this production.

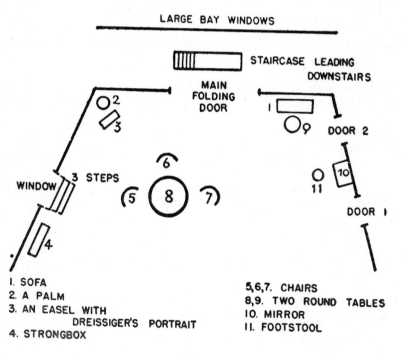

1. SOFA
2. A PALM
3. AN EASEL WITH
         DREISSIGER'S PORTRAIT
4. STRONGBOX

5,6,7. CHAIRS
8,9. TWO ROUND TABLES
10. MIRROR
11. FOOTSTOOL

On stage Mrs. Dreissiger and Mrs. Kittelhaus, the Pastor's wife. They are sitting on Chairs 5 and 7.

MRS. DREISSIGER (*In tears*): Is it my husband's fault if business is bad?

A loud commotion is heard below: laughter, jeering shouts, whistling. Dreissiger dashes in excitedly through the Main Door.

DREISSIGER: Rosa, put your things on and get into the carriage. I'll be right with you.

He rushes over to the window and shuts the blinds. Then he opens the strongbox (4) and hastily takes from it money and valuables.
Both women have sprung up in alarm. The Pastor's wife backs up toward the staircase and listens to the commotion.
John, the old family coachman, enters stage right through Door 1. He remains standing by the door.

JOHN: Everything's ready! But come quickly, before they break down the back gate!

Terrified, Mrs. Dreissiger rushes over to John and throws her arms around his neck. She sobs:

John, oh, my good old John! Save us, save us, John, my dear old John! Save my children, oh, oh!

Dreissiger stamps his foot impatiently. He continues meanwhile to hunt feverishly for his valuables:

Will you please come to your senses, and let go of John!

John has stood by helplessly while Mrs. Dreissiger embraced him. Now that he is again free, he says:

Madam, madam! Calm yourself, please. Our horses are in good condition. Nobody'll catch up with 'em. And if anyone does get in our way, we'll run 'em down.

He exits stage right—Door 1. Mrs. Dreissiger stands there helplessly, sobbing quietly. Mrs. Kittelhaus, having waited in vain near the stairs

---

Leopold Jessner: "*Weber* Inscenierung IV, Act Die Plunderung," *Die Scene*, March 1928, 92–94.

for her husband to come, walks agitatedly toward Dreissiger. She speaks in a voice of frightened despair:

But my husband! Where's my husband? Mr. Dreissiger, where's my husband?

DREISSIGER (*As he stuffs his pockets with money and valuables*): Mrs. Kittelhaus, Mrs. Kittelhaus, he's all right now. Don't be upset: he's quite all right.

MRS. KITTELHAUS (*Losing her self-control*): Something terrible has happened to him. I know it. You won't tell me; you're trying to keep it from me!

DREISSIGER: Please, please, pull yourself together. (*Pointing menacingly at the window*) They'll be sorry for this. They won't get away with their shameless, their outrageous behavior! A congregation laying hands on its own preacher! (*With an outcry, Mrs. Kittelhaus staggers back*) Mad dogs, that's what they are, raging brutes! And that's how they'll be treated.

He snatches up a few more valuables and quickly crosses to stage right, where Mrs. Dreissiger is standing as if stunned.

Go now, Rosa, please go! And quickly!

From below comes the sound of fists pounding at the front door. Then the noise of shattered windowpanes. Mrs. Dreissiger, weeping, slumps onto the sofa. Dreissiger, laughing nervously:

Can't you hear? The mob is running wild.

Shouts and cries are heard from below. Dreissiger, furious with rage:

That mob has gone crazy! There's nothing else we can do; we've got to get away from here.

The outcries grow ever louder and more ominous. Many voices shout in a chorus: "Pfeifer, Pfeifer, we want Pfeifer!"
Mrs. Dreissiger, prostrate on the sofa, moans:

Pfeifer . . . Pfeifer . . . they want Pfeifer.

Pfeifer lurches through the door stage right. He is pale, trembling, out of breath. He is so frightened he can hardly stand up.

PFEIFER: Mr. Dreissiger, Mr. Dreissiger, they're at the back gate. (*He comes closer to Dreissiger*) The front door won't hold out much longer. The blacksmith's pounding at it with a heavy bucket.

Louder, more distinct shouts from below: "Send out Pfeifer! We want Pfeifer!"

Dreissiger picks his wife up from the sofa and pushes the two women through the door. Pfeifer, petrified with fear, follows him. He tries to stop Dreissiger, clinging to the latter's arms and hands:

Please, please, Mr. Dreissiger, I beg of you, don't leave me behind.

For a second the stage is empty. The loud noises continue from below, and off-stage right Pfeifer wails with terror. Dreissiger, off-stage, tears himself away from Pfeifer and then quickly crosses the stage to the strongbox. He has forgotten something. Pfeifer follows him:

I've always served you faithfully. And I've treated the workers good too. But I couldn't give them more pay than the fixed rate.

He flings himself to his knees before Dreissiger and clutches at him like a drowning man:

Don't leave me here, they'll kill me! If they catch me, they'll beat me to death! Oh God, God! My wife, my children! . . .

Dreissiger brutally tears himself loose:

It'll come out all right, I tell you, everything will turn out all right.

He exits right. Pfeifer follows him, pleading and sobbing. The stage remains empty.

A terrific din below. The house door is battered in; more window-panes are shattered. Jubilant shouts of "Hooray!" Then utter silence. A few seconds pass, then the sound of many running feet is heard. Again silence.

In the midst of this silence a titter is heard: "Tee-hee-hee!" Then cautious, muffled outcries: "Go to the left." "Go on up!" "Shhh, take it easy!" People come up the stairs—slowly, hesitantly, timidly. The first to appear on stage is the figure of a haggard young weaver dressed in tatters. He goes carefully up the stairs and remains standing timidly at the Main Door.

Behind him are men and women weavers—all poor, thin, dressed in ragged or patched clothing. Many of them are sickly looking. They seem afraid to go in. "All right, go in there!" "No, *you* go first!"

Wittig the blacksmith, a stout bucket in his hand, pushes his way through the group: "Out of my way!" He rushes into the room with five young weavers and then exits right.

An old woman enters the room and sees a coffee set on the table stage right. "Oh, look at that!" She sits down on the sofa and pours herself some coffee. Slowly the room fills with weavers. The blinds are thrown open and the windows opened wide. Bright sunlight floods the room.

Silently, almost ghostlike, the looting now takes place. Not a word is spoken, not a question asked, not an order given. The weavers have overcome their timidity: hatred and the desire for revenge have the upper hand. Pictures are ripped from the walls and flung out of the window and through the door. A woman comes to the table, sees the richly brocaded tablecloth, takes it off, sits down on a chair and, panting softly, tears the tablecloth into shreds. Everything Dreissiger has left behind in the strongbox is thrown on the floor. Curtains are torn down. Pieces of furniture are smashed; upholstery cut to pieces. All this occurs almost in silence. Only a little weaver's boy runs around, tinkling a hand-bell he has found on the table. Old Baumert sits on the footstool stage right and drinks coffee.

In this silence Old Hieber comes downstage:

No, no, I don't like what's goin' on here. There no sense to what you're doin'. I'm keepin' out of it; I'll have no part of such goings-on.

Shaking his head in disapproval, he exits right.

During the looting, "Red" Becker has taken Dreissiger's portrait down from the easel. Now he stands near the window and studies it mockingly: "So . . . here he is . . . here he is." He tosses the picture out the window.

Moritz Jaeger appears in the Main Door:

Where did he go?

BECKER (*Quietly, in a controlled voice*): Where's the slavedriver?

Wittig the blacksmith enters the door stage right:

He's gone! He got away!

BECKER: Pfeifer too?

All the weavers, not violently but with repressed emotion, quickly call out: "Get Pfeifer! Look for Pfeifer!"

Some of the weavers hastily exit right with Becker. On stage are Old Baumert, who is drinking coffee, Moritz Jaeger, Old Ansorge, who is gazing at the mirror in mute bewilderment, and several of the weavers' wives.

Baumert gets up from the footstool, lets the cup fall to the floor, and staggers stage left. He is half drunk:

Find Pfeifer! Tell him there's a weaver here for him to starve!

Moritz Jaeger holds a piece of the broken easel in his hand:

If we can't lay hands on that dirty dog Dreissiger (*smashing the large chandelier with a club*) at least we'll make him poor. Ya, we'll see to that!

BAUMERT: As poor as a church mouse . . . that's what we'll make him!

Old Ansorge sits down on a footstool in front of the mirror and seems to be in a daze as he looks at everything going on around him.

"Red" Becker enters Door 2 stage right with the other weavers: "Stop!" They all gather around him. He speaks in a low voice but with intense energy and concentration:

That's enough here. We've only just begun. From here we'll go straight to Bielau, to Ditrich's, where the power-looms are. These factories . . . they're the cause of all our troubles.

He exits through the Main Door. They all follow him. When they get outside, they begin to sing the weaver's song. Old Ansorge remains on stage, sitting in front of the mirror. Women come out of the next room with bolts of cloth, which they roll across the floor. When Ansorge begins speaking, they stop what they are doing and gaze blankly at him.

ANSORGE: Who am I? Anton Ansorge, the weaver. Has he gone crazy—Old Ansorge? Sure enough, my head's spinnin' round and round like a top. Be off with you, you rebel upstarts! Off with your heads, off with your legs, off with your hands!

He gets up, looks into the mirror, then says menacingly:

If you take my house, I'll take your house. (*He beats against the mirror with his fists*) Take this! And this!

He smashes the mirror to bits. Lights out.
(*Curtain*)

JEAN-LOUIS BARRAULT

(b. 1910)

Mise en Scène of *Phaedra*, Act II, Scene V

In Reflections on the Theatre, *Jean-Louis Barrault writes about* Phaedra: "*A classic is like a hidden treasure. Its core is buried under so many layers of varnish, so many polishings, that it can be reached only by patience and infiltration. But once it is reached—or once we think it is—there are dazzling riches to be discovered at every turn. Its resources are inexhaustible.*" With the "*methods and tenacity of a speleologist*" Barrault has explored the depths of Racine in his Mise en scène and Commentary for Phaedra (1944), *one of the excellent volumes in the French series* Mises en scène.

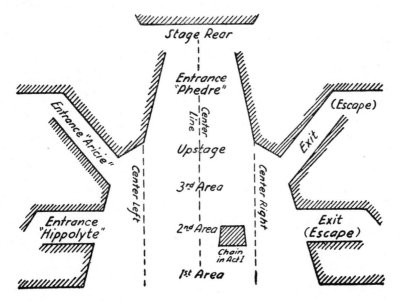

(HIPPOLYTUS, PHAEDRA, OENONE)

Third Part

Phaedra—Phaedra the widow, Phaedra the free—comes forward. Silence during which Hippolytus stands downstage left center like an attractive statue, like a young tiger with an inscrutable look.

> PHAEDRA (*To Oenone*):   Look, I see him!
>   My blood forgets to flow,—tongue will not speak
>   What I have come to say!

First Movement

Phaedra almost stumbles. Without looking at Oenone, but clinging to her, she murmurs her lines. Oenone supports her, standing face to face with her but without looking at her either. Oenone utters her reply out of the corner of her mouth.

> OENONE: Think of your son.
>   And think that all his hopes depend on you.

A pause during which Hippolytus bows while Phaedra advances, then straightens up again, mustering all his energy. This first phase of the scene is completely symmetrical with the first phase of the preceding scene. It is characterized by the effort made by the characters to maintain an "official" tone and to discuss "affairs of state."

> PHAEDRA: They tell me that you leave us, hastily.
>   I come to add my own tears to your sorrow,
>   And I would plead my fears for my young son.

Since Hippolytus had made use of his father, Phaedra now tries to plead for her son. Breathing pause. Inner conflict.

Jean Racine: *Phèdre, mise en scène et commentaires de Jean-Louis Barrault.* Paris: Editions du Seuil, 1946, 118–129. By permission of Editions du Seuil, Paris. (Translation of *Phaedra* text by Robert Henderson from *Masterworks of World Literature*, Vol. II, 362–366, Dryden Press, New York.)

He has no father, now; 'twill not be long
Until the day that he will see my death,
And even now, his youth is much imperiled
By a thousand foes.

Breathing pause. Inner conflict, change of timbre.

You only can defend him.

Breathing pause. Inner conflict, artificiality in the official tone.

And in my inmost heart, remorse is stirring,—
Yes, and fear, too, lest I have shut your ears
Against his cries; I fear that your just anger
May, before long, visit on him that hatred
His mother earned.

HIPPOLYTUS: Madam, you need not fear.
Such malice is not mine.

Hippolytus, motionless, is polite but cold. His having spoken makes
Phaedra draw closer to Oenone. She leans on the latter in order not
to collapse.

PHAEDRA: I should not blame you
If you should hate me; I have injured you.
So much you know;—you could not read my heart.

Phaedra's words give the impression that she no longer knows where
she is; that she is torn by inner conflict and is trying to control herself.

Yes, I have tried to be your enemy,
For the same land could never hold us both.
In private and abroad I have declared it;—
I was your enemy! I found no peace
Till seas had parted us; and I forbade
Even your name to be pronounced to me.

She smiles bitterly, then suddenly she grows serious and moving. This
whole scene must be played subtly. While exuding sensuality, the
characters must lose nothing of their grandeur and nobility; and even

when they give the impression of being "right next to each other," they are really from two to three feet apart. With this in mind, their explanations must come from within, yet they must not forget their sense of dignity.

> And yet, if punishment be meted out
> Justly, by the offense;—if only hatred
> Deserves a hate, then never was there woman
> Deserved more pity, and less enmity.

HIPPOLYTUS: A mother who is jealous for her children
> Will seldom love the children of a mother
> Who came before her. Torments of suspicion
> Will often follow on a second marriage.
> Another would have felt that jealousy
> No less than you; perhaps more violently.

Polite and cold, yet, in spite of himself, full of charm.

PHAEDRA: Ah, prince, but Heaven made me quite exempt
> From what is usual, and I can call
> That Heaven as my witness! 'Tis not this—
> No, quite another ill devours my heart!

During his reply, Hippolytus has been charming in his sincerity. Phaedra has turned around. She is lashed by her passion. Her voice is in her throat. All her blood literally races at the charm of Hippolytus' voice. The "Ah" she utters is a cry of suffering. She leans more and more on Oenone, who stands there stolidly like an executioner's stake.

HIPPOLYTUS: This is no time for self-reproaching, madam.

Seeing Phaedra's "drawn" features, which he misinterprets, Hippolytus takes a step toward her. In order to move out of his way, she turns lightly on herself . . . and faces forward.

> Perhaps your husband still beholds the light,
> Perhaps he may be granted safe return
> In answer to our prayers; his guarding god
> Is Neptune, whom he never called in vain.

Hippolytus' candor and purity are more and more alluring. This power of attraction is Phaedra's undoing. The latter utters virtually a curse against Theseus. Hard-faced, she expresses her regret which sounds like a wish.

> PHAEDRA: He who has seen the mansions of the dead
> Returns not thence. Since Theseus has gone
> Once to those gloomy shores, we need not hope,
> For Heaven will not send him back again.
> Prince,

Ten syllables for her to turn her head toward Hippolytus.

> there is no release from Acheron;—

A short pause during which the entire theatre—that is, reality, or better still, the present—reappears, tense and motionless. A change of timbre. Phaedra is drawn toward Hippolytus—where does she find the strength to tear herself away from Oenone and to advance slowly toward him? Their two faces are riveted to each other; their two breaths draw closer.

> It is a greedy maw,—and yet I think
> He lives and breathes in you,—and still I see him
> Before me here; I seem to speak to him—

Their two breaths are almost one.

> My heart—!

Her voice breaks off. Phaedra, terrified, flees wildly toward the imperturbable Oenone (who seems more and more like the statue of Fate). Clinging to her, Phaedra reminds one of a criminal who cannot, who dares not commit his crime.

> Oh, I am mad! Do what I will,
> I cannot hide my passion.
> HIPPOLYTUS: Yes, I see
> What strange things love will do, for Theseus, dead,
> Seems present to your eyes, and in your soul
> A constant flame is burning.

Hippolytus is now filled with compassion for this queen wracked with sorrow. He is all the more compassionate in that he himself is happy; he has not been happy for long, of course, but right now he feels a fresh access of happiness. Happiness makes people generous: hence

Hippolytus comes up to Phaedra, leans over her, his face above her face. Misinterpreting the situation, he is attentive to Phaedra, exciting her passion all the more.

PHAEDRA: Ah, for Theseus
          I languish and I long,

Phaedra, still leaning on Oenone, has only to turn her head to have her mouth and eyes right beneath Hippolytus' mouth and eyes. She does this slowly, sensually, as she utters the line: "Ah, for Theseus I languish and I long." At the same time, her eyes and the timbre of her voice cause Hippolytus to draw back slightly.

                                                            but not, indeed,
          As the Shades have seen him,

For the second time Phaedra can no longer resist Hippolytus' power of attraction. She advances as if magnetically drawn toward him. This is a situation in which the actors' movements are of great plastic interest. Phaedra, during this soliloquy which is not a "recitative" but a "period," does not advance *voluntarily* toward Hippolytus (which would give a confusing and uncalled-for impression of a threat); she advances because Hippolytus *voluntarily* draws back and *involuntarily* draws her toward himself. Hippolytus draws back, *then* Phaedra advances in spite of herself toward him. So Hippolytus has withdrawn slightly. She straightens up.

                                                      as the fickle lover
          Of a thousand forms, the one who fain would ravish
          The bride of Pluto;—but one faithful, proud,

She advances.

          Even to slight disdain,—the charm of youth

Hippolytus retreats.

          That draws all hearts, even as the gods are painted,—

He stops retreating. From a distance she observes him.

                    Or as yourself. He had your eyes, your manner,—
                    He spoke like you, and he could blush like you,
                    And when he came across the waves to Crete,
                    My childhood home, worthy to win the love

Of Minos' daughters,—what were you doing then?
Why did my father gather all these men,
The flower of Greece, and leave Hippolytus?

Again irresistibly drawn, she advances. Oenone begins quietly to move backstage right, from which position she will keep close watch.

Oh, why were you too young to have embarked
On board the ship that brought your father there?
The monster would have perished at your hands,
Despite the windings of his vast retreat.
My sister would have armed you with the clue
To guide your steps, doubtful within the maze.—
But no—

Phaedra is quite close to him, her face almost touching his; but their two bodies are still slightly apart from each other.

for Phaedra would have come before her,
And love would first have given me the thought,

Again he retreats.

And I it would have been, whose timely aid
Had taught you all the labyrinthine ways!

(If Hippolytus had accompanied Theseus, he himself would have triumphed over all the obstacles which Theseus had to overcome, for Phaedra would have replaced her sister Ariadne at his side and would have helped him in the episode of the labyrinth.)

The care

He stops retreating, she watches him.

that such a dear life would have cost me!
No thread could satisfy my lover's fears.
I would have wished to lead the way myself,
And share

She advances.

the peril you were sure to face.
Yes, Phaedra would have walked the maze with you,—
With you come out in safety, or have perished!

She is coming right up to him. Now, realizing only too well what is
going on, Hippolytus takes two quick steps back. She is silent and her
face hardens instantly. Hippolytus has come close to the footlights
about two-thirds of the way to the exit stage left. Phaedra stands
there—downstage slightly left.

There is an atmosphere of extreme sensuality in this portion of the
scene. Phaedra's femininity blossoms out to the outer limits of decency.
By a clever and perfidious subterfuge, she leaves us in doubt as to
whether she is speaking for herself when she puts herself in Ariadne's
place; we do not know if she is playing with Hippolytus or if she is
sincere. But we do know that she is displaying all her charm and trying to snare him sensually. Her extreme unrest infects everyone and
everything. The air is charged with her images and thoughts; her walk
is seductive and tantalizing; her voice is languorous and muffled. Her
flesh glistens with passion; the palms of her hands are damp. The air
is perfumed with her scent—one can almost perceive the "passion"
that grips her. She has just "secreted" all her reserves of seduction.

HIPPOLYTUS: Gods! What is this I hear? Have you forgotten
    That Theseus is my father and your husband?

Hippolytus, the pure and "puritanical" Hippolytus, can no longer believe his eyes. After retreating two steps, "bowled over," he speaks
these two lines with a maximum of prudence and caution, in order not
to re-arouse her abject passion.

PHAEDRA: Why should you fancy I have lost remembrance
    And that I am regardless of my honor?

Second Movement

Pause. Everyone on stage motionless. The second phase of the scene
begins.

It is hard to imagine without a shudder Phaedra's expression at this
moment. As a woman, she is now humiliated, crushed. As a queen,
she is dying of shame. Already half dead because of this passion which
is tearing at her insides, she now stands there, her eyes glassy, her features dangerously hard and implacable. Rigid in her dignity, the unhappy daughter of the Sun is now a potential menace.

If a snapshot of Phaedra were taken at this moment, one could at-
tach to it a sign reading: "Danger! Live Wire!"—like the warnings
displayed on high-tension wires. Ashen pale, she proffers her vague
and frightening threat.

> HIPPOLYTUS: Forgive me, madam! With a blush I own
> That I mistook your words, quite innocent.
> For very shame I cannot see you longer—

Hippolytus, the pure and candid Hippolytus, has been mistaken. Now
it is his turn to feel a sense of shame bordering on utter confusion.

> Now I will go—

He turns around to leave (taking three quick steps upstage).

> PHAEDRA: Ah, prince, you understood me,—

A single cry stops Hippolytus dead in his tracks. It is Phaedra's "Ah."
Then her voice grows hoarse, slightly choked up with suffering. But
save her maximum of strength for Act IV. Do not force the word
"prince"—let it be sufficient unto itself.

It is obvious that we are at the beginning of a recitative. The first
three lines of this speech should be spoken with full *emotion*.

> Too well, indeed! For I had said enough.
> You could not well mistake. But do not think
> That in those moments when I love you most

The phrase "I love you most" must long reverberate. As if physically
struck by this phrase, Hippolytus takes up his position at the very spot
where Aricia had taken refuge a few minutes previously; downstage
left, a dark warm corner in which he can conceal his disgust. He reminds one of a Saint Sebastian whom Phaedra is about to pierce with
her arrows.

Now comes a leveling-off of emotion.

> I do not feel my guilt. No easy yielding
> Has helped the poison that infects my mind.
> The sorry object of divine revenge,

After bringing Hippolytus to a halt, Phaedra moves freely about and
now finds herself in the center of the stage. Oenone is hidden against
the set—far upstage right.

I am not half so hateful to your sight
As to myself. The gods will bear me witness,—

Recitative

Here the recitative really begins. Must be spoken in a full, vibrant voice—a tragedienne's voice—but without false heroics. The grandeur must all come from within.

They who have lit this fire within my veins,—
The gods who take their barbarous delight
In leading some poor mortal heart astray!
Nay, do you not remember, in the past,

She goes toward him; but if he were not there, and she only imagined him present, she would speak no differently to him. Hippolytus can no longer check her flow of words. She speaks to him as to the passive object of her insane love. No one can stop Phaedra now. She is possessed. The fire is sweeping the palace.

How I was not content to fly?—I drove you
Out of the land, so that I might appear
Most odious—and to resist you better
I tried to make you hate me—and in vain!
You hated more, and I loved not the less,

Hippolytus, his eyes shut, his features distorted in disgust, the palms of his hands flattened behind him and resting against the wall, has turned his face away (so that he now faces the audience).
    Quite close to him now but slightly upstage, Phaedra twists around and now has her back three-quarters turned to the audience. She seeks out Hippolytus' eyes.

While your misfortunes lent you newer charms.
I have been drowned in tears and scorched by fire!
Your own eyes might convince you of the truth
If you could look at me, but for a moment!

With an abrupt and savage twist of his neck, Hippolytus turns his head (looking over her, toward the backdrop).

What do I say?

Now she speaks directly to Hippolytus' breast and heart—as if the latter will listen to her more readily than Hippolytus himself. Ah! If she could only speak as though the problem were solved! The few lines she utters (down through the line: " . . . and came to beg you not to hate him") will be all the more heart-rending if she really *speaks* them. At this moment Phaedra is a wretched woman groveling with desire. The pity she inspires is almost unbearable. This is the most painful moment of all, during which Hippolytus, dismayed, extends his arms as if trying to escape Phaedra vertically.

> You think this vile confession
> That I have made, is what I meant to say?
> I did not dare betray my son. For him
> I feared,—and came to beg you not to hate him.
> This was the purpose of a heart too full
> Of love for you to speak of aught besides.

She also extends her arms—but with longing; and she rears back. Then she straightens up and, about three feet away from him, her body wrenched like a twisted stalk, she says the lines "Take your revenge, and punish me my passion!" to "Does Theseus' widow dare to love his son?" We are at the high point of the recitative. Phaedra appears in all her splendor of a full-blown woman. Young, beautiful, ripe, she is altogether desirable.

> Take your revenge, and punish me my passion!
> Prove yourself worthy of your valiant father,
> And rid the world of an offensive monster!
> Does Theseus' widow dare to love his son?
> Monster indeed!

Finally she runs forward and plants herself right next to him. This time her stomach juts forward. The recitative now gradually declines.

> Nay, let her not escape you!
> Here is my heart!

The recitative has ended. Tragic reality reappears—like a hallucination. Feverish agitation returns. Extreme rapidity of speech. The orchestra plays furiously, the conductor finding it difficult to keep pace with the action.

Oenone slips out of her hiding place.

Phaedra is unchained. As she tears her garments, she uncovers a portion of her breast.

Hippolytus *must* remain absolutely motionless. He must show
absolutely no reaction. Perhaps his surprise accounts for his silence.

> Here is the place to strike!
> It is most eager to absolve itself!
> It leaps impatiently to meet your blow!—
> Strike deep!

While the rest of her speech is given with sweeping gestures, in the
last four lines Phaedra advances and turns slowly on herself, her right
arm extending toward Hippolytus' left side. As she starts to say "Or if,
indeed, you find it shameful . . . " she slowly unsheathes Hippolytus'
sword, and suddenly brandishes it; then she takes two steps and cries
with all her might: "Give it now!"

> Or if, indeed, you find it shameful
> To drench your hand in such polluted blood,—
> If that be punishment too mild for you,—
> Too easy for your hate,—if not your arm,
> Then lend your sword to me.—Come! Give it now!—

"Give it now!" must resound like a deafening gong.

> OENONE: What would you do, my lady? Oh, just gods!
> But someone comes;—go quickly. Run from shame.
> You cannot fly, if they should find you thus.

> (*Exeunt Phaedra and Oenone*)

"Give it now!" is the cue for Oenone to move forward. She rushes
toward Phaedra. At "Oh, just gods!" she grasps Phaedra's arms. At
"But someone comes" she whirls her around. At her physical contact
with Oenone, Phaedra seems somehow to become aware of the situation again. Unable to endure it any longer, she almost faints and allows herself to be moved about like a puppet. At "Run from shame"
Oenone fastens her grip. Then, as she speaks the last line, Oenone
takes (or rather: drags) her away. At " . . . find you thus" the two
women are well on their way out (diagonal exit upstage).

> (*End of Act II*)

BERTOLT BRECHT

(b. 1898)

Brecht Directs

The best example of the working methods of Bertolt Brecht in achieving the famed "alienation" effect would have been an excerpt from one of his "models." But Brecht's "models" are so dependent on hundreds of frames of sequence photography which fix for Brecht and others the line-by-line interpretation of his own version of the play that it was not feasible to reproduce a scene within the limits of this volume. The following account of Brecht at rehearsal by an anonymous colleague, drawn from a fascinating illustrated volume, Theaterarbeit (1952), *is the most recent and complete view of the work of this unusual playwright-director.*

———

D
URING rehearsals Brecht sits in the orchestra of the theatre. His directing is unobtrusive. When he intervenes, he does so almost unnoticeably and always "the way the wind is blowing"; he never disturbs the work, not even with suggestions for improvement. You do not get the impression that he wants his actors to "create something he sees in his mind's eye"; they are not his instruments.

He tries rather to work with them in finding the story told by the play, and he helps to bring out the strong points in every actor. His work with actors reminds one of the way in which a child takes a tree branch and propels tiny twigs from a stagnant pool on the riverbank into the mainstream of the river.

Brecht is not one of those directors who always knows more than the actors. His attitude toward the play is one of "not knowing"; he bides his time. You get the feeling that Brecht doesn't know his own play—not a single sentence in it. Nor does he want to know what is written down, but how the actor on the stage should convey it. If, for example, an actor asks: "Should I get up at this point?" Brecht will frequently answer in typical fashion: "I don't know." He really doesn't know, and only finds out in the course of rehearsing.

Brecht makes use of everything—positions, movements, gestures—to bring out the play's narrative.

The story of *Mother Courage and Her Children* is: The food peddler Anna Fierling, called Mother Courage, goes to the war [the Thirty Years' War] with her three children in order to do business. She loses her three children, one after another, and becomes destitute. Incapable of learning from experience, she continues to go her way alone. This story is shown in twelve scenes of the play, with each scene in turn broken up into a series of consecutive episodes. Brecht's stage direction is such that every one of these little episodes can be excerpted from the piece and played by itself. They are all scrupulously mounted, down to the smallest detail.

Brecht once wrote: "The creative writer's word is only as sacred as it is true. The theatre is not the servant of the dramatist but of society."

On Brecht's stage everything must be *true*. But there is a special kind of truth he likes most of all—that is, when truth comes as a discovery. Often during a rehearsal he points elatedly at one of the actors who has just revealed something unusual or unusually important in human nature or social living.

Man's social life is minutely studied. At the beginning of Scene 8 of *Mother Courage,* for example, a young peasant comes with his mother to the camp, in order to sell their blankets. What has to be shown is not only that peasants are selling their own blankets but that they are doing this in the fourteenth year of the war; and that it is nothing out of the ordinary. But it is hard for them to do this ordinary deed because the blankets are the last thing they have to sell and they really can't do without them. What are they going to use for covers at night? How does the mother look at the sack filled with blankets that are so important to the family? How does the son take this sack with its important contents from his shoulder? And how does he sling it across his shoulder again when he hears that peace has "broken out" and realizes that now the blankets will not have to be sold?

The teaching that the theatre offers must also entertain. On Brecht's stage everything must be good-looking. Pelagea Vlassova's shabby little hovel [in the Brecht production of Gorky's *Mother*] must be just as good-looking as the group scene of workers in the factory courtyard or the colors in the costumes of the middle-class ladies standing in line at the copper-collection station.

To be sure, all this is not always seen at first glance. But Brecht stages his plays in such a way that even at the tenth performance something new can still be discovered. The plays appear richer the more often one sees them. Even when the play itself is long familiar, the stage business, gestures, colors, etc., afford new pleasure.

Brecht acts out a good many things, but only very brief bits—and he will break off in the middle so as not to present anything ready-made. He does not dictate but stimulates the actors' imagination and creative power. He always imitates the actor for whom he acts out a part, but of course without pretending to be an actor. In this situation his attitude is: People of this type often do so-and-so in such-and-such a manner.

Every actor must catch the eye and ear of the audience for at least one moment. Brecht explains: No human being goes through life unobserved. Then how can we let an actor cross the stage unobserved? "This is *your* moment," he calls out to the actor. "Don't let it slip through your fingers. Now you're the important one—the devil with the play!" Of course, it must be a moment which the play calls for or allows. Then Brecht says: "It is in the interest of all the performers to present the play as a unit; it is also in your interest as an individual. But it is also in your interest to bring out certain contrasts. These contrasts are the lifeblood of the play." He never permits an actor—that is, a human being in the play—to be sacrificed "for the sake of" the play, for the sake of tension or tempo.

Brecht is the most appreciative member of his actors' audience. The actor is entitled to recognition for performing well. A joke remains a joke, even if it is used for the twentieth time. Then too the actor is entitled to a laugh. Otherwise he must assume that this time his joke fell flat.

Brecht always finds something to give to the actor at the right moment. There is no sense of confusion because something is missing; there are no heavy silences because something has to be discussed. The actor is kept busy even if the problem is not definitely solved. The rehearsal moves along without interruptions.

Brecht knows how to delve into his actors. They do not have to fit in with his mood; rather is it he who fathoms their individual moods. If an actor has "a good day," Brecht is insatiable; he gets the maximum out of him, but almost imperceptibly and without any straining on the actor's part. If the actor is in a bad mood, Brecht leaves him alone; he never insists on anything that cannot be performed smoothly.

Brecht works concentratedly but without tension. His cheerfulness during rehearsals is communicated to the actors. It is obvious that he means to have a good time.

His enjoyment of excellent gestures and authentic attitudes stimulates the actors; they outdo themselves because they look forward to his being entertained.

Brecht hates long discussions—particularly psychological discussions—during rehearsals. During the more than 200 rehearsal hours of Lenz's *Hofmeister*, there were altogether not more than perhaps fifteen minutes' discussion between director and actors. At the same time, he tries out every suggestion. He says: "Why tell me the reasons for it; just show me your suggestion," and "Don't talk about it, act it out." If it is a good suggestion, it is accepted. Lack of applause does more to convince actors that the suggestion is a bad one than any long-winded arguments about it.

Brecht always speaks in a loud voice and shouts his suggestions, usually from his seat in the orchestra, so that everyone can hear them. Yet this does not interfere with the unobtrusiveness of his suggestions. During the staging he is surrounded by students. He immediately passes on good suggestions, always naming the one who made it: "X says, Y thinks. . . . " In that way the work becomes everybody's work.

He explains to his students of direction: "If we cannot get out of a play or a scene what is in it, we must be careful not to put into it something that doesn't belong there. You must not overwork plays and scenes. Something may be of minor importance; but it is still of importance. If, however, you give it too much, the little (but genuine) importance is destroyed. In every play there are weak scenes (and weaknesses in general). If the play as a whole is fairly good, it contains a balance that is often hard to discover but easy to disturb. Often, for example, the playwright achieves a special effect from a scene as a result of the weakness of preceding ones. Frequently too the weakness of a scene serves to high-light something other than what is said. The speech of Coriolanus' mother, in which she faces her son as he marches against his native Rome, was, I believe, made deliberately weak by Shakespeare—he did not want Coriolanus to be dissuaded from his plan because of the real reasons involved or because of deep inner emotion but as a result of a certain inertia with which he succumbs to his old habits. Hence it would be wrong to give Volumnia better arguments and thereby make her speech more convincing. On the other hand, our actors often have too little confidence in the play, in an interesting moment of the story that is being told, in an effective line, etc.; so they do not allow this intrinsically interesting moment to achieve its full effect by itself. Besides, a play should have fewer spots in which it strains for effects. No spectator can follow an entire performance with the same amount and degree of attention; and this factor must be taken into consideration."

ELIA KAZAN

(b. 1909)

Notebook for *A Streetcar Named Desire*

> *The vitality of the characterizations in both the stage and screen versions of* A Streetcar Named Desire *derives in large part from a minute analysis of the life of each character before as well as during the actual events of the play. Elia Kazan, originally a versatile Group Theatre actor, applied the Stanislavskian principle of seeking the "spine" of each character. The following selection from the director's private notebook dated August 1947 was kept before and during the rehearsals of the play. Never intended for public perusal, these unedited creative memoranda reveal a director's intimate search for the inner spirit of a play.*

A thought—directing finally consists of turning Psychology into Behavior.

Theme—this is a message from the dark interior. This little twisted, pathetic, confused bit of light and culture puts out a cry. It is snuffed out by the crude forces of violence, insensibility and vulgarity which exist in our South—and this cry is the play.

Style—one reason a "style," a stylized production is necessary is that a subjective factor—Blanche's memories, inner life, emotions, are a real factor. We cannot really understand her behavior unless we see the effect of her past on her present behavior.

This play is a poetic tragedy. We are shown the final dissolution of a person of worth, who once had great potential, and who, even as she goes down, has worth exceeding that of the "healthy," coarse-grained figures who kill her.

Blanche is a social type, an emblem of a dying civilization, making its last curlicued and romantic exit. All her behavior patterns are those of the dying civilization she represents. In other words her behavior is *social*. Therefore find social modes! This is the source of the play's stylization and the production's style and color. Likewise Stanley's behavior is *social* too. It is the basic animal cynicism of today. "Get what's coming to you! Don't waste a day! Eat, drink, get yours!" This is the basis of his stylization, of the choice of his props. All props should be stylized: they should have a color, shape and weight that spell: style.

An effort to put poetic names on scenes to edge me into stylizations and physicalizations. Try to keep each scene in terms of Blanche.

1. Blanche comes to the last stop at the end of the line.
2. Blanche tries to make a place for herself.
3. Blanche breaks them apart, but when they come together, Blanche is more alone than ever!
4. Blanche, more desperate because more excluded, tries the direct attack and makes the enemy who will finish her.
5. Blanche finds that she is being tracked down for the kill. She must work fast.
6. Blanche suddenly finds, suddenly makes for herself, the only possible, perfect man for her.
7. Blanche comes out of the happy bathroom to find that her own doom has caught up with her.
8. Blanche fights her last fight. Breaks down. Even Stella deserts her.
9. Blanche's last desperate effort to save herself by telling the whole truth. The *truth dooms her*.
10. Blanche escapes out of this world. She is brought back by Stanley and destroyed.
11. Blanche is disposed of.

The style—the real deep style—consists of one thing only: to find behavior that's truly social, significantly typical, at each moment. It's not so much what Blanche has done—it's how she does it—with such style, grace, manners, old-world trappings and effects, props, tricks, swirls, etc., that they seem anything but vulgar.

And for the other characters, too, you face the same problem. To find the Don Quixote character for them. *This is a poetic tragedy, not a realistic or a naturalistic one. So you must find a Don Quixote scheme of things for each.*

Stylized acting and direction is to realistic acting and direction as poetry is to prose. The acting must be styled, not in the obvious sense. (Say nothing about it to the producer and actors.) But you will fail unless you find this kind of poetic realization for the behavior of these people.

BLANCHE

"Blanche is Desperate"

"This is the End of the Line of the Streetcar Named Desire"

Spine—find Protection: the tradition of the old South says that it must be through another person.

Her problem has to do with her tradition. Her notion of what a woman should be. She is stuck with this "ideal." It is her. It is her ego. Unless she lives by it, she cannot live; in fact her whole life has been for nothing. Even the Alan Gray incident as she now tells it and believes it to have been, is a necessary piece of romanticism. Essentially, in outline, she tells what happened, but it also serves the demands of her notion of herself, to make her *special* and different, out of the tradition of the romantic ladies of the past: Swinburne, Wm. Morris, Pre-Raphaelites, etc. This way it serves as an excuse for a great deal of her behavior.

Because this image of herself cannot be accomplished in reality, certainly not in the South of our day and time, it is her effort and practice to *accomplish it in fantasy.* Everything that she does in *reality* too is colored by this necessity, this compulsion to be *special*. So, in fact, *reality becomes fantasy too*. She makes it so!

The variety essential to the play, and to Blanche's playing and to Jessica Tandy's achieving the role demands that she be a "heavy" at the beginning. For instance: contemplate the inner character contradiction: bossy yet helpless, domineering yet shaky, etc. The audience at the beginning should see her bad effect on Stella, want Stanley to tell her off. He does. He exposes her and then gradually, as they see how genuinely in pain, how actually desperate she is, how warm, tender and loving she can be (the Mitch story), how freighted with need she is—then they begin to go with her. They begin to realize that they are sitting in at the death of something extraordinary . . . colorful, varied, passionate, lost, witty, imaginative, of her own integrity . . . and then they feel the tragedy. In the playing too there can be a growing sincerity and directness.

The thing about the "tradition" in the nineteenth century was that *it worked then*. It made a woman feel important, with her own secure positions and functions, her own special worth. It also made a woman at that time *one with her society*. But *today* the tradition is an anachronism which simply does not function. *It does not work.* So while Blanche must believe it because it makes her special, because it makes her sticking by Belle Reve an act of heroism, rather than an absurd romanticism, still *it does not work.* It makes Blanche feel *alone, outside of her society*. Left out, insecure, shaky. The airs the "tradition" demands isolate her further, and every once in a while, her resistance weakened by drink, she breaks down and seeks human warmth and contact where she can find it, not on her terms, on theirs: the merchant, the traveling salesman and the others . . . among whom the vulgar adolescent soldiers seem the most innocent. Since she cannot integrate these episodes, she rejects them, begins to forget them, begins to live in fantasy, begins to rationalize and explain them to herself thus: "I never was hard or self-sufficient enough . . . men don't see women unless they are in bed with them. They don't admit their existence except when they're love-making. You've got to have your existence admitted by someone if you are going to receive someone's protection," etc. As if you had to apologize for needing human contact! Also n.b. above—the word: protection. That is what she, as a woman in the tradition, so desperately needs. That's what she comes to Stella for, Stella and her husband. Not finding it from them she tries to get it from Mitch. *Protection*. A haven, a *harbor*. She is a refugee, punch drunk, and on the ropes, making her last stand, trying to keep up a gallant front, because she is a proud person. But really if Stella doesn't provide her haven, *where is she to go*. She's a misfit, a liar, her "airs" alienate people, she must act superior to them which alienates them further. She doesn't know how to work. So she can't make a living. She's really helpless. She needs someone to help her. Protection. She's a last dying relic of the last century now adrift in our unfriendly day. From time to time, for reasons of simple human loneliness and need she goes to pieces, smashes her tradition . . . then goes back to it. This conflict has developed into a terrible crisis. All she wants is a haven: "I want to rest! I want to breathe quietly again . . . just think! If it happens! I can leave here and have a home of my own. . . . "

If this is a romantic tragedy, what is its inevitability and what is the tragic flaw? In the Aristotelian sense, the flaw is the need to be superior, special (or *her* need for protection and what it means to her), the "tradition." This creates an apartness so intense, a loneliness so gnawing that only a complete breakdown, a refusal, as it were, to contemplate what she's doing, a *binge* as it were, a destruction of all her standards, a desperate violent ride on the Streetcar Named Desire can break through the walls of her tradition. The tragic flaw creates the circumstances, inevitably, that destroy her. More later.

Try to find an entirely different character, a self-dramatized and self-romanticized character for Blanche to play in each scene. She is playing 11 different people. This will give it a kind of changeable and shimmering surface it should have. And all these 11 self-dramatized and romantic characters should be out of the romantic tradition of the Pre-Bellum South, etc. Example: Sc. 2 Gay Miss Devil-may-care.

There is another, simpler and equally terrible contradiction in her own nature. She won't face her physical or sensual side. She calls it "brutal desire." She thinks she sins when she gives in to it . . . yet she does give in to it, out of loneliness . . . but by calling it "brutal desire," she is able to separate it from her "real self," her "cultured," refined self. Her tradition makes no allowance, allows no space for this very real part of herself. So she is constantly in conflict, not at ease, sinning. *She's still looking for something that doesn't exist today, a gentleman,* who will treat her like a virgin, marry her, protect her, defend and maintain her honor, etc. She wants an old-fashioned wedding dressed in white . . . and still she does things out of "brutal desire" that make this impossible. *All this too is tradition.*

She has worth too—she is better than Stella. She says: "There has been some kind of progress. . . . Such things as art—as poetry and music—such kinds of new light have come into the world . . . in some kinds of people some kinds of tenderer feelings have had some little beginning that we've got to make *grow!* And cling to, and hold as our flag! In this dark march toward whatever it is we're approaching . . . don't . . . don't hang back with the brutes!" And though the direct psychological motivation for this is jealousy and personal frustration, still she, alone and abandoned in the crude society of New Orleans back streets, is the *only voice of light.* It is flickering and, in the course of the play, goes out. But it is valuable because it is unique.

Blanche is a butterfly in a jungle looking for just a little momentary protection, doomed to a sudden, early violent death. The more I work on Blanche, incidentally, the less insane she seems. She is caught in a fatal inner contradiction, but in another society, she *would* work. In Stanley's society, no!

This is like a classic tragedy. Blanche is Medea or someone pursued by the Harpies, the Harpies being *her own nature.* Her inner sickness pursues her like *doom* and makes it impossible for her to attain the one thing she needs, the only thing she needs: a safe harbor.

An effort to phrase Blanche's spine: to find *protection,* to find something to hold onto, some strength in whose protection she can live, like a sucker shark or a parasite. The tradition of *woman* (or all women) can only live through the strength of someone else. Blanche is entirely dependent. Finally the doctor!

Blanche is an outdated creature, approaching extinction . . . like the dinosaur. She is about to be pushed off the edge of the earth. On the other hand she is a heightened version, an artistic intensification of all women. That is what makes the play universal. Blanche's special relation to all women is that she is at that critical point where *the one thing above all else that she is dependent on: her attraction for men, is beginning to go.* Blanche is like all women, dependent on a man, looking for one to hang onto: only *more so!*

So beyond being deeply desperate, Blanche is in a hurry. She'll be pushed off the earth soon. She carries her doom in her character. Also, her past is chasing her, catching up with her. Is it any wonder that she tries to attract each and every man she meets. She'll even take that protected feeling, that needed feeling, that superior feeling, for a moment. Because, at least for a moment, that anxiety, the hurt and the pain will be quenched. The sex act is the opposite of loneliness. Desire is the opposite of Death. For a moment the anxiety is still, for a moment the complete desire and concentration of a man is on her. He clings to you. He may say I love you. All else is anxiety, loneliness and being adrift.

Compelled by her nature (she must be special, superior) she makes it impossible with Stanley and Stella. She acts in a way that succeeds in being destructive. But the last bit of luck is with her. She finds the only man on earth whom she suits, a man who is looking for a dominant woman. For an instant she is happy. But her past catches up with her. Stanley, whom she's antagonized by her destructiveness aimed at his home, but especially by her need to be superior, uses her past, which he digs up, to destroy her. Finally she takes refuge in fantasy. She must have protection, closeness, love, safe harbor. The only place she can obtain them any longer is in her own mind. She "goes crazy."

Blanche is a stylized character, she should be played, should be dressed, should move like a stylized figure. What is the physicalization of an aristocratic woman pregnant with her own doom? . . . Behaving by a tradition that dooms her in this civilization, in this "culture"? All her behavior patterns are *old-fashioned, pure tradition.* All as if jellied in rote——

Why does the "Blues" music fit the play? The Blues is an expression of the loneliness and rejection, the exclusion and isolation of the Negro and their (opposite) longing for love and connection. Blanche too is "looking for a home," abandoned, friendless. "I don't know where I'm going, but I'm going." Thus the Blue piano catches the soul of Blanche, the miserable unusual human side of the girl which is beneath her frenetic duplicity, her trickery, lies, etc. It tells, it emotionally reminds you what all the fireworks are caused by.

Blanche—Physically. Must at all times give a single impression: her social mask is: *the High-Bred Genteel Lady in Distress.* Her past, her destiny, her falling from grace is just a surprise . . . then a tragic contradiction. But the mask never breaks down.

The only way to understand any character is through yourself. Everyone is much more alike than they willingly admit. Even as frantic and fantastic a creature as Blanche is created by things you have felt and known, *if you'll dig for them and be honest about what you see.*

STELLA

Spine—hold onto Stanley (Blanche the antagonist).

One reason Stella submits to Stanley's solution at the end, is perfectly ready to, is that she has an unconscious hostility toward Blanche. Blanche is so patronizing, demanding and superior toward her . . . makes her so useless, old-fashioned and helpless . . . everything that Stanley has got her out of. Stanley has made a woman out of her. Blanche immediately returns her to the subjugation of childhood, younger-sister-ness.

Stella would have been Blanche except for Stanley. She now knows what, how much Stanley means to her health. So . . . no matter what Stanley does . . . she must cling to him, as she does to life itself. **To** return to Blanche would be to return to the subjugation of the tradition.

The play is a triangle. Stella is the Apex. Unconsciously, Stella wants Blanche to go to Mitch because that will take Blanche off Stella.

And there is a Terrific Conflict between Blanche and Stella, especially in Stella's feelings. Blanche in effect in Sc. 1 *Resubjugates* Stella. Stella loves her, hates her, fears her, pities her, is really through with her. Finally rejects her for Stanley.

All this of course Stella is aware of only unconsciously. It becomes a matter of conscious choice only in Sc. 11 . . . the climax of the play as it is the climax of the triangle story.

Stella is a refined girl who has found a kind of salvation or realization, *but at a terrific price.* She keeps her eyes closed, even stays in bed as much as possible so that she won't realize, won't *feel* the pain of this terrific price. She walks around as if narcotized, as if sleepy, as if in a daze. She is waiting for night. She's waiting for the dark where Stanley makes her feel *only him* and she has no reminder of the price she is paying. She wants no intrusion from the other world. She is drugged, trapped. She's in a sensual stupor. She shuts out all challenge all day long. She loafs, does her hair, her nails, fixes a dress, doesn't eat much, but prepares Stanley's dinner and waits for Stanley. She hopes for no other meaning from life. Her pregnancy just makes it more so. Stanley is in her day and night. Her entire attention is to make herself pretty and attractive for Stanley, kill time till night. In a way she is actually narcotized all day. She is buried alive in her flesh. She's half asleep. She is glazed across her eyes. She doesn't seem to see much. She laughs incessantly like a child tickled and stops abruptly as the stimuli, the tickling, stops and returns to the same condition, a pleasantly drugged child. Give her all kinds of narcotized business.

She has a paradise—a serenely limited paradise when Blanche enters—but Blanche makes her consider Stanley, judge Stanley and find him wanting, for the first time. But it is too late. In the end she returns to Stanley.

Stella is doomed too. She has sold herself out for a temporary solution. She's given up all hope, everything, just to live for Stanley's pleasures. So she is dependent on Stanley's least whim. But this can last only as long as Stanley wants her. And *secondly* and *chiefly*— Stella herself cannot live narcotized forever. There is more to her. She begins to feel, even in the sex act, *taken*, unfulfilled—not recognized . . . and besides she's deeper, needs more variety. Her only hope is her children and, like so many women, she will begin to live more and more for her children.

She tries to conceal from herself her true needs through hiding and drugging herself in a sex relationship. But her real needs, for tenderness, for the several aspects of living, for realization in terms of herself—not only in terms of Stanley, *still live . . . she can't kill them* by ignoring them. Blanche, despite apparent failure, makes her realize certain things about Stanley. She hugs Stanley in Sc. 4 out of desperation, and out of a need to silence her doubts by the violence of sexual love (the "old reliable") . . . but Blanche has succeeded in calling Stella's attention to her own "sell-out" . . . she never sees Stanley the same again—or their relationship.

Stella, at the beginning of the play, won't face a *hostility* (concealed from herself and unrecognized) toward Stanley. She is *so* dependent on him, so compulsively compliant. She is giving up so much of herself, quieting so many voices of protest. She is Stanley's slave. She has sold out most of her life. Latent in Stella is rebellion. Blanche arouses it.

Stella is plain out of her head about Stanley. She has to keep herself from constantly touching him. She can hardly keep her hands off him. She is setting little traps all the time to conquer his act of indifference (he talks differently at night, in bed). She embarrasses him (though he is secretly proud) by following him places. They have a game where he tries to shake her all the time and she pursues him, etc. He makes her a panther in bed. He is her first man, really; he made her a woman. He fulfilled her more than she knew possible and she has to stop herself from *crawling* after him. She's utterly *blind* as to what's wrong with Stanley. She's blind to it and she doesn't care, *until* Blanche arrives. At the end of the play, her life is entirely different. It will never be the same with Stanley again.

Note from Tennessee Williams on the fourth day of rehearsal: "Gadge—I am a bit concerned over Stella in Scene One. It seems to me that she has too much vivacity, at times she is bouncing around in a way that suggests a co-ed on a benzedrine kick. I know it is impossible to be literal about the description 'narcotized tranquillity' but I do think there is an important value in suggesting it, in contrast to Blanche's rather feverish excitability. Blanche is the quick, light one. Stella is relatively slow and almost indolent. Blanche mentions her 'Chinese philosophy'—the way she sits with her little hands folded like a cherub in a choir, etc. I think her natural passivity is one of the things that makes her acceptance of Stanley acceptable. She naturally 'gives in,' accepts, lets things slide, she does not make much of an effort."

STANLEY

Spine—keep things his way (Blanche the antagonist).

The hedonist, objects, props, etc. Sucks on a cigar all day because he can't suck a teat. Fruit, food, etc. He's got it all figured out, what fits, what doesn't. The pleasure scheme. He has all the confidence of resurgent flesh.

Also with a kind of naïveté . . . even slowness . . . he means no harm. He wants to knock no one down. He only doesn't want to be taken advantage of. His code is simple and simple-minded. He is adjusted *now* . . . later, as his sexual powers die, so will he; the trouble will come later, the "problems."

But what is the chink in his armor now, the contradiction? Why does Blanche get so completely under his skin? Why does he want to bring Blanche and, before her, Stella *down to his level?* It's as if he said: "I know I haven't got much, but no one has more and no one's going to have more." It's the hoodlum aristocrat. He's deeply dissatisfied, deeply hopeless, deeply cynical . . . the physical immediate pleasures, if they come in a steady enough stream quiet this *as long as no one gets more* . . . then his bitterness comes forth and he tears down the pretender. But Blanche he can't seem to do anything with. She can't come down to his level so he levels her with his sex. He brings her right down to his level, beneath him.

One of the important things for Stanley is that Blanche *would wreck his home.* Blanche is dangerous. She is destructive. She would soon have him and Stella fighting. He's got things the way he wants them around there and he does *not* want them upset by a phony, corrupt, sick, destructive woman. *This makes Stanley right!* Are we going into the era of Stanley? He may be practical and right . . . but what the hell does it leave us? Make this a removed objective characterization for Marlon Brando.

Choose Marlon's objects . . . the things he loves and prizes: all sensuous and sensual—the shirt, the cigar, the beer (how it's poured and nursed, etc.).

The one thing that Stanley can't bear is someone who thinks that he or she is better than he. His only way of explaining himself—he thinks he stinks—is that everyone else stinks. This is symbolic. True of our National State of Cynicism. No values. There is nothing to command his loyalty. Stanley rapes Blanche because he has tried and tried to keep her down to his level. This way is the last. For a moment he succeeds. And then, in Scene 11, he has failed!

Stanley has got things his way. He fits into his environment. The culture and the civilization, even the neighborhood, etc., etc., the food, the drink, etc., are all his way. And he's got a great girl, with just enough hidden neuroticism for him—yet not enough to even threaten a real fight. Also their history is right: he conquered her.

Their relationship is right: she waits up for him. Finally God and Nature gave him a fine sensory apparatus . . . he enjoys! The main thing the actor has to do in the early scenes is make the physical environment of Stanley, the *props* come to life.

Stanley is deeply indifferent. When he first meets Blanche he doesn't really seem to care if she stays or not. Stanley is interested in his own pleasures. He is completely self-absorbed to the point of fascination.

To physicalize this: he has a most annoying way of being preoccupied—or of busying himself with something else while people are talking with him, at him it becomes. Example, first couple of pages Scene 2. Stanley thinks Stella is very badly brought up. She can't do any of the ordinary things—he had a girl before this that could really cook, but she drank an awful lot. Also she, Stella, has a lot of airs, most of which he's knocked out of her by now, but which still crop up. Emphasize Stanley's love for Stella. It is rough, embarrassed and he rather truculently *won't show it*. But it is there. He's proud of her. When he's not on guard and looking at her his eyes suddenly shine. He is grateful too, proud, satisfied. But he'd never show it, demonstrate it.

Stanley is supremely indifferent to everything except his own pleasure and comfort. He is marvelously selfish, a miracle of sensuous self-centeredness. He builds a hedonist life, and fights to the death to defend it—but finally it is *not* enough to hold Stella

and

this philosophy is not successful even for him—because every once in a while the silenced, frustrated part of Stanley breaks loose in unexpected and unpredictable ways and we suddenly see, as in a burst of lightning, his real frustrated self. Usually his frustration is worked off by eating a lot, drinking a lot, gambling a lot, fornicating a lot. He's going to get very fat later. He's desperately trying to squeeze out happiness by living by *ball and jowl* . . . and it really doesn't work . . . because it simply stores up violence and stores up violence, until **every *bar in the nation is full of Stanleys ready to explode.*** He's desperately trying to drug his senses . . . overwhelming them with a constant round of sensation so that he will feel nothing else.

In Stanley sex goes under a disguise. Nothing is more erotic and arousing to him than "airs" . . . she thinks she's better than me . . . I'll show her. . . . Sex equals domination . . . anything that challenges him—like calling him "common"—arouses him sexually.

In the case of Brando, the question of enjoyment is particularly important. Stanley feeds himself. His world is hedonist. But what does he enjoy. Sex equals sadism. It is his "equalizer." He conquers with his penis. But objects too—drunk. Conquest in poker, food . . . sweat. *Exercise.* But Enjoy! Not just cruel and *unpleasant* . . . but he never graduated from the baby who wants a constant nipple in his mouth. He yells when it's taken away.

As a character Stanley is most interesting in his "contradictions," his "soft" moments, his sudden pathetic little-tough-boy tenderness toward Stella. Scene 3 he cries like a baby. Somewhere in Scene 8 he almost makes it up with Blanche. In Scene 10 he *does* try to make it up with her—and except for her doing the one thing that most arouses him, both in anger and sex, he might have.

MITCH

Spine—get away from his Mother (Blanche the lever).

He wants the perfection his mother gave him . . . everything is approving, protective, *perfect for him.* Naturally no girl, today, no sensible, decent girl will give him this. But the tradition will.

Like Stella, Mitch hides from his own problem through mother-love.

Mitch is the end product of a matriarchy . . . his mother has robbed him of all daring, initiative, self-reliance. He does not face his own needs.

Mitch is Blanche's ideal in a comic form, 150 years late. He is big, tough, burly, has a rough southern voice and a manner of a homespun, coarse, awkward, overgrown boy, with a heart of mush. He's like that character (who cries easy) in *Sing Out Sweet Land*. He is a little embarrassed by his strength in front of women. He is straight out of Mack Sennett comedy—but Malden has to create the reality of it, the truth behind that corny image. Against his blundering strength there is shown off the fragility and fragrance of a girl. Her delicacy. "Lennie" in *Mice and Men*.

Mitch, too, is most interesting in his basic contradictions. He doesn't want to be Mother's Boy. Goddamn it he just can't help it. He does love his Mother, but is a little embarrassed at how much. Blanche makes a man out of him, makes him important and grown-up. His Mother—he dimly realizes—keeps him eternally adolescent, forever dependent.

Violence—he's full of sperm
                 energy
                 strength
the reason he's so clumsy with women is that he's so damn full of violent desire for them.

Mitch's Mask: He-man *mama's-boy*. This mask is a traditional, "corny" one in American dramatic literature. But it is true.

This play contains the crucial struggle of Mitch's life. For Mitch instinctively and even consciously, to a degree, knows what's wrong with him. He is jibed at often enough. And in his guts he knows they're right. Mitch, in his guts, hates his Mother. He loves her in a way—partially out of *early habit*, partially because she is clever—but much more fundamentally he *hates her*. It is a tragedy for him when he returns to her absolute sovereignty at the end. He will never meet another woman who will need him as much as Blanche and will need him to be a man as much as Blanche.

HAROLD CLURMAN

(b. 1901)

Some Preliminary Notes for
The Member of the Wedding

(November-December 1949)

"To put it as simply as possible, the function of the stage director is to translate a play text into stage terms: that is, to make the play as written, clear, interesting, enjoyable, by means of living actors, sounds, colors, movement." With these words Harold Clurman defines the task of the director. From his earliest productions as a mentor of the Group Theatre, interpretation has always been the creative keynote of this sensitive, articulate director. How he initiates and develops the process of interpreting the language of the script in theatrical terms is revealed in this specimen of the personal notes he prepares for himself during the formative period of production. To accompany their publication here, Mr. Clurman has written a retrospective postscript which indicates the manner in which he employs the notations he makes in his "little book."

What is the audience to enjoy?

The poetry of first impulses expressed naïvely, sweetly, directly. The first "shoots" of life and emotion (adolescent longing) appreciated by grownups thinking back on the purity of their first contact with life.

The production style

Poetic—which means concentrated: every moment visually significant of the inner state.

311

The *main action of the play*: to get "connected."

It all happens in a hot summer atmosphere. The world is "dead"—the people suspended. Everything is slightly strange, not altogether real.

"Less us have a good time" says John Henry. He seeks "connection" but there's so little to connect with in this environment.

People who seek connection and aren't able to—ache. Frankie aches all the time. Her sobbing in the first act is the climax of an ache delicately indicated all through . . . part of the loneliness inherent in the main action.

(Frankie has no one to talk to about her resolve—so she talks to strangers: the Monkey Man or to a cat. . . . She wants connection with the whole wide world of experience.)

A stage direction reads: "Frankie scrapes her head against door." These strange gestures of children make one think that they are re-enacting man's past living through the ages—animal-like, weird, primitive. More of such "gestures" must be invented for Frankie. "Flying around the world together"—Frankie will "fly" through the kitchen.

A mighty loneliness emanates from this play. It is as if all the characters were separated from the world—as if the world were only a mirage in a vaporous space making wraiths of the people.

The Main Actions for the Leading Characters

Frankie

Her main action—*to get out of herself.*

Getting out of herself means *growth.* . . . She has "growing pains": she is both tortured and happy through them. . . . The juices of life are pouring through her. She is a fragile container of this strange elixir.

Growth twists and turns her—as it does us—gives us new shapes. Frankie twists and turns. The play is the lyric drama of Frankie's growth. At the end of the play, she runs or twirls out—"to go around the world." She has achieved her aim—imaginatively. She is ready "to get out of herself."

The Main Characteristics

1) Frankie is tomboyish. (She puts on no shows with kissing. Her father is a "widowman" with his nose to the grindstone. She has no mother, no "social" environment.)

2) Frankie is crazy with first love: literally head over heels: the love of the *wedding*.

3) She is intense. She's trying to see underneath everything, seize its essence, "cozen it in her mind"; she even tries to seize the atmosphere of heat as a unique experience. "The kitchen's the hottest place in the U. S." she says.

   Thus she is a "poetic" character. She is terribly aware of every little thing: Berenice's fur, Frankie says, has "a sad, foxwise face."

4) All the above produces an awkwardness that is weird and occasionally graceful.

5) Frankie is hostile. You hate what you can't connect with and want to hurt it. Or you want to hurt yourself for failing to make the connection.

6) She is given to self-examination. She is self-absorbed in relation to her desire for connection and wanting to "get out."

7) Her torture comes from a sense of a past vaguely remembered, troubled and painful—and the future—wondrous, void, unrealized and therefore frustrating. "I have this feeling," she moans.

8) She is imaginative. Her mind and spirit leap: they stretch, lift, dart, fly . . . to whatever place she wants to go. When the destination is too vague, she explodes or drifts in all directions.

   (Remind Julie Harris: The main action makes her a very active character. She is straining to get out. When she fails, she has one sort of emotion; when she almost succeeds, another.)

Frankie is fascinated by Honey. He is romantic, exciting, lightfoot. He's been "out."

Berenice Sadie Brown

To do her deed (*work*) . . . *"normally."*

For her to live is to be connected.

A woman who is naturally and easily connected. Once she was connected with Ludie Maxwell Freeman. He died. "It leaves you lonesome afterward." After that, she sought connection with scraps and bits of what she loved—even to a madman. Now she's alone, relatively unconnected. But she manages somehow to connect with her community, with T.T., with Honey, with John Henry—but some people she doesn't desire connection with (Mrs. West, "them Germans and Japs," Mary Littlejohn.) Of John Henry she says, "We enjoys him." It's as simple as that. Everything is approached without fuss, without sentimentality, without "eloquence."

She is plain—direct, earthy, quiet. Hers is the poetry of the "prosaic!" She's basic: "Two is company" she says.

Her life "We just talks and passes the time of the day"—that's enough.

"Stop commenting about it" she tells Frankie. She does not need to "comment" to make things real to herself.

"Sunday will come." Sufficient unto the day——

When people want to go away from her—John Henry or Frankie or Honey—she just lets them go.

Unnaturalness ("freaks") give her the creeps.

She rarely tries to prevent anything from happening that seems to have to happen: when Frankie wants to take a splinter out of her foot with a kitchen knife, when Frankie smokes, when Honey needs a stimulant, when Frankie rushes out to the town, she cautions, but does not fight. ("I'm just trying to head this thing off, but I see it's no use.")

This is her wisdom: the acceptance of the pain and sorrow of life. All this is, as she puts it, a "thing known and not spoken."

Her movement is quiet, solid, strong. Her eyes look deep with a slight slanting glance—so that she may see better out of her one good eye.

And suddenly——

She too feels the loneliness, the fear, the terror of life . . . and needs consolation from John Henry or anyone else. This pain of life is always sensed by her, but she lives on despite it. She knows the irony of life—John Henry's death—she didn't believe he was sick—a rebuke to her "practicality," to her too-sensible nature.

She ends alone—tragic, majestic, patient, waiting . . . while Frankie dashes out joyously to learn—some of the things Berenice knows.

This contrast in their destinies (that of Frankie and Berenice) must be clear in action at the end. They change "colors"—Frankie becomes more "extroverted" and "superficial" at the end. Berenice more quietly profound than ever.

John Henry

To learn to connect.

The pathos of the child is that it imitates the process of life as it beholds life being lived. There is mystery and comedy in this, too.

The child repeats a pattern of behavior without realizing its significance. The child has hardly any conscious tastes, appetites, or desires (they all seem automatic).

The child develops conscious appetites and ideas through imitation.

Hence it is likely to imitate bad things as well as good, it might kill or die almost as easily as live and love. The environment teaches the

child through its tendency to imitate, its capacity to be formed unconsciously.

The child's imitation is a species of attachment: hence the child appears to be "loving." It loves to repeat what it sees and hears—and
since most life is an effort to "connect"—the child is always learning
to connect and so grows to be a man.

"Me too" is the keynote. But since this is just the sign of a desire to
follow or imitate a pattern without any reason or justification beyond
what appears to be merely an imitative impulse—it strikes us (grownups) as funny.

John Henry says "how pretty" about Frankie's dress, but repeats
Berenice's less flattering description; that is, he imitates Berenice, at-
taching himself or reflecting her . . . so that Frankie calls him "a dou-
ble-faced Judas."

The child reflects life: it reflects connection, attachment, but it has to
learn to develop a conscious connection which it doesn't possess at
first.

The child's lack of consciousness makes much of its behavior seem
meaningless and mysterious. Hence there is something sad as well as
funny, and, from a conscious point of view, oddly pathetic about the
child.

The child is fragile: death is "natural" to it . . . it is always close to
death. The "realest" thing John Henry does is to say he is sick, but because he says such things as a reflex he is not taken seriously.

A child is like the light of a flickering candle—bright, gay, pretty, sad,
extremely sensitive to the atmosphere around it—easy to intensify or
to extinguish.

Frankie wants to get out of herself so that she can connect, even more
with the world. Berenice connects because she has learned to live and
John Henry is learning the process in the unconscious way of a child—
but he stops (dies) before he has gone very far in the process. . . . In

a word, he presents the image of the fragility of the whole process—hence our tender feeling toward him. How susceptible he is (the life process) to destruction—disappearance—"the ghost in the arbor with a little silver ring!"

The first step in connection after imitation is attachment and from the attachment, "love" develops which we observe in John Henry's consolation of Frankie and Berenice.

When the child's connection is sharply cut off, it becomes afraid—"scarey." It has become used to the connection. The child isn't a bit lonesome (as John Henry says) but comes running to get together—connected—with what he has become used to.

The child "studies" to be a man. Observe the rapt look of a concentrated child. This "study" is the essence of the child's activity—the study and the action that follows—sometimes slow and hesitant, sometimes sudden as if inspired.

Addams (Frankie's father)

To keep in touch.

He can barely make it. . . . His connection is faltering, bleak. "Marriage is a sacred institution," he says, but it's a long time since he's been married. He keeps on going, but he has connection only with memories and the little mechanisms—watches—to which he has set, automatic responses.

Life is queer, a little strange or "funny" to him—he has a trace of humor—— Life is sad for him because its objects are dim, sweet because he realizes no evil, sour because he's pushed into a corner and his area of nourishment is limited.

He's widowed of life. "A good provider"—he works without aim. He pets life (Frankie) in passing, and wanders off into bleakness—and rest.

All that remains to him is his "white superiority." Even his porter doesn't show up to work for him. People don't pay attention to him—because he's not there for them. ("Answer me when I call.")

Handling people who are "alive" embarrasses him. He's "evasive"—constantly clearing his throat in embarrassment.

A baffled man.

Jarvis

To make the simplest connection . . .
  with the first thing that's nice—a girl.

He's an ordinary boy—rather unimaginative—his father's son—proper, good-natured, conventional, cautious—pleasant and inconspicuous—except to Frankie and people who admire his looks.

He smiles a lot, friendly, even sentimental, normally affectionate, but without much expression. He is comparatively "mute"—awkward in expressing his feelings. Affectionate gibberish is the best he can manage in response to Frankie's adoration.

T.T.

To make as much connection as he can find.

Modest, resigned, soft, unhappy. He hasn't enough energy for his unhappiness to develop into resentment. He is acquiescent.

He is self-effacing, "understanding," honorable—"understanding" in a mediocre, practical way. Hence his deaconish fat. "Respected"—walking in a state of grace. He is almost "womanish" (or eunuch-like.)

He would take a blow, quietly, hurt, unangry. ("I'm not particular—whichever way is convenient.")

He's even afraid—or at least shy—of being unseemly in front of Frankie. . . .

Yet he is not obsequious—honorable in a way, dignified, understanding and kindly—slightly depressed.

Honey Brown

To force connection—(or die).

Rejected, humiliated, his only connection is through violence, hostility (defiance) or mad escape ("snow," liquor, the protection and romance of jazz.)

He is depressed and crazed by his own violence.

He's always on the verge of breaking loose or getting into a stupor of sadness—followed by an outbreak toward escape. He's repentant about hurting John Henry—for a second—tries to make up for it by playing with him, giving him money.

He has a kind of hysterical lyricism about him—(his movements are dance-like in their nervousness).

A kind of terrified joy in being pursued. He takes a kind of mad pleasure in his violent connection through pistol or razor. . . .

Explanation of the Above (December 1952)

Such notes set down for my own use when I have read a play at least a half-dozen times are never communicated to the actors in the form which they take in my "little book." They would be unintelligible to actors in this form as well as practically useless. They serve to make the thought and sentiments I experience in reading the script somewhat more specific than they might be if I allowed them to remain inchoate within myself. They are springboards and tracers for my own feelings. They lead me on and point to the objectives I hope to attain.

(What folly it would be to "explain" my notes on John Henry to a seven-year-old actor. But I found things for Brandon de Wilde to *do* which were a concrete embodiment of my "abstract ideas.")

With these notes as a basis, I am able to approach the actor. In rehearsal (by careful study and observation of my actors) I find the best way of directing—stimulating, leading—the actors—by allusion, suggestion, explanation, encouragement, demonstration, criticism. The method of reaching the actor varies with the gifts, character and total personality of each actor. There is no right way—except the way that brings results.

More decisive than any of these notes is my line by line "breakdown" of the script, which indicates the aim of each scene and what particular actions and adjustment (mood) moment by moment the actor must carry out and convey. These actions—what the character wants to do and why—together with any physical action (or "stage business") which might result from the character's purpose are duly noted by the director or, in most cases in my own work, they may be left to the actor's nature and imagination—under the director's guidance—to accomplish.

My working script is packed with notations for almost every moment of the play, but this does not delude me into believing that the entire direction of a play can be written down or that I, or anybody else, can direct from the written notes alone. The play on the stage is written with and through the actor's being. One works with flesh, blood and spirit much more than with the words one has written or spoken to the actor.

SELECTED BIBLIOGRAPHY

BIBLIOGRAPHY

The following selected bibliography, centering on the figures represented in this volume, contains (I) books by and about individual directors, (II) pertinent general volumes and periodicals, and (III) historical studies of special value in the preparation of the introduction "The Emergence of the Director."

I

Antoine, André: "Causerie sur la mise en scène." *La Revue de Paris,* X, April 1, 1903, 596-612.

Antoine, André: *Mes Souvenirs sur le Théâtre Antoine et sur L'Odéon.* Paris: Bernard Grosset, 1928.

Antoine, André: *Mes Souvenirs sur le Théâtre Libre.* Paris: Artheme Fayard, 1921.

Antoine, André: *Le Théâtre.* 2 vols. Paris: Les Editions de France, 1932.

Antoine, André: *Le Théâtre Libre.* Paris: May 1890.

Thalasso, A.: *Le Théâtre Libre.* Paris: Mercure de France, 1909.

Waxman, Samuel M.: *Antoine and the Theatre Libre.* Harvard University Press, 1926.

"Adolphe Appia: A Memorial." *Theatre Arts Monthly,* XVI, August 1932.

Appia, Adolphe: *Art vivant ou nature morte?* Milan: Bottegia di Poesia, 1923. (This essay is available in English translation in the *Theatre Annual,* 1943)

Appia, Adolphe: "Comment reformer notre mise en scène." *La Revue* (*Revue des Revues*), L, June 1, 1904, 342-349.

Appia, Adolphe: *Goethes Faust: Erster Teil als Dichtung Dargestellt.* Bonn: Fritz Klopp Verlag, 1929.

Appia, Adolphe: *La mise en scène du drame Wagnérien.* Paris: L. Chailley, 1895. (An unpublished English translation by Robert Sencer of the above titled *Staging Wagnerian Drama* was made available to the editors.)

Appia, Adolphe: *Die Musik und die Inscenierung.* Munich: F. Bruckmann, 1899. (The above work, originally written in French, is available in that language in manuscript at the Main Reference Branch of the New York Public Library.)

Appia, Adolphe: *L'Oeuvre d'art vivant*. Paris: Atar, 1921.

Appia, Adolphe: "The Staging of Tristan and Isolde." Translated by Lee Simonson. *Theatre Workshop*, I, April-July 1937, 61-72.

Artaud, Antonin: *Le Théâtre et son double*. Paris: Gallimard, 1938.

Barrault, Jean-Louis: *Phèdre de Jean Racine, mise en scène et commentaires de Jean-Louis Barrault*. Paris: Editions du Seuil, 1946.

Barrault, Jean-Louis: *Reflections on the Theatre*. Translated by Barbara Wall. New York: Macmillan, 1952.

Barrault, Jean-Louis: *Une Troupe et ses auteurs; extraits et commentaires à propos de; Shakespeare, Molière, Marivaux, Claudel, Gide, Kafka, Feydeau, M. Archaud et J. P. Sartre*. Paris: Compagnie M. Renaud—J. L. Barrault, et J. Vautrain, 1950.

Baty, Gaston: *Le Masque et l'encensoir; introduction à une esthétique du théâtre*. Paris: Bloud & Gay, 1926.

Baty, Gaston: *Théâtre nouveau; notes et documents*. Paris: A la Société des Spectacles, 1927.

Baty, Gaston: *Rideau Baisse*. Bordas, 1949.

Blanchart, Paul: *Gaston Baty*. Paris: Editions de la Nouvelle Revue Critique, 1939.

Belasco, David: *The Theatre Through Its Stage Door*. Edited by Louis V. Defoe. New York: Harper and Brothers, 1919.

Huneker, James Gibbons: "David Belasco," American Producers, III. *Theatre Arts Magazine*, V, October 1921, 259-267.

Winter, William: *The Life of David Belasco*. 2 vols. New York: Moffat, Yard, 1918.

Bentley, Eric: "Discovering a Play; Directing Lorca's House of Bernarda Alba at the Abbey Theatre, Dublin," in *In Search of Theater*. New York: Alfred A. Knopf, 1953.

Brahm, Otto: *Kritische Schriften über Drama und Theater*. Berlin: S. Fischer, 1913.

Henze, Herbert: *Otto Brahm und das Deutsche Theater in Berlin*. Berlin: E. S. Mittler und Sohn, 1930. (An abridged adaptation of this work in English by Frank Freudenthal under the title "Otto Brahm and Naturalist Directing" appears in the *Theatre Workshop*, I, April-July 1937, 13-28.)

Newmark, Maxim: *Otto Brahm: The Man and the Critic*. New York: G. E. Stechert, 1938.

Brecht, Bertolt: *Antigonemodell.* Berlin: Gebrueder Weiss, 1949.

Brecht, Bertolt: A *Little Organum for the Theatre.* Translated by Beatrice Gottlieb. *Accent,* IV, winter 1951, 13-40.

Brecht, Bertolt: "A Model for Epic Theatre." Translated by Eric Bentley. *The Sewanee Review,* LVII, summer 1949, 425-436.

Brecht, Bertolt: *Mutter Courage Modell.* Frankfurt: Suhrkamp, 1952.

Brecht, Bertolt: "A New Technique of Acting." Translated by Eric Bentley. *Theatre Arts,* XXXIII, January 1949, 38-40.

Brecht, Bertolt: "Notes for *The Three-Penny Opera*" in *From the Modern Repertoire,* Series One, edited by Eric Bentley. University of Denver Press, 1949, 391-400.

Brecht, Bertolt: *Theaterarbeit.* Dresden: VVV Dresdner Verlag, 1952.

Bentley, Eric: "German Stagecraft Today." *Kenyon Review,* XI, autumn 1949.

Gorelik, Mordecai: "Epic Realism: Brecht's Notes on the *Three-Penny Opera.*" *Theatre Workshop,* I, April-July 1937, 29-40.

Browne, Maurice: "The New Rhythmic Drama." *Drama,* IV, November 1914, 616-630, V, February 1915, 146-160.

Roeder, Ralph: "Maurice Browne," American Producers, I. *Theatre Arts Magazine,* V, April 1921, 113-124.

Clurman, Harold: "The Director's Job." *New Republic,* Vol. 121, August 8, 1949, 20-22, August 15, 20-21.

Clurman, Harold: *The Fervent Years: The Story of the Group Theatre and the Thirties.* New York: Alfred A. Knopf, 1945.

Clurman, Harold: "In A Different Language." *Theatre Arts,* XXXIV, January 1950, 18-20.

Clurman, Harold: "Interpretation and Characterization." *New Theatre,* III, January 1936, 21, 44.

Copeau, Jacques: "L'ecole du Vieux Colombier," *Les Cahier du Vieux Colombier,* November 2, 1921. Paris: Editions de la Nouvelle Revue Française.

Copeau, Jacques: *Etudes d'art dramatique, critiques d'un autre temps.* Paris: Editions de la Nouvelle Revue Française, 1923.

Copeau, Jacques: *Les Fourberies de Scapin de Molière, mise en scène et commentaires.* Préface de Louis Jouvet. Paris: Editions du Seuil, 1951.

Copeau, Jacques: "La mise en scène." *Encyclopédie Française,* December 1935, 17'64, 1-5.

Copeau, Jacques: *Souvenirs du Vieux-Colombier*. Paris: Nouvelle Edition Latine, 1931.

Frank, Waldo: *The Art of the Vieux Colombier*. Paris: Editions de la Nouvelle Revue Française, 1918.

Kurtz, Maurice: *Jacques Copeau*. Paris: Les Editions Nagel, 1950.

Roeder, Ralph: "Copeau 1921." *Theatre Arts Magazine*, V, October 1921, 279-292.

Craig, Edward Gordon: *The Art of the Theatre*. London: T. N. Foulis, 1905.

Craig, Edward Gordon: *On the Art of the Theatre*. Chicago: Browne's Bookstore, 1912.

Craig, Edward Gordon: *A Production—Being Thirty-Two Collotype Plates of Designs Projected or Realized for The Pretenders of Henrik Ibsen*. London: Oxford University Press, 1930.

Craig, Edward Gordon: *Scene*. London: Oxford University Press, 1923.

Craig, Edward Gordon: *The Theatre—Advancing*. Boston: Little, Brown & Co., 1919.

Craig, Edward Gordon: *Towards a New Theatre: Forty Designs with Critical Notes*. London: J. M. Dent and Sons, Ltd., 1913.

Leeper, Janet: *Edward Gordon Craig: Designs for the Theatre*. London: Penguin Books, 1948.

Rose, Enid: *Gordon Craig and the Theatre*. London: S. Low, Marston & Co., 1931.

Dullin, Charles: *L'Avare de Molière, mise en scène et commentaires de Charles Dullin*. Paris: Editions du Seuil, 1946.

Dullin, Charles: *Cinna de Pierre Corneille, mise en scène et commentaires de Charles Dullin*. Paris: Editions du Seuil, 1948.

Dullin, Charles: *Souvenirs et notes de travail d'un acteur*. Paris: O. Lieutier, 1946.

Crozier, Eric: "Charles Dullin and the Atelier." *Theatre Arts Monthly*, XX, March 1936, 197-200.

Fuchs, Georg: *Die Revolution des Theaters*. Leipzig: Georg Mueller, 1909.

Gémier, Firmin: *Le Théâtre*, Entretiens réunis par Paul Gsell. Paris: B. Grosset, 1925.

Gielgud, John: *Early Stages*. New York: Macmillan, 1939.

Gielgud, John: "Staging *Love for Love*." *Theatre Arts*, XXVII, November 1943, 662-668.

Gilder, Rosamond: *John Gielgud's Hamlet: A Record of Performance, With Notes on Costume, Scenery and Stage Business by John Gielgud.* New York: Oxford University Press, 1937.

Granville-Barker, Harley: *The Exemplary Theatre.* London: Chatto and Windus, 1922.

Granville-Barker, Harley: "Rehearsing a Play." *Theatre,* XXX, September 1919, 142, 204, October, 236.

Granville-Barker, Harley: *Shakespeare's Comedy of Twelfth Night; An Acting Edition with a Producer's Preface.* London: 1912.

Granville-Barker, Harley: *The Winter's Tale . . . an Acting Edition Prepared with a Preface.* London: 1912.

Guthrie, Tyrone: "The Producer's Job." *Listener,* March 20, 1941, 419-420.

Guthrie, Tyrone: "Some Notes on Direction." *Theatre Arts,* XXVIII, November 1944, 649-653.

Guthrie, Tyrone: *Theatre Prospect.* London: Wishart & Co., 1932.

Hopkins, Arthur: *How's Your Second Act?* New York: Philip Goodman Company, 1918.

Hopkins, Arthur: *Reference Point.* New York: Samuel French, 1948.
  Eaton, Walter Prichard: "Arthur Hopkins," American Producers, II. *Theatre Arts Magazine,* V, July 1921, 230-236.

Jessner, Leopold: "*Weber* Inscenierung IV, Act Die Plunderung." *Die Scene,* March 1928, 92-94. (This is a special issue of *Die Scene* devoted entirely to the work of Jessner.)
  Bluth, K. T.: *Leopold Jessner.* Berlin: Oesterheld, 1928.
  Grabbe, C. D.: *Hannibal: Bühneneinrichtung von Leopold Jessner.* Berlin: Oesterheld Verlag, 1926.
  Ziege, Felix: *Leopold Jessner und das Zeit-Theater.* Berlin: Eigenbroedler Verlag, 1928.

Jouvet, Louis: "Problemes de la mise en scène des chefs-d'oeuvre classiques; le point de vue du metteur en scène." *Revue d'Histoire du Theatre,* No. 4, 1951, 378-387.

Jouvet, Louis: "The Profession of the Producer." *Theatre Arts Monthly,* XX, December 1936, 943-949, XXI, January 1937, 57-64.

Jouvet, Louis: *Reflexions du comédien.* Paris: Editions de la Nouvelle Revue Critique, 1938.

Jouvet, Louis: *Temoignages sur le théâtre.* Paris: Flammarion, 1952.

Cezan, Claude: *Louis Jouvet et le théâtre d'aujourd'hui*. Paris: Editions Emile-Paul Freres, 1938.

"Louis Jouvet, 1887-1951 Notes et Documents." *Revue d'Histoire du Theatre*, No. 1, 1952.

Kazan, Elia

Isaacs, H. R.: "First Rehearsals: E. Kazan directs a modern legend: *Jacobowsky and the Colonel* by F. Werfel." *Theatre Arts*, XXVIII, March 1944, 143-150.

Kommisarjevsky, Theodore: *Myself and the Theatre*. New York: E. P. Dutton, 1930.

Kommisarjevsky, Theodore: "The Producer in the Theatre." *Drama*, XIII, November 1934, 19-21, December, 35-37.

Lugne-Poe, Aurelie: *Sous les étoiles, souvenirs de théâtre, 1902-1912*. Paris: Gallimard, 1933.

Jasper, Gertrude R.: *Adventure in the Theatre: Lugne-Poe and the Theatre de l'Oeuvre to 1899*. New Brunswick: Rutgers University Press, 1947.

Meyerhold, Vsevolod: "The Booth." Translated by A. Bakshy. *Drama*, No. 26, May 1917, 203-216, No. 27, August 1917, 425-447.

Meyerhold, Vsevolod: "Na repetitzia Revizora." *Teatr i Dramaturgia*, February 1934, 40-42.

Meyerhold, Vsevolod: *O Teatre*. Petrograd: 1913.

Alpers, B.: *The Theatre of the Social Mask*. Translated by Mark Schmidt. New York: The Group Theatre, 1934.

Bely, A. and Others: *Gogol i Meyerkhold*. Moscow: 1927.

Fagin, Bryllian: "Meyerhold Rehearses a Scene." *Theatre Arts Monthly*, XVI, October 1932, 833-836.

Lozowick, Louis: "V. E. Meyerhold and his Theatre." *Hound and Horn*, IV, October-December 1930, 95-105.

Strasberg, Lee: "The Magic of Meyerhold." *New Theatre*, I, September 1934, 14-15, 30.

Volkov, Nikolai: *Meyerkhold*. 2 vols. Moscow: Academia, 1929.

Nemirovich-Danchenko, Vladimir: "Danchenko Directs: Notes on *The Three Sisters*." *Theatre Arts*, XXVII, October 1943, 603-606.

Nemirovich-Danchenko, Vladimir: *Julius Caesar: Publikatsiia Rezhisserskoi Partituri (Publication of the Director's Promptbook of Julius Caesar)* in *Moscow Art Theatre Yearbook*, 1944, 551-670. Moscow: Museum of the Moscow Art Theatre, 1947.

Nemirovich-Danchenko, Vladimir: *My Life in the Russian Theatre*.

Translated by John Cournos. Boston: Little, Brown & Co., 1936.
Okhlopkov, Nikolai: See *Moscow Rehearsals* by Norris Houghton and *Theatre in Soviet Russia* by Andre Van Gyseghem.
Piscator, Erwin: "Objective Acting," in *Actors on Acting*. Edited by Toby Cole and Helen Krich Chinoy. New York: Crown Publishers, 1949, 285-291.
Piscator, Erwin: *Das Politische Theater*. Berlin: Adalbert Schultz, 1929.
Pitoëff, Georges: *Notre Théâtre*. Paris: Messages, 1949.
Reinhardt, Max
    Carter, Huntly: *The Theatre of Max Reinhardt*. New York: Mitchell Kennerly, 1914.
    Fleischmann, Benno: *Max Reinhardt; Die Wierdererweckung des Barocktheaters*. Vienna: P. Neff, 1948.
    Herald, Heinz: *Max Reinhardt; Ein Versuch über das Wesen der Modernen Regie*. Berlin: F. Lehmann, 1915.
    Jacobsohn, Siegfried: *Max Reinhardt*. Berlin: Erich Reiss, 1910.
    Rothe, Hans: *Max Reinhardt 25 Jahre Deutsches Theater*. Munich: R. Piper & Co., 1930.
    Sayler, Oliver M., editor: *Max Reinhardt and his Theatre*. New York: Brentano's, 1924.
Sakhnovski, V.: *Rezhissura i Metodika ee Prepodavanie (Directing and Methods of Teaching It)*. Moscow: Iskusstvo, 1939.
Saxe-Meiningen, George II, Duke of
    Grube, Max: *Geschichte der Meininger*. Stuttgart: Deutsche Verlags-Anstalt, 1926.
    See also *The Stage is Set* by Lee Simonson and *New Theatres for Old* by Mordecai Gorelik.
Shaw, George Bernard: *The Art of Rehearsal*. New York: Samuel French, 1928.
Shaw, George Bernard: *Dramatic Opinions and Essays*. 2 vols. New York: Brentano's, 1928.
Shaw, George Bernard: *Our Theatres in the Nineties*. 3 vols. London: Constable & Co., 1932.
D'Angelo, Evelyn: "Shaw's Theory of Stage Representation." *Quarterly Journal of Speech*, XV, June 1929, 330-349.
Stanislavsky, Konstantin S.: *An Actor Prepares*. Translated by Elizabeth Reynolds Hapgood. New York: Theatre Arts, 1936.
Stanislavsky, Konstantin S.: *Building a Character*. Translated by

Elizabeth Reynolds Hapgood. New York: Theatre Arts Books, 1949.

Stanislavsky, Konstantin S.: *My Life in Art.* Translated by J. J. Robbins. New York: Theatre Arts Books, 1948.

Stanislavsky, Konstantin S.: *Na Dne: Rezhisserskii Ekzempliar* (*The Lower Depths: Director's Copy*) in *Moscow Art Theatre Yearbook*, 1945, 4-279. Moscow: Museum of the Moscow Art Theatre, 1948.

Stanislavsky, Konstantin S.: *The Seagull Produced by Stanislavsky.* Translated by David Magarshack. New York: Theatre Arts Books, 1952.

Stanislavsky, Konstantin S.: *Stanislavsky on the Art of the Stage.* Introduced and translated by David Magarshack. London: Faber and Faber, Ltd., 1950.

Stanislavsky, Konstantin S.: *Stanislavsky Produces Othello.* Translated by Dr. Helen Nowak. London: Geoffrey Bles, 1948.

Clurman, Harold: "Conversation with Two Masters." *Theatre Arts Monthly,* XIX, November 1935, 871-876.

Cole, Toby, editor: *Acting: A Handbook of the Stanislavsky Method.* New York: Crown Publishers, 1947.

Gorchakov, N.: *Rezhisserskiie Uroki Stanislavskovo* (Directing Lessons of Stanislavsky). Moscow: 1951.

Magarshack, David: *Stanislavsky: A Life.* New York: Chanticleer Press, 1951.

Toporkov, V.: *K. S. Stanislavskii na Repetitzii* (Stanislavsky at Rehearsal). Moscow: Iskusstvo, 1950.

Strasberg, Lee: "The Director," in *The Theatre Handbook,* edited by Bernard Sobel. New York: Crown Publishers, 1948, 219-220.

Tairov, Alexander: *Zapiski Rezhissera* (*Notes of a Régisseur*). Moscow: 1921. (More widely available in the German edition *Das Entfesselte Theater,* Potsdam, G. Kiepenheuer, 1923)

Vakhtangov, Eugene: *Zapiski, Pisma, Stati* (Notes, Letters, Articles). Moscow: Iskusstvo, 1939.

Webster, Margaret: "Credo of a Director." *Theatre Arts Monthly,* XXII, May 1938, 343-348.

Webster, Margaret: *Shakespeare Without Tears.* New York: Whittlesey House, 1942.

Zakhava, B. E.: *Igor Bulichov i Drugie, Rezhisserskii Kommentarii*

(*Yegor Bulichev and Others, Director's Comments*). Moscow: 1937.

Zakhava, B. E.: "Principles of Directing." *Theatre Workshop*, I, April-July 1937, 43-58, September-October 1937, 14-33.

Zavadsky, Yuri: "Conversation with a Young Regisseur." *Theatre Arts Monthly*, XX, September 1936, 726-730.

II

Art of Directing Issue, *Theatre Workshop*, I, April-July 1937.

Bab, Julius: *Das Theater der Gegenwart*. Leipzig: Weber, 1928.

Ben-Ari, R.: "Four Directors and the Actor." *Theatre Workshop*, I, January-March 1937, 65-74.

Bentley, Eric: *The Playwright as Thinker*. New York: Reynal & Hitchcock, 1946.

Blanchart, Paul: *Histoire de la mise en scène*. Paris: Presses Universitaires de France, 1948.

Blanck, Karl and Heinz Haufe: *Unbekanntes Theater; Ein Buch der Regie*. Stuttgart: J. G. Gotta'sche Buchhandlung Nachfolger, 1940.

Brassilach, Robert: *Animateurs de théâtre*. Paris: Corrêa, 1936.

Bricker, H. L., editor: *Our Theatre Today*. New York: Samuel French, 1936.

Carter, Huntly: *The New Spirit in the European Theatre, 1914-1924*. New York: George H. Doran, 1925.

Carter, Huntly: *The New Spirit in the Russian Theatre, 1917-1928*. New York: Brentano's, 1929.

Cheney, Sheldon: *The Art Theatre*. New York: Alfred A. Knopf, 1925.

Cheney, Sheldon: "The Most Important Thing in the Theatre." *Theatre Arts Magazine*, I, August 1917.

Cheney, Sheldon: *The New Movement in the Theatre*. New York: Mitchell Kennerly, 1914.

Clark, Barrett H. and George Freedley: *A History of the Modern Drama*. New York: D. Appleton-Century, 1947.

Cole, Toby and Helen Krich Chinoy, editors: *Actors on Acting*. New York: Crown Publishers, 1949.

D'Amico, Silvio: *La Regia Teatrale*. Rome: Angelo Belardetti Editore, 1947.

Dickinson, Thomas H.: *The Theatre in a Changing Europe*. New York: Henry Holt, 1937.

Eustis, Morton: "The Director Takes Command." *Theatre Arts Monthly*, XX, February, March, April 1936. (A series of interviews with George Abbott, Guthrie McClintic, Max Reinhardt, Robert Sinclair, John Murray Anderson and Harold Clurman.)

Fergusson, Francis: *The Idea of a Theatre*. Princeton University Press, 1951.

Fuerst, Walter Rene and Samuel J. Hume: *Twentieth Century Stage Decoration*. 2 vols. London: Knopf, 1928.

Gassner, John: *Producing the Play*. New York: The Dryden Press, 1952.

Gervais, A. C.: *Propos sur la mise en scène*. Paris: Editions Françaises Nouvelles, 1943.

Gorchakov, N.: *Besedi o Rezhissure* (Discussions on Directing). Moscow: Iskusstvo, 1941.

Gorelik, Mordecai: *New Theatres for Old*. New York: Samuel French, 1948.

Gyseghem, Andre Van: *Theatre in Soviet Russia*. London: Faber and Faber, Ltd., 1943.

Hagemann, Carl: *Die Kunst der Bühne*. Vol. I: *Regie*. Berlin: Deutsche Verlags-Anstalt, 1922.

Houghton, Norris: *Moscow Rehearsals: An Account of Methods of Production in the Soviet Theatre*. New York: Harcourt, Brace & Co., 1936.

Ihering, Herbert: *Reinhardt, Jessner, Piscator oder Klassikertod*. Berlin: Ernst Rowohlt Verlag, 1929.

Isaacs, Edith J. R., editor: *Theatre: Essays on the Arts of the Theatre*. Boston: Little, Brown & Co., 1927.

Kutscher, Artur: *Grundriss der Theater-Wissenschaft*. Munich: Verlag Kurt Desch, 1936.

Legband, Paul: *Der Regisseur*. Hamburg: J. P. Toth Verlag, 1947.

Macgowan, Kenneth and Robert Edmond Jones: *Continental Stagecraft*. New York: Harcourt, Brace & Co., 1922.

Macgowan, Kenneth: *Theatre of Tomorrow*. New York: Boni and Liveright, 1921.

Moderwell, Hiram Kelly: *The Theatre of Today*. New York: Dodd, Mead & Co., 1927.

Moscow Art Theatre Yearbooks, 1943, 1944, 1945, 1946, 1947, 1948. Moscow: Museum of the Moscow Art Theatre.

Owen, Alice C.: *The Art of Play Directing: A Tentative Bibliography*. Boston: Simmons College, 1943.

Rouché, Jacques: *L'Art théâtrale moderne*. Paris: Edouard Cornily, 1910.

Sayler, Oliver M.: *Inside the Russian Theatre*. New York: Brentano's, 1925.

Sayler, Oliver M.: *The Russian Theatre*. New York: Brentano's, 1922.

Simonson, Lee: *The Stage is Set*. New York: Harcourt, Brace, 1932.

Tolmacheva, Galina: *Creadores del teatro moderno—los grandes directores de los siglos XIX y XX*. Buenos Aires, 1946.

Vardac, A. Nicholas: *Stage to Screen*, Harvard University Press, 1949.

Winds, Adolf: *Geschichte der Regie*. Berlin: Deutsche Verlags-Anstalt, 1925.

Young, Stark: *Theatre Practice*. New York: Charles Scribner's Sons, 1926.

Periodicals

Gesellschaft für Theater Geschichte (Berlin)
Mask (Florence, Italy)
Revue d'Histoire du Théâtre (Paris)
Teatr (Moscow)
Theatre Annual (New York)
Theatre Arts Monthly (New York)
Theatre Workshop (New York)
Die Scene (Berlin)

III

Adams, John Cranford: *The Globe Playhouse*. Harvard University Press, 1942.

Bruford, W. H.: *Theatre, Drama and Audience in Goethe's Germany*. London: Routledge and Kegan Paul Ltd., 1952.

Campbell, L. B.: *Scenes and Machines on the English Stage During the Renaissance*. Cambridge University Press, 1923.

Clark, Barrett H.: *European Theories of the Drama*. New York: Crown Publishers, 1947.

Cohen, Gustave: *Histoire de la mise en scène dans le théâtre religieux français du moyen age*. Paris: H. Champion, 1926.

Cohen, Gustave: *Le Livre de conduite du régisseur et le compte des depenses pour le mystère de la Passion joué à Mons en 1501.* Paris: Société d'Edition, 1925.

Downer, Alan: "Macready's Production of Macbeth." *Quarterly Journal of Speech*, XXXIII, April 1947, 172-181.

Goethe on the Theatre. Edited by John Oxenford. Dramatic Museum of Columbia University, 1919.

Haigh, A. E.: *The Attic Theatre*. Oxford at the Clarendon Press, 1917.

Isaacs, J.: "Shakespeare as a Man of the Theatre," in *Shakespeare Criticism*, edited by Anne Bradby. Oxford University Press, 1936.

Mantzius, Karl: *A History of Theatrical Art in Ancient and Modern Times*. 6 vols. New York: Peter Smith, 1937.

Morley, Henry: *The Journal of a London Playgoer*. London: George Routledge, 1891.

Moses, Montrose and John Mason Brown: *The American Theatre as Seen by its Critics*. New York: W. W. Norton, 1934.

Nagler, A. M.: *Sources of Theatrical History*. New York: Theatre Annual, 1952.

Nicoll, Allardyce: *The Development of the Theatre*. New York: Harcourt, Brace, 1937.

Nicoll, Allardyce: *World Drama*. London: George G. Harrap, Ltd., 1949.

Petit de Julleville, Louis: *Les Mystères*. 2 vols. Paris: Librairie Hachette, 1880.

Wagner, Richard: *Essays*. Translated by William Ashton Ellis. New York: The German Publication Society, 1914.

Watson, Ernest Bradlee: *Sheridan to Robertson*. Harvard University Press, 1926.

Zola, Emile: *The Experimental Novel and Other Essays*. New York: Cassell Publishing Company, 1893.

INDEX

INDEX

Abbey Theatre, 143
Aeschylus, 14, 47, 156, 158, 178
Alexandrinsky Theatre, 136 f.
Andreyev, Leonid, 37, 163
Anthony, 165
Antigone, 92, 93, 94, 95, 96, 139
Antoine, André, 13, 27, 29, 30, 31, 32, 33, 63, 79-91
Appia, Adolphe, 13, 16, 40, 41, 42, 43, 46, 48, 60, 111-119, 155
Aristophanes, 158
Aristotle, 300
Arms and the Man, 146
Atelier, 63

Bab, Julius, 61
Baron, Michel, 91
Barrault, Jean-Louis, 63, 64, 65, 279-290
Baty, Gaston, 63
Bear, The, 55
Beaumarchais (Pierre-Augustin Caron), 178
Becque, Henri François, 29
Beer-Hoffman, Richard, 52
Belasco, David, 38, 39, 40, 65, 98-110
Bel Geddes, Norman, 65, 242
Bells, The, 33
Ben-Ari, R., 52
Berlin State Theatre, 273
Bio-mechanics, 56
Blok, Alexander, 164
Booth, The, 164
Bouchet, Jean, 17
Boucicault, Dion, 38

Brahm, Otto, 31, 32, 33, 45, 46, 54, 60, 61, 92-97
Brando, Marlon, 307, 309
Brecht, Bertolt, 61, 62, 291-295
Bridie, James, 200
Browne, Maurice, 65
Burbage, Richard, 95
Burlador de Sevilla, El, 139

Cartel des Quatre, 63
Carter, Huntly, 54
Chaliapin, Feodor, 164
Charley's Aunt, 199
Chekhov, Anton, 35, 36, 55, 57, 161, 164
Chekhov, Michael, 165
Cheney, Sheldon, 40, 46
Chicago Little Theatre, 65
Chikamatsu-Monzaimon, 138
Chronegk, Ludwig, 26, 33, 34
Cid, Le, 81
Clurman, Harold, 54, 65, 66, 311-320
Cohen, Gustave, 14
Comédie-Française, 29, 83, 89, 138
Conducteurs de secrets, 17, 18
Conservatoire, 80, 90
Copeau, Jacques, 13, 14, 40, 45, 47, 48, 49, 63, 64, 65, 148-159
Coquelin, Constant, 80
Coriolanus, 295
Corneille, Pierre, 136, 138, 178
Così Fan Tutte, 200
Craig, Gordon, 13, 14, 15, 37, 40, 43, 44, 45, 46, 48, 60, 65, 120-135, 173
Crawford, Cheryl, 65

337

Cromwell, 81
Curel, François de, 30, 31
Czar Fyodor, 34, 164

Darling of the Gods, The, 101
Davydov, Vladimir, 261
Decroux, Etienne, 64
Delechiere, Jehan and Guillaume, 17
Deutsches Theater, 31, 32, 92, 93, 95, 96, 97
Devrient, Emil, 96
Diderot, Denis, 159
Dionysus, 16
Don Juan (Byron), 139
Don Juan (Molière), 136, 137, 139, 140
Downer, Alan, 25
Drama of Life, The, 163
Drury Lane, 22
Du Barry, 101
Dullin, Charles, 63
Dumas, Alexandre, 81
Dupuis, Adolphe, 89
Duse, Eleonora, 164
Dybbuk, The, 164

Easiest Way, The, 40, 106
Ekhof, Konrad, 22, 23
Epic Theatre, 61
Euripides, 178
Eustis, Morton, 51, 52
Evans, Edith, 203
Eysoldt, Gertrude, 52

Federal Theatre, 65
Fehling, Juergen, 61
Fergusson, Francis, 16
Fortuny, Mariano, 114 f.
Fossiles, Les, 30
Fouquet, Jean, 14
Fourberies de Scapin, Les, 64
Freie Buehne, 31, 32

Freytag, Gustav, 95
Fuchs, Georg, 60

Garrick, David, 22, 23, 25
Gémier, Firmin, 14, 63
Gesamtkunstwerk, 41, 63
Gielgud, John, 65
Giradoux, Jean, 177
Girl of the Golden West, The, 40, 100
Globe Theatre, 18
Goethe, Johann Wolfgang von, 23, 72, 95, 132, 180
Gogol, Nikolai, 55, 165, 259, 262, 263, 269
Gorky, Maxim, 36, 163, 293
Got, Edmond, 80
Governor's Lady, The, 40
Gozzi, Carlo, 165
Grand Guignol Theatre, 115
Granville-Barker, Harley, 65, 147, 152, 153
Gregory, Lady Augusta, 143
Gremislavsky, I. Y., 223
Griboyedov, Alexander S., 139
Grosses Schauspielhaus, 53, 207
Group Theatre, 65, 296, 311
Guthrie, Tyrone, 65, 199-209

Hachmann, Carl, 32
Hamlet, 14, 45, 95, 110, 112, 123, 199, 200
Harris, Julie, 313
Hofmeister, Der, 294
Hopkins, Arthur, 65, 166-174
Houghton, Norris, 55, 57
Hugo, Victor, 81
Humperdinck, Engelbert, 242

Ibsen, Henrik, 26, 45, 159
Impromptu at Versailles, 15

Inspector-General, The, 55, 165, 259-272
Iphigenie auf Tauris, 72
Irving, Henry, 28, 65

Jacques Damour, 29
Jedermann, 52
Jessner, Leopold, 60, 61, 273-278
Jones, Robert Edmond, 65, 174
Jonson, Ben, 16
Jouvet, Louis, 47, 63, 64, 175-182
Jubilee, The, 55

Kahane, Arthur, 50, 52, 53
Kainz, Josef, 96, 97
Kamerny Theatre, 58
Kazan, Elia, 296-310
Kean, Charles, 25, 26
Kemble, John Philip, 24, 25
King Lear, 124
Kleist, Heinrich von, 94
Koonen, Alice, 58
Kotlubai, K. I., 160-165
Kunstler Theater, 60

La Grange, Charles Varlet, 15
Laube, Heinrich, 32
Lekain, Henri Louis, 91
Lemaître, Frédéric, 82
Lenz, Jacob M., 294
Lessing, Emil, 32
Lessing Theatre, 45
Life of Man, The, 163
Lilina, Maria Petrovna (Mme. Stanislavsky), 165
Livre de conduite du régisseur, Le, 14, 17
Logan, Joshua, 210-217
Loutherbourg, P. J. de, 22
Lower Depths, The, 33, 36, 163
Lozowick, Louis, 57

Macbeth, 25
MacKaye, Steele, 65
Macready, William Charles, 24, 25
Maeterlinck, Maurice, 116
Magarshack, David, 37
Maître de jeu, 14, 16, 17
Maksheyev, 261
Malade Imaginaire, Le, 180
Malden, Karl, 310
Marivaux, Pierre-Carlet de Chamblain de, 178
Masefield, John, 147
Masse Mensch, 61
Mazarin, Cardinal, 16
Member of the Wedding, The, 311-320
Mendelssohn, Felix, 92, 93
Meyerhold, Vsevolod, 13, 14, 36, 37, 40, 47, 54, 55, 56, 57, 59, 60, 136-141, 160, 161, 162, 164, 259-272
Midsummer Night's Dream, A, 25, 179
Miracle, The, 52, 242-258
Misanthrope, Le, 91
Molière (Jean-Baptiste Poquelin), 14, 15, 16, 18, 28, 31, 47, 55, 83, 136, 137, 138, 139, 140, 141, 158, 178
Montigny, M., 80
Morley, Henry, 25
Moscow Art Theatre, 35, 37, 45, 57, 58, 160, 162, 163, 164, 210, 221
Moses, Montrose, 39
Mother, 293
Mother Courage, 292
Musset, Alfred de, 178

Nathan, George Jean, 39
Nemirovich-Danchenko, Vladimir, 57, 58
No plays, 137

Odéon, 31
Oedipus at Colonus, 94
Oedipus Rex, 54, 94
Of Mice and Men, 310
Okhlopkov, Nikolai, 60
Old Vic, 65
Olivier, Laurence, 65
Ononu-Otsu, 138
Othello, 33, 221-241

Palais Royal, 136, 141
Parisienne, La, 29, 91
Parsifal, 115
Passion Play at Mons (1501), 14, 17, 18
Passion Play at Poitiers (1508), 17
Passion Play at Valenciennes (1547), 14
Perrin, M., 80
Petit-Bourbon, 136, 141
Phaedra, 279-290
Phelps, Samuel, 25
Picasso, Pablo, 57
Piscator, Erwin, 61
Pitoëff, Georges, 63
Porel, M., 79, 82
Poulsen, Johannes, 45
Prasch, Aloys, 26, 27
Pretenders, The, 26, 45
Proposal, The, 55
Pushkin, Alexander, 37, 164

Racine, Jean, 90, 159, 178, 279
Realistic Theatre, 60
Reinhardt, Max, 13, 14, 45, 47, 50, 51, 52, 53, 54, 60, 65, 173, 207, 208, 242-258
Réjane, Gabrielle, 89
Richard III, 61
Ring of the Nibelung, The, 115
Robertson, Tom, 38
Romeo and Juliet, 72, 73, 124, 129

Sadler's Wells Theatre, 25
Saint-Denis, Michel, 63
Salle des Machines, 16
Salvini, Tommaso, 164
Sarcey, Francisque, 29, 87
Satsumo-Joun, 138
Saxe-Meiningen, George II, Duke of, 25, 26, 27, 29, 32, 33, 34, 60, 71-78, 93
Schiller, Friedrich, 73, 94, 95
Schroeder, Friedrich, 23
Sea Gull, The, 33, 35, 57
Seneca, 178
Sennett, Mack, 310
Shakespeare, William, 14, 23, 24, 25, 31, 37, 47, 94, 95, 124, 143, 156, 158, 164, 178, 179, 180, 200
Shaw, George Bernard, 142-147
Siegfried, 117, 118
Simonson, Lee, 26, 27
Sing Out Sweet Land, 310
Sommi, Leone de, 20
Sonnenthal, Adolph, 96
Sophocles, 92, 93, 94, 139, 178
Stanislavsky, Konstantin, 13, 27, 33, 34, 35, 36, 37, 38, 45, 46, 54, 57, 59, 60, 66, 160, 161, 162, 164, 165, 210, 221-241, 296
Strasberg, Lee, 19, 65
Streetcar Named Desire, A, 296-310
Sumurun, 52

Tairov, Alexander, 58, 59
Talma, François Joseph, 23, 82, 91
Tandy, Jessica, 299
Tartuffe, 87, 137
Tempest, The, 115
Théâtre Antoine, 115
Théâtre Athénée, 64
Théâtre Libre, 29, 31, 32, 84
Theodora, 116
Three Sisters, The, 160

Tieck, Ludwig, 92
Toller, Ernst, 61
Tolstoy, Alexei, 34
Troilus and Cressida, 115
Turandot, 164, 165

Vakhtangov, Eugene, 59, 160-165, 185, 193
Vakhtangov Theatre, 59
Valéry, Paul, 176
Venice Preserved, 46
Vieux Colombier, 47, 48, 49, 63
Violin-Maker of Cremona, 73
Volkov——, 165
Volksbuehne, 61
Vollmoeller, Karl, 242
Voltaire, 159

Wagner, Richard, 40, 41, 54, 111, 116, 155
Waxman, Samuel, 32
Weavers, The, 273-278
Weimar Court Theatre, 23, 96
Wilde, Brandon de, 319
Wilhelm Tell, 73
Williams, Tennessee, 306
Winter, William, 39
Woe from Wit, 139
Wolff, P. A., 23

Yeats, William Butler, 143

Zakhava, Boris E., 59, 160-165, 183-198
Zavadsky, Yuri, 56
Zola, Emile, 28, 29, 40